FOULSHAM'S

NEW

FUN BOOK

A GREAT GUIDE TO
HOME AMUSEMENT

256
PAGES

2560
LAUGHS

CONTENTS

SECTION		PAGE
I.	HA! HA! HA! . . . . Jokes, Funny Stories, Perverted Proverbs, Humorous Advertisements, Curious Epitaphs.	7
II.	AMUSING POSERS . . . . A collection of interesting "tests" that will set you and your friends thinking.	16
III.	PARTY GAMES FOR ALL . . . . Games to play not only at parties but also during the Winter Evenings, at home. Including a selection of Forfeits.	28
IV.	CONUNDRUMS WORTH ASKING . . . Not only to ask your friends, but also, to ask yourself.	67
V.	PUZZLES . . . . All kinds to suit all tastes.	80
VI.	AMUSING CARD GAMES . . . . . The games you want to learn rather than those you already know. There are included some good Patience Games.	97
VII.	MAGIC AND TRICKERY . . . . . Things you can do without being a Magician, and without a great deal of rehearsing.	131
VIII.	COMMUNITY SINGING . . . . . The words of songs of which you already know the tunes.	169
IX.	FORTUNE TELLING AND CHARACTER READING . Teacup Fortune Telling, Fortune Telling with Cards, Dice, Dominoes, The Magi's Tablet, Handwriting.	183
X.	THEATRICALS . . . . Monologues, Humorous Recitations, Acting Charades.	196

CONTENTS

SECTION		PAGE
XI.	JUNIOR SECTION	219
	The Boys' and Girls' Own Section.	
XII.	MISCELLANEOUS SECTION	236
	The General Knowledge Game, Table Tennis, Three Good Games of Dominoes. A Game of Dice, etc.	

HA! HA! HA!

Mabel "Have you heard I'm engaged to an Irish boy?"
Violet: "Oh, really!"
Mabel: "No, O'Riley."

Saturday Night: "Did the children behave when you bathed them?" enquired the mistress of the new French nurse, when she returned home from the card party.

"All but ze biggest boy, and sapristi how he fight and kick before I get him in ze water," replied the nurse.

"Which biggest boy? We've only one boy, Freddy, and he's not two years old."

"Et is not leetle Freddy, I mean. Et is ze big boy with glasses and curly hair."

"Good gracious! That's not my boy, that's my husband."

When a man and a girl get married they become one. Then they discover which one.

THE DRAMA OF LIFE
Act I: "Oh, boy!"
Act II: "Obey!"
Act III: "Oh, baby!"

One Cat: "You'd never believe how all the boys ran after me."
Another Cat: "No, I wouldn't."

Next-door Neighbour's Little Boy: "Father says 'could you lend him your gramophone, for to-night?'"
Gramophone Enthusiast: "Have you a party on?"
Little boy: "Oh, no; Father only wants to go to bed."

First Cruise Enthusiast: "What's the best cure for seasickness?"
Second Ditto: "Give it up."

Counsel: "Is it true that your wife was, at one time, thinking of taking up the law before she married you?"

Henpecked One: "Yes, but now she is satisfied to lay it down."

Timid Little Gent: "But, why do you call me, Mr. Harris, Miss Bursting?"

Miss Bursting (*coyly and forty-five*): "Because I don't know your other name."

Timid Little Gent: "Well, it's Mr. Smith."

"Why do you call your maid, Dawn?"
"Because she is continually breaking."

Doctor: "Good, you have no temperature now."
Patient: "No, Nurse took it just now."

A man summoned his neighbour for calling him a rhinoceros. In court, he admitted that the description had been levelled at him five years previously.

"But, why have you only just thought of invoking the aid of the law?" enquired the Magistrate.

"Well, you see," replied the man, "I only went to the Zoo last week."

Small Boy (*snivelling*): "I don't want to go to school to-day. I feel ill."

Mother (*without sympathy*): "Where do you feel ill?"

Small Boy: "In school."

"So, you are writing a book."

"Yes. It is to be called 'How to Rear Your Baby.'"

"Don't you find the writing an awful tie, with your own baby to look after?"

"Oh, no. You see the baby is at its grandmother's, so that I can get on with the book."

Wife: "I saw the dinkiest little hat in a shop to-day."

Husband: "Well, put it on and let me see how you look in it."

From a Young Ladies' Journal: "How to keep your Youth." Our advice is, don't introduce him to your girl-friends.

He was on the point of being refused. Dramatically, he exclaimed, "If you will marry me, darling, I will lay my fortune at your feet."

"Oh, but," she said smilingly, "you have only a very, very little money."

"Ah, yes," came the quick reply, "but think what a lot it will look beside those tiny feet of yours!"

The banns were read a third time last Sunday.

The other day, at school, a boy was asked where the capital of England was. He should have got full marks for his answer, for he said it was in the U.S.A.

They say that you can cure a person of stammering by making him sing. It's a pity, sometimes, that the reverse is not equally true.

In Scotland, fathers don't object to their sons sowing wild oats, as long as they sow them in the back garden. There, they can be turned to some account.

In the year 2000.
Landlady: "And this is the bathroom."
Modern Miss: "Yes. Now show me the television arrester."

He (*in telephone kiosk*): "I want a box for two."
Voice at the Other End: "Sorry, but we don't have boxes for two."
He: "But, aren't you the box-office of the Non-Stop Cabaret?"
Voice: "No, we are Deadman's, the Undertakers."

"Youth is stranger than fiction."

A Yankee newspaper recently printed an article in which it said that the Englishman was a white man. Should it not have said "bled-white"?

Here is a story about Lord Birkenhead in his early days at the Bar when he was representing a railway company, one of whose vehicles had run down a boy. The boy's case was that his arm was so badly injured that he could no longer lift it above his head. "F.E.'s." cross-examination of the boy was carried out very, very quietly—and very, very effectively :—

"Now, my boy," he said. "Your arm was hurt in the accident?"

"Yes, sir," said the boy.

"And you cannot lift your arm high now?"

"No, sir."

"Would you mind," said "F.E.," very gently, "just showing the jury once more how high you can raise your arm since the accident?"

The boy lifted it with an apparent effort just to the shoulder level.

"And how high could you lift it before the accident?" asked "F.E.," in the most innocent manner, and up went the arm straight over the boy's head. (*John O'London's Weekly*)

Darwin had been invited to a friend's house and, when he arrived, the two small sons of the host rushed into the room and asked the great scientist if he could identify a creature they held out to him. The creature was one they had artfully concocted by sticking the wings of a bluebottle on the body of a butterfly, and adding trifles of the anatomy of a daddy long-legs, a grasshopper and a black beetle.

Darwin eyed the thing and then eyed the two boys. "Did the creature hum when you caught it?" he asked the boys, solemnly.

"Yes, it did," they answered in unison.

"Then," said the great man, "its a humbug."

Mac arrived at the office half an hour late. "What's this mean?" enquired the chief.

"Well, it was like this," replied Mac. "I squeezed the tube of toothpaste too much, and it took a good half hour to get the stuff back into the tube."

Newspaper item : A small girl, named Sally Jones, swallowed a glass marble.

Not Sally in our Alley ; but alley in our Sally.

A provincial newspaper published in its news column that a well-known local resident had been seen kissing his kitchenmaid. The paper was careful to give no name. All the same, twenty-nine men called at the newspaper office next day, and threatened proceedings.

A POINTED ONE

Somebody has worked it out that the average family in England now consists of 3.1 people. Needless to say the " point one " is father.

Whistler, the painter, was at a dinner one night, and an awful bore came up to him and said, " Do you know, old chap, I passed your house last night."
" Thanks," said Whistler.

Mrs. A. and Mrs. B. met outside the Pig and Whistle. Mrs. A. did not exactly love Mrs. B. and Mrs. B. was no admirer of Mrs. A.
" I'm moving next week," said Mrs. A., " and then I shall be livin' in a much better place."
" And, next week, I shall be livin' in a much better place, too," retorted Mrs. B.
" What day are yer movin' ? " queried Mrs. A.
" I'm not movin'," was Mrs. B's. final reply.

Recently, a father of twins was heard humming that song, " How happy could I be with either."

Although wives are supposed to have the last word, they don't, really. It's the husbands who have it. What they say is, " Very well, then ; go and buy it."

Mark Twain once called on a neighbour and asked him to lend a certain book. The neighbour said he would be extremely pleased to lend the book, but he would have to adhere to his rule that the book should be used on the premises and not taken away.
A little later, the neighbour called on Mark Twain and asked him if he would lend his lawn-mower. Mark Twain said he would be delighted ; but he, too, had a rule. The mower would have to be used on the premises and not taken away.

Jim had a frightful black eye. "How did you get that?" asked John.

"Well, you know that charming girl who lives in the big house, at the bottom of the lane," said Jim.

"Yes," replied the other.

"And you know," went on Jim, "that her young man is in South America? Well, he isn't!"

A gushing lady once said to Sir James Barrie, "I do so love your play *Peter Pan*. Are all your other plays equally successful?"

Barrie looked dryly at her. "Madam," he said, "the other plays either Peter out or they Pan out."

Interfering Old Gentleman: "That's a bonnie baby of yours, madam. I trust he will grow up to be a man of credit and renown."

Mother (*pushing the pram*): "Tain't likely."

I.O.G.: "Madam, why do you say that? It all depends on how you bring him up."

Mother: "I can't bring *him* up, because the him's a her."

A doctor says that sherry is good for seasickness. But, surely, port is much better!

They say that it requires three hundred miles for a new car to be run in. We have known the same thing to happen to new drivers in much less than three hundred miles.

Counsel (*to Medical Witness*): "And even doctors, I suppose, make mistakes sometimes."

Medical Witness: "Yes, just as lawyers do."

Counsel: "But, the mistakes doctors make are often buried beneath the ground."

Medical Witness: "And lawyers mistakes often swing in the air."

Two soldiers were out in no man's land, during the last war. A bullet screeched past them and they both bolted for their lives. When they were somewhat composed, one said to the other, "Did you hear that bullet?"

"Yes," came the reply. "I heard it twice. Once when it passed me, and once when I whizzed past it."

Of many tortures thrust on man,
The vilest, I assert,
Is to wear a fifteen collar
On a sixteen shirt.

NOT EXACTLY

"As Mr. Robinson was returning home last night, a savage dog attacked him and bit him in the public square."

"While Samuel Jones was painting the front of a house, he slipped off the ladder and struck himself on the porch."

"Mary Brown was opening a tin of sardines last night and accidentally cut herself in the pantry."

"While on her yacht, the Bounder, Lady Rich was badly scratched by a cat amidships."

"As Farmer Williams was harnessing a restless pony, it kicked him on his corn patch."

If money is the root of all evil, the people in this country must be growing better and better, every week.

Nice Sister: "If I had been offered a dish with two apples on it, I would have taken the smaller one."

Nasty Brother: "Well, you've got it, so what's all the fuss about?"

In a Government Blue Book, it says somewhere that a pound note lasts seven months. Husbands should remind their wives of this.

Many men could escape the charge of being intoxicated if they just sat tight.

In a certain mining village, up north, there was a competition to see who could eat the most in the shortest time. There was one man who easily outdistanced all the other competitors. During the time allowed, he put away a beefsteak, a pound of sausages, a hefty meat pie and about a yard of suet pudding. For this remarkable performance he was roundly fêted and, of course, he was adjudged the winner.

Just as he was proceeding to leave the scene of his glory, he turned round and said, "I say, you lads, don't let my missus know or I shan't get no dinner."

Commercial Traveller (*to Landlady*) : " Are these sheets on the bed perfectly clean ? "

Voluble Landlady : " Perfectly clean, perfectly clean. I should just think they was. Why, they've only just this minute come from the laundry. 'Old 'em in yer 'and ; you can feel they're still damp."

Lots of things had mysteriously disappeared from the works, so the boss sent for the foreman, who was a native of the Irish Free State.

" Look here," he said, " if anything more goes, just stop the men, as they are leaving at night, and search them."

About a week later, the boss happened to be going across the yard, just as the " leaving off " hooter was sounding. There was the foreman, with all the men lined up.

" Take yer coats off ! " he ordered, in an aggressive tone.

" What's disappeared, now ? " whispered the boss.

" A wheelbarrow," was the husky reply.

First Electrician : " You put me in mind of William the Conqueror."

Second Electrician : " How's that ? He didn't know anything about electricity."

First Electrician : " That's why."

Swank (*entering a multiple store*) : " What have you got in the shape of motor tyres ? "

Shopwalker : " Funeral wreaths, life-belts, children's hoops and doughnuts."

Saleswoman : " These stockings, Modom, are the finest you can buy. Fast colour, latest shade, won't shrink, won't ladder and the yarn is excellent."

Incredulous Woman : " Yes, the yarn *is* excellent."

" Why is Phyllis looking so worried ? "

" I suppose it's because she looks every bit of six months older in the last two or three years."

Maisie : " Do you know, I wouldn't trust Tony too far."

Daisy : " I wouldn't trust him too near."

Enthusiastic little boy: "Father, when I grow up may I be an actor?"
Fed-up father: "It all depends."
Enthusiastic little boy: "What does it depend on?"
Fed-up father: "On how long you can go without food."

Sonny: "Mother, Dolly is using fearful swearwords."
Mother: "What did she say?"
Sonny: "She said she wouldn't wear those darned stockings any more."

Auntie: "And how did Jimmy do his history examination?"
Mother: "Oh, not at all well, but there, it wasn't his fault. Why, they asked him things that happened before the poor boy was born!"

"Ma," said a little girl who was reading a geography book, "where is the state of matrimony?"
"That," said the mother, "is one of the united states."

Hotel visitor (*at breakfast*): "Waiter, this coffee tastes remarkably funny."
Waiter: "Well, sir, it was ground only half an hour ago."
Hotel visitor (*fed-up*): "I see, it was ground a few minutes ago, and now it's mud."

The dear old lady approached the bed where a soldier lay almost hidden in a mass of bandages.
"Oh, poor man," she said, "have you been wounded?"
"Oh, no, mum, I bin kicked by a canary."

The young bride had promised her fond mother that she would send a daily telegram to report all was going well on the honeymoon.
On the third morning, at breakfast, the mother looked up horrified, and said to her husband:
"Oh, John, it's too bad. Jack and Milly are quarrelling already. Look at this."
"This" was a telegram which read: "Jack and I had a long row before breakfast."
It was not till some time after that she tumbled to the idea of a boating expedition.

AMUSING POSERS

Everybody likes to wrestle with a difficulty, especially if it is not too difficult. Here are some posers, set out in the form of mental tests, which will be found sufficiently hard to be interesting and yet amusing. Go through them, yourself, when you are alone, and then test your friends with them, when they gather round your fireside.

Where answers are needed, they will be found towards the end of the chapter.

1

You are allowed two minutes for solving these four questions. Here the words are given in the wrong sequence. You have to write them out in their correct order and reply to the question asked by each sentence.
1. Is which ice or hot fire?
2. Stamp penny a red is?
3. First Sunday comes Monday or which?
4. In pence many a shilling there are how?

2

Some people are very good at guessing the number of beans there are in a glass jar; but a guess, pure and simple, is seldom of any use. What is far better is an intelligent estimate. Here is something that will show whether you are any good at estimating. On the opposite page are several crosses. Look at them for ten seconds and then write down how many you think there are.

When you have estimated the total number, further useful trials may be made by placing a sheet of paper over part of the diagram and covering up some of the crosses. You can continue the tests then as often as you wish.

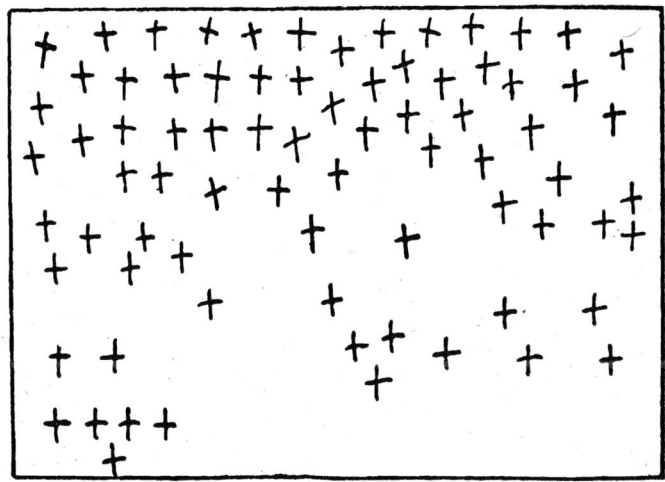

3

Below, a passage is taken from a standard author, but it is not printed exactly as originally written. True, the letters are all given in the order that the authors wrote them. The only difference is that the letters are not split up into their proper words. The last one or two letters of a word may be tacked on to the next word, and so on. You are allowed two minutes to write out the passage so that it makes proper sense. All the stops are omitted and you may do the same.

" Th isisi ndee dan othe rmis tak esai dDo nQu ixo tein tow hic hman yha vebe enl eda nd inse ver alco mpa nie sih avem an yt ime sha docca siont ovin dic atet hat manif estt rut hfr omt heal mos tun ivers alerr ortha ti sent ertai nedto it spre jud ice."

4

This is not as easy as it appears, and quite a number of people fail to give perfectly correct solutions. You are asked to write down the answers to the six questions, given below, in one minute; but, and here comes the difficulty, you must spell each word backwards. The first letter to be written down must be the last needed in the answer, and so with all the other letters. To make this quite clear, suppose you

have to write the word *ink*, the *k* must be set down first, followed by the *n*, and the *i* placed last.
1. On what river does London stand?
2. What is the King's Christian name?
3. What are the wooden supports used by people who are lame?
4. What is twice eight?
5. What colour is a nigger?
6. What is the capital of Belgium?

5

The following test is a purely mechanical one, and one minute is allowed for writing out the solution. There are six mutilated words, set down. Where letters have been omitted, a star is placed. You have to decide what same letter will replace all the stars in each word, but it is as well to note that a different letter is concerned in each of the six cases.
1. ✶HA✶
2. ✶HI✶
3. ✶EVE✶
4. ✶I✶ID
5. ✶X✶T✶R
6. ✶ARS✶.

6

Six pictures are drawn by an artist to depict a certain incident. Below each picture is given the description which is set out here. The descriptions, however, are not given in their proper order; they do not represent the facts as they must have occurred. You are allowed half a minute to decide what is the real order and to write down the numbers of the pictures as they should have been arranged.
1. The lady tells the conductor of her loss.
2. As soon as she sits down, the conductor comes to collect her fare.
3. She asks the conductor to stop the bus, so that she may alight.
4. A bus pulls up and a lady enters it.
5. Just as she stands up, the purse falls from her lap on to the ground.
6. She opens her bag and finds that she has lost her purse.

7

In this case, you are required to find your way through the maze below, from the star to the dagger, without

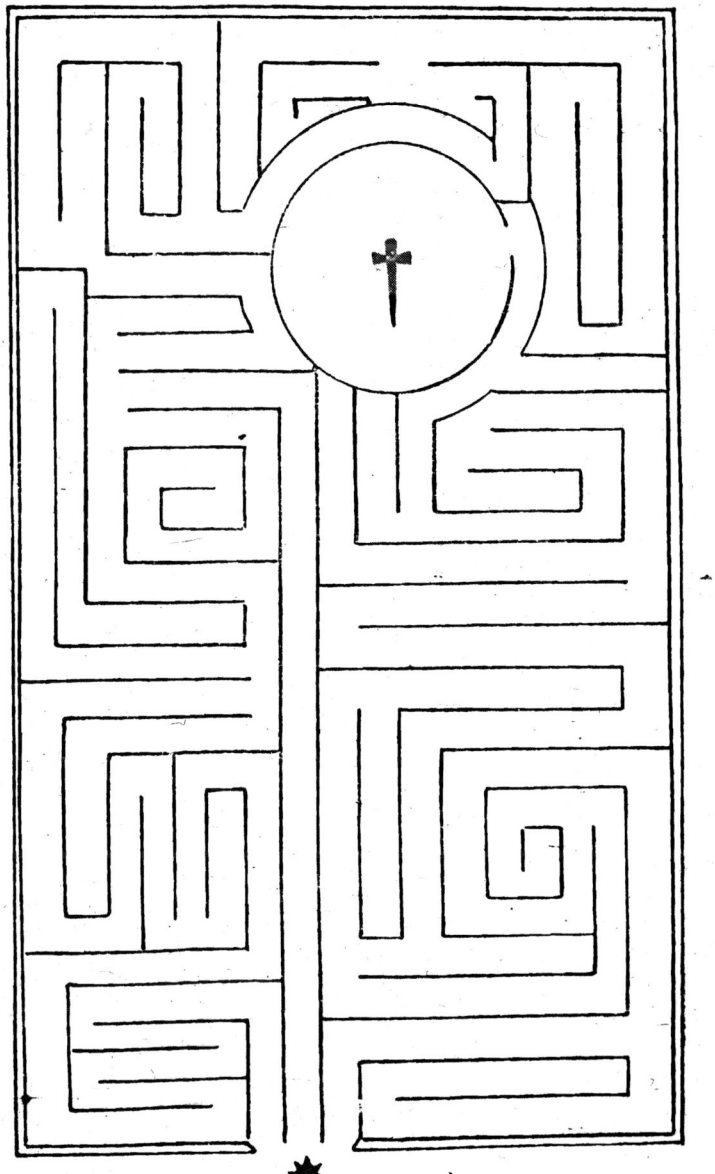

20   FUN BOOK

crossing over any of the black lines. There is one stipulation ; should you find that your way is barred at any point, you must not retrace your steps. You are required to go back to the star and begin all over again. One minute is allowed.

8

In the diagram, eight circles are given. Each is a different size. The test consists in putting them in their correct order, the largest one first, the smallest last. As they are

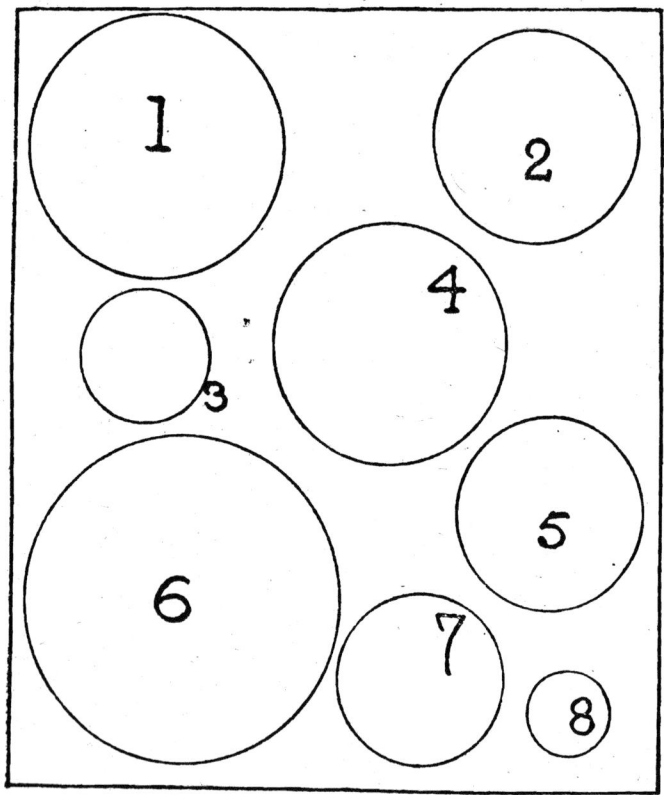

all numbered, it will be sufficient to jot down the figures in whatever order you think proper. You are allowed thirty seconds.

AMUSING POSERS

9

There is nothing very difficult about this, yet many people stumble over some of the items. Ten words are given in the left-hand column, but two letters are missing in each instance. The missing letters, however, are to be found in the right-hand column, though not opposite the appropriate word. In the space of one minute, you have to write out the words of the left-hand column, replacing the stars by letters found in the other column. No pair of letters may be used more than once.

1. RA✶✶IT   EU
2. PL✶✶HT   NG
3. N✶✶TER   IN
4. ✶✶IFLE   CL
5. THI✶✶S   BB
6. LIN✶✶G   ST
7. HU✶✶AR   TI
8. EME✶✶C   IG
9. DAM✶✶K   SS
10. ✶✶UTCH   AS

10

The following test is quite simple if you think before you begin to draw. You are allowed three minutes.
1. Draw any square you like, and then draw another one half the area of the first.
2. Draw any square you like, and then draw another one twice the area of the first.
3. Draw any triangle you like, and then draw another one half the area of the first.
4. Draw any square you like, and then draw a triangle equal to it in area.

11

There is no value in knowing that such and such an advertiser uses a particular sign or mark to single out his goods; but if you happen to know his sign it shows that you keep your eyes open and absorb information unconsciously. That, of course, is a valuable quality because it means that you

FUN BOOK

AMUSING POSERS

will get to know about all sorts of things in the world without any effort. Just to test your ability in this direction, on page 22 we give a number of silhouettes. Each represents a sign used frequently to advertise some well-known article. Make out a list, number it and state beside each item the name of the firm or the goods represented by each silhouette. Do not refer to any newspapers, etc. You are allowed two minutes.

12

This test shows how much you can concentrate your mind on a thing. You are required to spell certain words, but in each word a selected letter has been changed. For instance, suppose the word *book* is chosen and you are told to put down an F wherever an O occurs, you will accordingly, write the word thus *bffk*.

The time allowed is one minute.

1. Write down the Christian name of the King, putting the letter X instead of G.
2. Write down the name of this country, putting the letter M instead of N.
3. Write down what a man is who purposely kills another, putting the letter Z instead of R.
4. To what figures do the hands of a clock point at noon? Write down the word, putting the letter X instead of E.
5. Write down the name given to December 25th, putting the letter P instead of S.

13

Here are six sets of words. Each set consists of several articles which are much alike, but there is one article in each set that has nothing in common with the others. For instance, suppose one of the sets contained the words, Black, green, blue, pink, daisy, purple. It is clear that *daisy* is the only word not denoting a colour. In the same way, there is an article in each group which cannot be attached to the other articles. You are allowed one minute to make a list of the one word in each group which stands by itself.

1. Road, street, avenue, house, square, crescent.
2. Tin, iron, steal, brass, gold, silver.

3. Lion, tiger, cat, horse, ostrich, cow.
4. Tea, coffee, beer, hops, ale, lemonade.
5. London, Manchester, Liverpool, Bristol, Chester, Devon.
6. Milk, ink, turpentine, petrol, water, ice.

14

Write down the four amounts given below, then add them up. But you must put the " unit " figures on the left, the " tens " figures in the centre and the " hundreds " on the right. Moreover, each figure has to be written backwards. Thus, when the whole sum is finished and held up to a mirror, it will appear to be set out ordinarily. Two minutes allowed.
1. Five hundred and six.
2. Three hundred and twenty-four.
3. Nine hundred and seventy-eight.
4. Six hundred and twenty-three.

15

Most people have very inaccurate ideas about time and distance, although they are things that affect us considerably. Just see whether you are a " super " individual at this game. There are two things to do. First, mark off what you consider to be two and a quarter inches on a piece of paper, then, time yourself with a watch for a space of two and a half minutes. If possible, get a friend to help you with the latter test. Let him tell you when to start and you tell him when you think the time is up. If you come within an eighth of an inch in the first test, and within fifteen seconds, in the other, you are better than the average person in your judgment of time and distance.

ANSWERS

1

1. Which is hot, ice or fire ? Fire.
2. Is a penny stamp red ? Yes.
3. Which comes first, Sunday or Monday ? Sunday.
4. How many pence are there in a shilling ? Twelve.

3

This is indeed another mistake said Don Quixote into which many have been led and in several companies I have many times had occasion to vindicate that manifest truth from the almost universal error that is entertained to its prejudice.

4

1. Semaht.
2. Egroeg.
3. Sehcturc.
4. Neetxis.
5. Kcalb.
6. Slessurb.

5

1. That.
2. Ohio or Chic.
3. Level.
4. Vivid.
5. Exeter.
6. Harsh.

(Other suitable words may be found, and must, of course, be accepted, if offered by a competitor.

6

The correct order is 4, 2, 6, 1, 3, 5.

8

The correct order is 6, 1, 4, 2, 5, 7, 3, 8.

9

1. Rabbit.
2. Plight.
3. Neuter.
4. Stifle.
5. Things.
6. Lining.
7. .Hussar.
8. Emetic.
9. Damask.
10. Clutch.

10

(1) First draw the original square, then mark the centre points of each side and join them. The square formed inside the original square will be half the area.

(2) First draw the original square, then put in the two diagonals by joining the corners. After that, draw a square outside the original square so that its sides pass through the corners of the original square and are parallel to the diagonals. The outside square will be twice the area of the original square.

(3) First draw the original triangle, then halve the base line and join this point to the apex or top point of the triangle. Two new triangles will be formed and each is half the area of the original triangle.

(4) First draw the original square and then draw another one equal to it in area using one side of the original as a side of the new square. Join two opposite corners of the rectangle formed by the two squares, and the triangle formed on either side of this line will be equal in area to the original square.

11

1. Player's Navy Cut. 2. Wolsey Underwear. 3. His Master's voice (The Gramophone Co., Ltd.). 4. Wrigley's chewing gum. 5. Black Cat cigarettes. 6. Mr. Therm. 7. Jenkyn (Kensitas cigarettes). 8. Johnnie Walker whisky. 9. Force (Sunny Jim). 10. White Horse whisky.

12

The required spellings are: 1. Xeorxe. 2. Emglamd. 3. Muzdezez. 4. Twxlvx. 5. Chriptmap.

13

1. House. 2. Steal. 3. Ostrich (all the other animals have four legs). 4. Hops. 5. Devon. 6. Ice.

14

This is how the sum should appear when looked at in a mirror.

$$506$$
$$324$$
$$978$$
$$623$$
$$\overline{2431}$$

THE LATEST CRAZE

BLACKARTS are the latest craze. You simply cut a piece of black paper into a few shapes, according to your fancy, and then form them into some weird article.

It is not as easy as it looks, but it is much more fascinating than it appears. Once the craze gets hold of you, there will be a run on the scissors. Try it for yourself.

Here we have eight shapes of black paper, and the office boy has assembled them so that they represent a sandwich-man or Henry VIII, whichever you prefer.

Why not see what you can do with the pieces, and then go ahead with other sets of black shapes of your own making?

PARTY GAMES FOR ALL

Here is an excellent collection of party-games for big and little people. It does not matter whether you have fifty visitors under your charge, or there is just the family circle sitting round the table ; the games set out in this chapter will prove highly enjoyable. Some are regular old favourites that no gathering can do without, but many will be quite new to you. Try them.

THAWING GAMES

Every host knows the terrible feeling that things may not warm up quickly enough—the visitors stand round and they will not break through the ice. Start right away with this ; it may sound silly in print, but it has just the necessary effect.

Stand all the guests in a ring, the host included. When all is ready, the latter goes to the left round the ring, and shakes hands with everyone in turn, saying " Hello ! " As soon as he reaches the third person, the guest who was standing on the left of the host follows suit ; in the same way, the one standing on his left follows up, and so on, in " follow my leader " fashion, until everyone has shaken hands and exchanged " Hello ! " with each other.

This has to be done as quickly as possible so that much fun is caused by quick " players " following behind those who are not so rapid.

Thus, everyone in the circle takes a turn at the business. At the end, there is usually a roar of laughter, and the ice is broken.

ANOTHER

Line up all the men and boys, one behind the other, with one hand on hip. The first does this with his left hand, the second with his right, and so on, alternately. The ladies and girls then form a ring around the men. The music strikes up and the ladies proceed to march around. As soon as the strains cease, every lady has to grab one of the bent arms of the men. All those who are surplus and cannot find an arm have to stand out. The game continues like musical chairs. Of course, if the men are in excess of the ladies, they have to form a ring, and the ladies stand in file.

YET ANOTHER

Sit all the players, except one, around a table cloth, which they hold tightly. On the cloth, a small feather is placed. At the word "go," everybody sitting blows at the feather and the lone player tries to lean over and grab it. As he tries, they blow to get it away from him. The whole thing is so ludicrous that the roars of laughter have the desired effect of breaking the ice.

HARVEST FESTIVAL

The company is divided into halves, each half sitting on chairs facing one another a few yards apart. At the commencement of each row a basket of small parcels is placed and at a signal given by the M.C. the first person of each row picks up a parcel, unwraps it and passes the article on down the line. The last person at the end of each row places the article in a basket provided at the end of each row. The fun in this game lies in the funny objects contained in each parcel as it is unwrapped. For instance the first parcel may contain a huge parsnip, and the next a wee grape, then an onion, then perhaps a stick of rhubarb and so on. The row which finishes passing the articles correctly and in order first, is of course the winning row.

BOGIE

All lights are put out for this game and two circles are formed one of boys and one of girls, the same number of each sex, and the ring of girls stand just inside that of the boys. The piano is started and the circles move in opposite directions, the boys to the right and the girls to the left. When the music stops, the circles halt and the girls take hold of the arm of the boy next to them, and a flashlamp is suddenly shone upon one couple (by one of the party who beforehand has stationed himself on a chair in the centre of the circles). The couple thus spotted goes out of the ring and the music starts again. This goes on until there is only one couple left, who are usually presented with a small "spot" prize.

This game is unusual and much fun is caused owing to its being played in darkness.

CONFESSIONS

The players sit round a table and each is given a strip of paper and a pencil. The High Priest then commands everybody to write his or her name on the top line and, that done, the paper is folded over two or three times so that the name will not be revealed.

Next, the H.P. commands everybody to pass his paper around the circle of players in a left-hand direction. After they have travelled a good way round, he cries "halt" and they stop. Each player, then, has a paper, and he should not be able to guess who was the original owner.

The H.P. now commands everyone to write a confession, in short, the worst thing he has ever done. This is written below the portion which has been folded over.

A second time the papers are folded and passed on, and, when they are halted, the thing is to write "why he did it."

A third time the papers continue their journey and, when the H.P. calls a final halt, each person unfolds the paper in his possession and in turn, reads aloud the three sections. Naturally, some of them are screamingly funny. Such entries as this are obtained: Ann Winterton—stole a motor car—because I didn't care two hoots.

TWO BY TWO

Each lady is paired off with a man, or a girl with a boy, and the men or boys take stock of their partners. Then, they go out of the room, where they are blindfolded. On being led back into the room, they are given the word "go," and it is their business to find their partners, who are standing still in various parts of the room. The first to find his quarry is the winner.

Sometimes each pair is allotted the name of an animal and a lady may, then, assist her partner in discovering her by giving the cry or call of the animal. But she must only do so twice.

The ladies, of course, can take their turn at being blindfolded.

How to use this Face.—Look at the face for sixty seconds, then shut the book; draw another face on a scrap of paper and see if you can indicate where the letters are placed. How you draw the face does not matter: it is a question of getting the letters right.

HAT CHANGING

Players all sit in a circle and each is given some kind of hat, the funnier the better. A collection of these hats is made beforehand and should include an old tall silk hat, a baby's straw hat, a policeman's helmet, a sombrero, and such like; a small bowler hat, too, looks extremely funny on a big head. The game is played in the same way as musical chairs, but instead of changing chairs the hats are passed round and put on when the music stops. There is one hat taken away each time, but the chairs remain. The players leave the circle as they become " out " or hatless.

HIT OR MISS

Stand all your players but one evenly over the room and make them understand that on no account may they move their feet, except perhaps to turn round. The one player can dart about just as he fancies.

Next, you take some soft article and tie it up to form a ball. Hand the ball to one of the " fixtures " and cry " go." The person with the ball has to throw it at the player who may dart about, endeavouring to hit him and he, naturally must try to avoid being hit. The other " fixtures " catch the ball or pick it up and do their level best to hit the " darter," who has to be very spry when the game is well played.

If the " darter " is hit, he changes place with the one who puts him out, and the game proceeds.

PASSING THE PARCEL

Wrap up a small gift (as funny as possible, say a baby's dummy) in a large well padded parcel. Seat the company round the room while someone goes to the piano. One of the players is given the parcel and when the music starts she passes it to her neighbour, and so it goes round the ring, until the music stops. The player then in possession of the parcel drops out of the game. The music starts again and the procedure is gone through. As the players become fewer in number the fun waxes faster. When the players are only two in number the parcel becomes the property of the person who was *not* in possession of it when the music stopped.

The opening of the parcel creates roars of laughter.

THE DANGER ZONE

A boisterous game is often very useful for livening things up. Here is one. The players form a ring and hold hands. In the middle of the floor, a sheet of newspaper is put; it is the danger zone. The music strikes up and the ring begins to move round. As it goes, the players bump against each other and each makes an effort to push his neighbour on to the paper. The slightest step with the foot, on the paper, and the victim is out. The ring reforms, minus the victim, and proceeds. The last in is the winner.

"THUS" AND "SO"

This may seem a nonsensical game, but we have tried it many times with small children, and the way their eyes have sparkled has shown us plainly that it is something well within their liking. A leader is chosen and she stands on a chair, while all the other little faces are turned towards her. The leader chooses some favourite character such as "Peter Pan," "Alice in Wonderland," or "Cinderella," and then goes through various actions, at the same time remarking either, "Thus does Cinderella" or "So does Cinderella." Now, the rule is that when she begins her remark, with "Thus," the youngsters are to imitate her; but when she begins with "So," they are to stand stiffly at attention with their hands at their sides. It is great fun watching the kiddies get muddled and do the wrong thing, and the kiddies themselves enjoy their confusion. All sorts of actions will suggest themselves to the leader. The following may be offered as examples:

(1) Holding the face, as if suffering from toothache.
(2) Rubbing the eye, as if dirt is in it.
(3) Pretending to comb her hair.
(4) Blowing her nose.
(5) Crying.
(6) Coughing.
(7) Eating.
(8) Pretending to wash her face and hands.
(9) Rubbing her arm, as if hurt.
(10) Lifting her foot, as people do when trodden on.
(11) Marking time with feet.
(12) Yawning, as if tired.

B

WHAT IS WRONG?

This game will provide endless fun and amusement for a small party of players. First of all, lots are drawn to see who shall begin the play, and, when this matter has been decided, everybody goes out of the room except the chosen individual. He or she then closes the door and changes the position of some obvious thing in the room. That done, the search party is called in and asked what is wrong? The game is to spot the changed article first. Whoever finds out quickest takes his or her turn in changing some article in the same way as before. Note that the thing which is wrong must be quite apparent, say a picture turned round, a statuette placed facing the wall, or all the fire-irons on one end of the fender, etc.; but it would be hardly fair to place some insignificant ornament where it does not ordinarily stand. And it is well to remember that such things as clocks and delicate articles must not be touched at all.

WITH OPERA GLASSES

Have you ever tried this game? It is screamingly funny. Arrange a line to run the length of the floor. A piece of tape pinned to the carpet, at intervals, will do quite well and, as a makeshift, the edge of two big hearthrugs, put end to end, will serve admirably.

The next thing is to get your competitors to walk along the line, putting one foot before the other, so that each tread is made on the line. So far, there is nothing alarming about all this; but, and here is the fly in the ointment, each competitor is required to look through a pair of opera-glasses turned round the wrong way!

For some inexplicable reason, each person, as he looks through the glasses and proceeds on his way, lifts up his legs in a most curious manner, so much so that the whole company is bound to roar.

THE TRAVELLER'S ALPHABET

A leader is selected and she or he sits in the middle of the circle of players and pointing to any individual says, " I hear you are going on a journey to [any place with the initial A]; what will you do there?" The person must give an answer containing at least three words beginning with A. The leader then points to another player and repeats the same remark

PARTY GAMES FOR ALL 35

but mentions a place beginning with B. The answer, as before, must contain three words beginning with B. And in the same way progress is made throughout the alphabet, though it will be permissible to omit X and Z. Anyone not being able to give a proper reply must pay a forfeit.

The following sample question and answer was given in the writer's presence :

Austere Lady—I hear you are going on a journey to Cambridge. What will you do there?

Nasty little Boy—I shall catch caterpillars and let them crawl on my collar.

WHERE AM I?

This game is suited to a party of grown-up players, but not small children. Those who take part sit in a circle and someone leads off by describing any place he chooses. " I am standing on the edge of a cliff, the sea is far below me ; there is a pier, and close to it a few people are whirling round on roller skates. Near me and on my level is a band-stand and people are listening to the music " . . . and so on. The person is here endeavouring to describe Folkestone. The game is to see how quickly someone can hit on the place selected. Naturally, it is of little use referring to some unknown spot that the company cannot vizualise ; but there are so many places which everybody will know that the game need not be spoiled by a poor choice of locality. Given a reasonable spot and a party of people with imagination, the game has much to recommend it.

YOUR POWERS OF OBSERVATION

It is rare that the following contest fails to prove popular. You tell your company that you will presently bring into the room a tray bearing a number of objects and you will give a prize to the member who can recall the greatest number of them. A dozen articles are about the maximum number youngsters can remember, but two dozen are often recalled by adults. Now you bring in the tray and leave it where all can see it for two minutes. The tray being removed, pencils and paper are provided and the competitors start to write down what they can still see in their mind's eye. Nobody may talk or otherwise receive assistance. Give two minutes for the making of the lists and then call them in. It is a really good game that might well be indulged in not only at parties but at other times, as it is a fine memory trainer. A fountain pen or some other small article may well serve as the prize for the best list.

PICK AND CUP

This is an excellent game and must be played very fast. Form sides, equal numbers; sit down on the floor opposite each other, about two yards apart. The first player is a Pick the next a Cup, the next a Pick, and so on alternately, but the first and last player must be a Pick. The cups hold their hands together so as to form a cup. Place on the floor at the same end of each column an apple, button, marble, stone, orange, and a bean or any other trifling articles that may be at hand. The articles at the end of each column must be identical in number and kind. An umpire must be chosen who starts the race—for race it is. At the word "Go!" the end player of each column picks up one of the articles from the floor and places it in the cup next to him or her. The next pick must take it out of the cup and place it in the next cup, and so on, until the last player, who is a pick, places it on the floor.

Directly the first player has picked up one article and placed it in a cup, he or she must pick up another immediately and pass it in the same way, until all the articles are set going. The picks must work at lightning speed, else the other side will win. The side that first has all the articles on the floor at the opposite end of the column from which they started, wins. Each article must be handled separately throughout.

THE PARLOUR POTATO RACE

An ordinary potato race indoors would not provide much fun, but variations of it are decidedly amusing. For instance, a number of oranges are placed on the floor in a line, and around each is slipped an elastic band. The players are provided with a piece of wood, say a meat skewer, and they are required to lift an orange by slipping the skewer through its elastic band and carry it to a basket placed some distance away. The basket may very well be situated in an adjoining room. The task will perhaps appear easy, but it is not. While the skewer is being inserted, the elastic band has an unhappy knack of flying off the orange—a matter which disqualifies the player. Or the orange may bounce out of the band while it is being carried along, and again the unfortunate individual is disqualified. There will be some jostling as the players try to pass through the doorway, which adds to the difficulty of the task. Of course, no player may touch his orange.

CAT AND MOUSE

In playing this game, first form a circle holding hands up to make an arch between each player. One player, called the "Cat," goes round outside the circle and touches anyone he pleases. The one touched becomes a "Mouse," and must dart away in any direction he wishes in and out of the arches. The cat follows in exactly the same track. Should the cat go through a wrong arch he must pay a forfeit; but he still remains a cat. Should he catch his mouse, he becomes a mouse himself, the one caught then becoming the cat.

TWIRLING THE TRENCHER

A good deal of fun can be derived from this simple game. A leader is chosen who designates to each of the players a number, starting with one and progressing as far as there are players. Next, a trencher or wooden bread platter is obtained, and, while the leader is spinning it on the floor, she calls out a number—say, No. 3. Player No. 3 must rush out, grasp the platter before it sinks to the ground, give it another twirl and, at the same time, call out another number. The player bearing this latter number must immediately run to the platter and catch it, as before. She, in her turn, calls a number, and so the game proceeds until someone allows the trencher to fall flat on the ground. This unlucky individual, having failed, is called upon to pay some suitable forfeit.

THE BLIND MAN'S STICK

First form a circle of your friends. Then let one be blindfolded and stood in the centre, with a stick in his hand. The circle must be kept moving round. The one in the centre keeps the stick low, and with it touches one of the circle. The player touched at once takes hold of the stick, when the whole circle must stand still. The blind man now vocally imitates some animal or call, such as "Milko!" "Co-als!" "Rags and Bones!" etc., and this must be at once copied by the player holding the stick. The blind man then guesses who it is. If successful, they change places.

ALL BEARS

If you would like to play a trick on the company, as well as amuse your guests, try this game. Stand all the players in a circle and place in the centre, on the floor, some article such as a book. Then announce that you are going to assign to everybody the name of an animal. Naturally, the impression is that each person will be allotted a different animal, but you go round and whisper to each in turn, " bear." Of course, speaking is forbidden.

Now, you announce that the moment a person hears his animal called, he must rush to the centre and pick up the object on the floor. Let there be a certain amount of mystery about what will ensue.

When all is ready, call out, " owl." Not a soul will stir. You hesitate a moment and look puzzled. " Very well," you say, " that's not a good beginning." Then you pick up the book and replace it by a bun. " Bear," you shout, and the whole company as one man, darts at the unfortunate bun.

Your best plan is to get to the door, when you announce " bear," and then to make yourself scarce for the next few minutes.

MOTHER MACGEE

It is perfectly absurd to read of this game, but get it going properly and the room becomes convulsed with laughter. The players sit in a ring and the leader says to the individual next to him, " Mother MacGee is dead." " How did she die ? " queries this second individual. Then comes the answer, " With her mouth open." As soon as this is said, the second person must open his mouth and keep it so to the end. But it is his turn and, with open mouth, he says to the next player, " Mother MacGee is dead." This is followed by the two other remarks, stated above. It is now the turn of player No. 3 and he, with open mouth, tells No. 4 about Mother MacGee. No. 4 must continue the story, with open mouth, to No. 5.

When all have their mouths open, the leader begins again, but this time the story is varied, " She died with one eye shut " or " With her hand on her head," and so on. The players have to go through these contortions, retaining the old ones as well as the new.

PARTY GAMES FOR ALL

Suddenly, someone looks at another player and bursts out laughing, or fails to preserve the required actions. Such a player is ruled out. The game ceases when only one person is left.

WHO'S PIG?

One player is blindfolded and all the others sit or stand round him in as large a circle as possible. The person blindfolded then makes his way to the ring and, using only one hand, touches somebody. Once he touches another player, he must not move his hand, but keep it perfectly still. Then he says "Is this Mike's pig?" and the person touched must reply by giving three disguised grunts. The questioner listens and, if he can detect the player by the grunts, the bandage is removed from his eyes and he changes places with the grunter. On the other hand, if he makes a wrong guess, he must pass on to someone else. It is as well to turn the person round three times as soon as he is blindfolded, in order that the location of the other players may not be noted by him. Better still, let all the other players change places.

MIND THE STEP

Halve your players and send one section out of the room. As far as possible, the players sent out should not know the game.

Form up the players, left inside, in two equal rows. Let them face inwards and tell them to extend the left foot, so that the toes of opposite players meet.

Now, call in someone from outside and conduct him to the head of the line. Explain to him that he is about to be blindfolded and that he is required to go down the avenue. Suggest that he takes good stock of the feet, so that he may know how and where to step over them.

When he is blindfolded, the avenue of players draw in their feet and away goes the victim, carefully stepping over—nothing. His ludicrous antics provide the fun. When he reaches the end, you untie his bandage and call in the next.

THE HAND OF THE MUMMY

Send the players, who do not know this game, out of the room or, alternatively, let about half of them go out. Line up the others in the room and bring in the outsiders, one by one. These latter are blindfolded just before entering.

On coming in, a leader guides the blindfolded player to the head of the line and tells him to go down the line and shake hands with each person in turn.

The sightless man does as he is told and proceeds, somewhat timidly, to shake hand after hand. While he is doing this, the leader creeps down to the end of the line and holds out a glove, previously rammed full with wet sand or sawdust. The sightless one, finally, reaches the dummy hand and grips it before he realises anything is amiss. What he does next may be surmised.

His bandage is removed, he is given a place among the hand-shakers and a new victim is led in, to be similarly treated.

AS YOU WERE (?)

For this game, the players have to stand in a circle, with the leader in the centre. Plenty of space is required. The leader calls out any command he pleases, but it must be one that permits of a directly opposite performance, and it is the opposite that the players must perform. For instance, should the leader give the command, "A pace to the rear," the players must take a step forward. Should he say, "Right turn," they must turn left. If he says, "Raise the right foot," it is the left that must be lifted. And so on.

No second shots, however quickly done, are admitted, and anyone who goes wrong is dismissed from the company. The game continues until only one player, beside the leader, is left in the squad.

NOAH'S ARK

Line up the players, then give to each the name of a well-known animal. You must so arrange matters that every animal is allotted to two different people, but nobody may know the identity of any animal but their own. Therefore, it is usual to whisper the names as you go round.

The players may not speak but, on a signal from you, they proceed to make such noises as they think will reveal the animals for which they serve. As they roar and crow and hoot, they wander round the room, looking for somebody who is likely to pair off with them.

Having discovered their mate or whoever they think must be the one, they hold hands and come to you for verification. If correct, they fall out of the game, and the pair left in last has to submit to forfeits.

This is a capital game for bringing your guests together.

WHO'S MISSING?

Where there are twenty or more players, the following is a good game for thawing the company. Form all the players in a circle and let them march round the room two or three times; for preference, they should be singing to the music of a piano or gramophone. Suddenly the music stops and the order to break up the circle is given. As everybody leaves his position, a crowd is formed. Simultaneously, the lights are switched off and the leader or host spirits away one of the players without creating any notice. That done, the lights are put on again and the thing for the remaining company to do is to guess who is missing. The first to name or describe the absentee is the winner.

MOTORING

This is a form of musical chairs. A leader is chosen and all the other players are given a seat. They should be set out in a circle. Next, the leader assigns to each player the name of a part of a motor car. He chooses such names as index-plate, head lamp, steering column, clutch, axle, hooter, and windscreen wiper.

When everyone is quite clear about his own particular part, the leader walks round within the circle of chairs and, as he proceeds, he calls out one of the names of the parts. Immediately, the person concerned must jump up and follow him. As soon as he has collected a goodly following of players, he calls out " breakdown " and all make a scramble for the seats.

Naturally, the leader sees to it that he can obtain a seat, so somebody else is left standing. This individual then becomes the leader and commences the round over again. When played in this way, there is no finality to the game; accordingly, some people prefer to keep their same leader throughout, to remove one chair after each " breakdown," and to rule out the person left standing.

B*

HOPPING STORKS

Select two players about equal merit and, if children, of much the same age. Place them about three yards apart and tell them to stand on one foot. When ready, give the word "go." The two then hop towards each other and endeavour to push their opponent, so that the raised foot has to touch the ground. If one of them finds it necessary to put the second foot on the ground, in order to preserve his balance, he loses. Note that the pushing can only be done with one hand, i.e. the one on the side of the raised foot. No tugging, pulling or holding is allowed.

If the players are all of much the same ability, it is good fun to arrange for the winners to compete amongst themselves, and to continue the rounds until one is the final champion.

STEPPING STONES

Two pairs of players are selected, each a man and lady, or a boy and girl. The two female players are stood side by side at one end of the room, and they are required to race to the other end of the room, where a rug is placed to denote the finishing line.

The two male players are each given three sheets of newspaper, folded into four (in half, and in half again). The male players bend down, holding their papers. On the word "go," each man puts down his three folded sheets of paper in a line ahead of his partner. The lady players have to race across the room, but each must only step on the folded sheets of paper entrusted to her male partner. Thus, it is his work to provide the "stepping stones," and she moves along as quickly as he can bring a rear paper forward. Obviously a lady player who allows any part of her foot to touch the floor must be disqualified.

HOW MANY BEANS?

While all the players are out of the room, secrete a number of haricot beans—dry ones, of course—in all sorts of places. Use about a hundred for ten players and for other players, in proportion.

Then, call in those who are taking part in the game and give them two minutes to find all they can. He or she who produces the greatest number is the winner.

Give the players to understand that no object is to be moved in order to discover the beans; otherwise the room will be turned upside down.

PAIRING OFF

Decide on about twenty questions and answers that are not too hard for the average ability of the players. Then, make out a list of the forty items in such a way that the questions and answers are given in a jumbled order. Either duplicate a number of the lists, one for each player, or read out the items and tell the players to write them on a blank piece of paper. If the latter course is followed, it is advisable not to explain the competition before the lists have been written down.

When all is ready, give the players five minutes in which to decide how the questions and answers should be paired off. They can register their selections by assigning the same number to a question as to the answer.

The questions may deal with matters of general knowledge, current events, family history, and so on.

CHINESE TOUCH

Divide the players into two equal camps, arranging for each camp to have, as far as possible, half boys and half girls.

Next, set two rugs on the floor, parallel to each other, with their nearest edges about ten feet apart; if this is impossible, as far away as possible.

Play proceeds in this way: A girl on one side takes up her position on the edge of her hearthrug and stands on one foot, whichever she pleases. She must not put the raised foot on the ground, nor may she step over the rug, not even a fraction of an inch. A boy of the other side then comes forward and he tries to touch the edge of the girl's hearthrug, without her touching any part of him. The fact that she can only use one foot gives him a good opportunity of approaching safely; he may dash up and chance his luck, he may wriggle along the floor and stretch out his arm; but he must avoid being touched, if he can.

As soon as the issue is decided, a girl from the boy's camp comes forward and is matched against a boy from the girl's camp. So the game goes on until all the pairs have finished and the side with the most successes is adjudged the winner.

MUSICAL MAGIC

Someone is told to go out of the room and re-enter when the piano is played. Before the music strikes up, the company decides that the absent one is to come in and do a certain act. It may be that he has to pick up a cushion on the sofa and put it on a particular chair, or take a book from the shelf and put it under the settee. When all is ready, the piano begins to play loudly and in comes the individual. He looks round rather aimlessly and then picks up some object. If it is the thing he has to deal with, the music becomes soft; but if, as is at first probable, it is not the right article, the piano grows louder. According to the musical strains being soft or loud so he keeps to an article or leaves it. When at last he alights on the proper thing he is made aware that he is on the right track by the soft pedal. He now takes the object, looks around, and walks, perhaps, towards the door. The increasing sounds of the piano tell him that that move is wrong, and he turns about and goes up to a chair. The piano grows soft, for that, we will say, is what he has to do. In this way the fun continues, and according to the strains of the music, so he is directed to perform the act required.

BIRDS OF THE AIR

All the competitors must face the leader, or speaker, as he is called, in this game. They must stand with the right hand placed upon the left arm. Each time the speaker mentions the name of a bird, the right hands of all the players must be raised and fluttered in the air to imitate a bird; should *birds* in general be mentioned both hands must be fluttered by all. When an animal or anything that cannot fly is mentioned the right hand must remain on the left arm. Of course, the speaker tries to make the players go astray, as a forfeit must be paid by anyone doing the wrong thing. All being ready, he begins to tell them a story after this style:

"I had just turned out of bed and was on my way to the bathroom. It was a beautiful spring morning, and the *birds*" (here all hands should flutter) "were singing charmingly. I opened the window, and on the lawn was a lovely *thrush*, trying to pull a *worm* out of the ground. A *blackbird* darted out of a bush and made a rush, but neither of them obtained the *worm*. When I went out the air was full of song from all kinds of *birds*; and in the tree on my right a *squirrel* was leaping about."

Let us review this little speech:

"It was a beautiful spring morning and the *birds*" (all hands must flutter in the air) . . . "on the lawn a *thrush*" (all the right hands must flutter). . . . "A *blackbird*" (right hands flutter again) . . . "obtained the *worm*" (right hands must again be resting on the left arms) . . . "songs from all kinds of *birds*" (all hands again flutter) . . . "a *squirrel*" (right hands once more replaced on left arms).

It is obvious that the more frequently the speaker varies his allusions from animals to birds and *vice versa*, the greater will be the number of forfeits he obtains.

THE CROSS MAKER

The company sits round a table, and each person should have twelve counters as "lives." Number One makes a number of crosses on a sheet of paper, in order to represent a word. Then in turn, each player names a letter of the alphabet; if this letter occurs in the word, the Cross-maker must insert it in place of one of the crosses. If not, the guesser forfeits one of his or her lives.

Then the turn goes to the next player, who also guesses a letter of the alphabet. So the game goes on, with this variation: After *three* correct letters have been discovered, any player is allowed to guess the whole word, instead of only naming a letter of the alphabet. Whoever first guesses the word, becomes Cross-maker in his turn.

If there are two or more letters alike in the word, and this letter is named, the Cross-maker can place the letter where he chooses. Thus in CANNON, if N is guessed, he can place it instead of the last cross. There is always a great possibility that players will overlook this point; if N is guessed and proved successful, most players will avoid naming it a second time.

COCK FIGHTING

For boys, this is an admirable little contest. The floor is cleared for a considerable space and two of the noisiest youngsters are invited to take part in a cock-fight. They are placed on the floor, with their knees drawn up: their ankles

Cock Fighting

are tied together with a handkerchief, and they are told to grasp their knees. A walking-stick is then thrust under their knees and over their arms. Trussed in this way, the two combatants are pushed or lifted towards each other, so that their toes easily touch. At the word "Go," they have to endeavour to capsize each other by inserting the feet under those of the opponent, and on lifting them up, overthrowing the adversary.

FEEDING THE BLIND

This is an amusing game for bright young people, but it is advisable to have a loose cloth or sheet on the ground.

Two hassocks are placed about a foot apart; two performers—or victims—are selected, and both are blind-folded. One of them receives a bowl of sugar, or flour, and a dessert spoon, and is told to feed his or her companion, who is allowed to open his mouth and move slightly, but not so as to touch the "feeder," as that would be unfair.

It is really very difficult to guess the position of another person's mouth, apart from the fact that the apparent height when sitting is very deceptive, as many short people are only short in the leg, and appear far taller when sitting than when standing. It is advisable for the partners to wear aprons, or some such adequate protection for their clothes.

THE TREASURE HUNT

Here is a capital game. The host prepares a short story which is written on a sheet of paper. At the proper moment, the paper is pinned up prominently in the main room and all the players gather round it and read the story. The story is so put together that it contains a number of clues and, by discovering these clues, the players are able to guess what the treasure is and in which part of the house it is hidden. Naturally, the person who is able to fix on the hidden article and find it first is the winner.

Treasure hunting provides an immense amount of fun; but, to make it absolutely successful, certain rules must be observed. For instance, the document providing the clues must not be removed from its fixed position. This law adds greatly to the merriment because it will cause the players to come racing back to refresh their memory, whenever their searchings are brought to a standstill.

The host will be advised to lock certain doors to prevent the guests wandering into rooms that must be kept private, and to explain that the treasure is not to be found in any place that is locked.

The story containing the clues may be built up on the following plan :

"It had vanished completely—the bright little article on which she had set such store. It was not that she valued it so highly on account of its actual worth; but because it had been given her by a dear friend, who had since passed out. Where could it be? As a matter of fact, she must have dropped it as she had been going to and fro. She sat down and thought over her movements. She had certainly rummaged, that morning, through the old oak chest, she had cut fresh blossoms and put them in the flower bowls. . . ." etc.

The story can be continued at length in this manner, making it as simple or as complex as desired. Perhaps, it may be added that these clues would serve for a penny piece, hidden under a bowl of flowers.

A CODED MESSAGE

The following makes an amusing and interesting word game. Present each player with a sheet of paper and a pencil: then proceed to explain that the numbers, letters and words which are given below, are the clues to an amusing verse. The player whose translation is nearest to being correct wins. Arrange a time limit of from 10 to 15 minutes.

> 2 U, O ! 2 U
> I vow 2 B true;
> 2 C U Y I
> In XTC HI !
> I H 8 LN G.,
> Always following me;
> 4 U, O ! U R
> NICR-looking by far!
> So when I C L N,
> My head I shall toss;
> & U, if U chance 2,
> B sure 2 look X.

Translation

To you, O! to you I vow to be true;
To see you, why I in ecstasy hie!
I hate Ellen G., always following me;
For you, O! you are nicer-looking by far!
So when I see Ellen, my head I shall toss,
And you, if you chance, too, be sure to look cross.

PARTY GAMES FOR ALL
PRINTERS' MISTAKES

Cut from a news article in a daily paper, an interesting paragraph of about fifteen lines. Then jumble up the lines and have the result duplicated, say on a typewriter, so that each guest has a copy. Note that the words of a line are not, themselves, jumbled. The puzzle is to arrange the lines in their correct order. The first to write out the whole passage, as given in the newspaper, is the winner of the competition.

The following example will show how it should be done

> be laid out by the amateur, whether
> In fact, the way is here pointed out
> the space at his disposal is large and
> would have the satisfaction, after
> which are given side by side throughout.
> photogravure plates and numerous
> The little volume is illustrated with
> sunny or cramped or badly shaded.
> diagrams. With its help gardens can
> recognition, and the householder
> Latin as well as more common names,
> Leicester could be transformed beyond
> whereby those unlovely backs in
> alpine and rockery plants by their
> close study, of being able to talk of his

Placed in correct order of lines, this reads as follows :

> The little volume is illustrated with
> photogravure plates and numerous
> diagrams. With its help gardens can
> be laid out by the amateur, whether
> the space at his disposal is large and
> sunny or cramped or badly shaded.
> In fact, the way is here pointed out
> whereby those unlovely backs in
> Leicester could be transformed beyond
> recognition, and the householder
> would have the satisfaction, after
> close study, of being able to talk of his
> alpine and rockery plants by their
> Latin as well as more common names,
> which are given side by side throughout.

ALPHABETICAL SENTENCES

This is an amusing and fascinating game, and it pleases either adults or juveniles, though the young people should be in their teens. Each person is provided with paper and pencil, and a time limit is fixed, after which all papers must be given up. A small prize, such as a box of chocolates, could be given for the best list.

The object is to make a list of as many words as possible, using only isolated letters of the alphabet, such as Q (Kew), T (Tea), or L ('Ell), though these are somewhat obvious. It is really startling, when you begin, as many curious combinations can be formed. Below we give some examples to make matters quite clear.

EGNC	Aegean Sea
ODV	Eau de Vie
FEG	Effigy
AQ	A queue
LEG	Elegy
XLNC	Excellency
NRG	Energy
OICURMT	Oh, I see you are empty
XPDNC	Expediency
AYZ	A wise head
LN	Ellen
SA	Essay
DK	Decay
KN	Cayenne
XQQ	Excuse
DDEE	Disease

NEWSPAPER PUZZLES

A good deal of fun for both old and young can be derived by making puzzles out of newspapers in the following way:

1. Purchase two identical copies of a comic newspaper. From one of the pages cut out, say, half a dozen separate squares, each about an inch in size. Paste each slip on a blank post card and hand one card to each competitor. Spread the unmutilated copy of the paper on a table with the appropriate pages in view. The winner is the person who first points out the exact spot on the complete paper which corresponds with his or her cutting. Much amusement is

PARTY GAMES FOR ALL 51

occasioned if squares are taken from unlikely portions of the illustrations.

2. Purchase two copies of the paper as before. From one of them cut out half a dozen lines of bold type. Paste each line on a separate card, and then sever the letters one from the other. Place each group of letters, forming a line, in an envelope. When all is ready, hand an envelope to each player, and spread out the unmutilated copy of the paper on a table. The winner is the person who re-forms his line of type in the shortest time.

3. Take another page from the same newspaper and cut out some of the pictures. Paste them on to separate cards and, when dry and flat, cut each of them into many pieces of grotesque shape. These jig-saw puzzles will cause endless amusement.

4. Cut out about two dozen articles from the pictures—say, a hat, a boat, a tree, a house, and so on. There is an endless variety of suitable things to choose from. Paste all the pictures on one large card. Assemble the players, let them look at the jumble of illustrations for one or two minutes, and then give a prize to the competitor who can write down the most complete list, from memory, of the things seen on the card.

5. Turn to the columns of print and cut them into blocks, each of twenty lines. Paste each block on a card. The players are required to choose one word from each line and so form a sentence. The person who composes the best sentence is adjudged the winner of a prize.

TELEGRAMS

A good deal of fun may be derived by getting the members of a party to write supposed telegrams. Here is one suggestion. Provide the players with pencils and sheets of paper and divide them into two groups of about a dozen people each. The first thing is for each player to print any letter he chooses on the paper in his possession and then to pass it on to the next individual. He then prints another letter on the paper in front of him and passes it on. In the end, each paper bears twelve letters written by as many different people. We must add that the letters should follow on in line, with a space of about an inch left blank between them. This done, the papers are handed on to the next player in the circle, and he has to use the twelve letters as initials for a telegram of twelve words. The wording should attempt at being funny, dramatic, terse, or anything else. Finally, the competitors listen to the telegrams and vote as to which effort is the best.

PAIRING OFF

A good game can be made out of the fact that there are many articles in common use which are associated in our minds in pairs. For instance, a hook and an eye go usually together, and so do a pen and ink, a brush and comb, a needle and cotton, a cup and saucer, a knife and fork, a sheet of notepaper and an envelope. When a large number of such things have been collected together they are wrapped in little parcels and every member of the party is served out with one. On a given signal each individual unwraps his package and immediately begins to search for his particular partner—the hook looks for the eye, the brush for the comb, and so on. The game must, of course, be explained to the players beforehand, and note is taken of the first pair to report their success and the last to pair off. It makes for more fun if one item of each pair is wrapped in, say, red paper and the other item in white, the gentlemen then being given the red parcels and the ladies the white ones.

DUMB CRAMBO

This is an old favourite which many people look upon as a necessary game for any well-conducted party. The players are divided into two equal groups, whether equal in numbers or in intelligence, and by the luck of a toss one group goes outside the room and the other remains within. The side staying in the room holds a hurried council and decides on a word. That being settled, a member is sent out to tell the opposing party that the chosen word rhymes with so-and-so. Say the word favoured is "eye," then the informant tells the outside people that the word they must seek rhymes with " pie."

Of course, the guessers will think of " my " " try," " lie," " fie," " guy," " sigh," " buy," " die," " high," etc. And to find out which it is they enter the room and act the possible words in turn. Every time they hit on the wrong one the sitting members hiss them in no half-hearted way, and the actors hurriedly retire, only to come in a few seconds later with another effort. When they eventually alight upon the correct word they are applauded, and the other side goes out to try their luck. It need hardly be added that most fun is derived from selecting a word that has quite a number of possible rhymes. Those with but few rhymes are unsatisfactory.

MUSICAL GLASSES

A great deal of fun can be obtained from unusual musical instruments, and the simplest of these takes the form of glasses. These can be of different sizes, as that naturally affects the tone, or the tumblers can all be alike, when the pitch can be varied by the amount of water poured into each glass. Twelve glasses with a varying amount of water in each makes a good keyboard, and anyone with a slight ear for music can give a splendid entertainment.

When playing the Musical Glasses, it is better to arrange them in two rows, the glasses in the right-hand row being slightly in advance of the others, so that the first right-hand glass comes about midway between the first and second glasses on the left. The lowest note of all should be nearest to the player.

The sound is produced by passing the moistened tip of the finger lightly round the edge of the glass. It is not necessary to go all round the edge of the tumbler—a quick gliding movement is sufficient to start the vibration, which should travel round by its own velocity. A little gum added to the water used for moistening the finger assures a closer grip, and gives a louder—not higher—note.

LOVE LETTERS

With the proper type of guest, this form of amusement is screamingly funny. Give each player a sheet of paper and a pencil and instruct him or her to write a really passionate love-letter. Ladies write a man's letter to a woman, and men write a girl's letter to a man. The name signed at the end, like the whole of the letter must be imaginary, but the writer's own name must be stated on the paper.

At the end of ten minutes, the letters are collected and dealt out one to each competitor, who is required to read the " screed " aloud. When each letter has been read, the author is required to admit that it is his or her unaided work.

OUTLINES

This is a splendid item for a party. A number of sheets of paper are prepared in advance, each bearing from six to a dozen simple outline strokes. One of these is required for each guest, and all should be alike. The duplication is easily done if the original is placed upon the glass of a window,

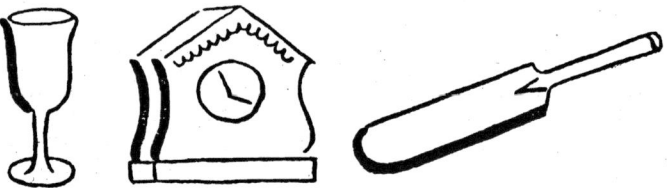

as these test outlines should be dark. The object of the game is to make a drawing of any article introducing the original outline in some way or other. The illustration given shows the idea. The heavy black lines were those given at the outset.

THE FEWEST STROKES

The idea behind this artistic competition is to make a suggestive design, that can be easily recognised as a definite

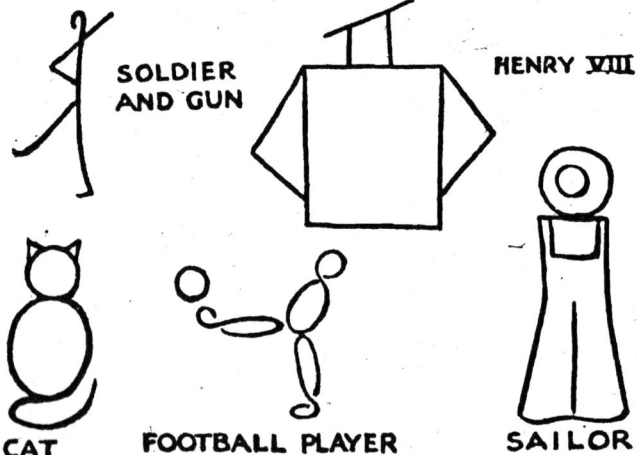

thing, with the fewest possible strokes of the pencil. Thus a circle, curve or square would count one stroke. The accompanying designs will show the idea, and we may mention that humour is essential.

PARTY GAMES FOR ALL

FUNNY FACES

This is a very amusing game. Give all your friends a piece of paper and a pencil. Tell them to draw a circle on it or, perhaps, you will feel disposed to put the circles on the sheets, before distributing them.

Then, allow your friends two minutes in which to turn the

circles into funny faces. They may do anything they like, put in as many lines as they please, and so on; the only rule is that they must stop at the end of two minutes.

The diagram given here may be shown to the competitors, before starting, as the kind of drawing that is wanted.

THE DWARF WITCH

Here, we have something which, if trouble is taken to prepare properly, will not only create laughter and bewilderment among the little ones, but will also mystify the grown-ups. Some time back we saw this " business " performed at a party, and the whole audience was amazed. Perhaps it would be well to relate it exactly as we witnessed it on that occasion.

The scene was a dining-room with a bay window, across which were drawn heavy curtains, meeting in the middle. A small table was placed where the curtains met, the leg of

the table being hidden by a table cloth, which was pinned
around. Two people performed the trick. One had his
face made up like an old witch with long grey hair and witch's
hat. The same person had placed a pair of socks on his hands
so that the upper part extended well over the wrists, and his
hands into slippers. A dark red pinafore was pinned round
to look like a skirt and bodice. He stood behind the table

CURTAIN

where the curtains met, putting his slippered hands on the
table. The curtains were pinned just behind his head, and
directly under the table, so that all the audience could see
was the head down to the hands, which were resting on the
table to represent feet. Now the witch was complete, all
but the arms and hands. The other person, standing behind,
then pushed his arms through the armholes of the pinafore,
but only just far enough to appear in keeping with the size

of the witch—just sufficient to enable the hands to reach the witch's face. A pair of long mittens were next placed on the wrists. We then had a perfect dwarf. The voice was disguised, and the hands moved in harmony with what was being said. Now and then the hand was raised to scratch the head or face; and when the witch coughed, the hand was raised to the mouth. Fortunes were told, people coming right up to the dwarf and placing their hands in hers without

Long Apron or Curtain

detecting the trick. The two actors used their imagination, and the old witch chuckled, laughed, and danced with her slippered hands, to the delight of all.

It is well to have a stage-manager, who might announce early in the evening that the hostess had engaged the famous witch "Zaza," measuring only two feet in height, and whose age was a hundred and fifty-six, to tell the fortune of anyone in the room. This will give rise to much speculation and wonderment, and all will be looking forward to the time when she will appear.

58 **FUN BOOK**

When this time arrives, set chairs for the grown-ups and a few for the children. The manager should then make an appropriate speech, and at its conclusion say, " Now I will introduce to you the wonder of the age—the renowned witch ' Zaza ' "—at the same time drawing back a little curtain, which you must fix over the witch previously. Of course, there will be much clapping of hands and roars of laughter, during which the witch must bow, chuckle and dance. Our advice is to have one or two rehearsals, when success will be certain.

A Giant may be staged in a similar manner.

ARTISTIC NONSENSE

Give each member of the party a sheet of paper and a pencil : then make all the players put five dots on their

papers, placing them anywhere they like. They must not be impossibly close, nor absurdly distant : but more or less similar to the five shown in the diagram.

When all the papers are ready, they should be collected and mixed up. Following this, they are dealt out, one to each player. The game is to draw a human being, man, woman, child or baby, using one dot for the mouth, two for the hands and two for the feet. The sketch gives a good idea of the really clever designs that can be made from almost hopeless diagrams.

DOTS, LINES AND HUMAN BEINGS

You can have a lot of fun by drawing silly little sketches, such as those we give here. You do not have to know any-

thing about the art of drawing to be able to produce some really amusing results.

Just take a soft pencil and a pad of smooth paper: then,

begin by making a dot for your victim's head, and follc
with the body. It is rather amazing how you can sugge
all sorts of effects by mere lines. Our first " study," und
which is written, *Off for the Week-end*, is obviously a ma
who is setting out with the one idea of having a good tim(
No. 2, entitled *The First Stroll*, shows him in the act of havin
that good time. The other pictures follow him through hi
week-end activities, until, at last, we see him *Homeward bound*
which reveals him "refreshed" as a result of the change

Do not copy these pictures, but make a continuous set o]
your own on a quite different theme. It will be a capital
way to have an hour's fun.

DRAWING-ROOM ACROBATICS

These simple acrobatic tricks are of more than usual interest, and they will pass a few moments very amusingly, especially if you have a few friends with you who are "keen on doing things."

Place something on the ground to form a rigid starting place, such as the edge of a carpet or a newspaper. Now, toe the line in turns : bend down, supported only by the left hand, and place a penny on the floor, with the right hand, as far away as possible. The coin must be *placed* on the floor, not tossed or thrown. Now get back to an upright position : bend down again and pick up the coin.

* * * * * * *

Toe a similar line, kneel down and get up again without touching the floor with the hands, and keeping the toes to the line.

* * * * * * *

Stand with the back against the wall, heels touching the skirting board, and pick up a shilling from the floor, placed about a foot in front. The heels and feet must not be moved.

* * * * * * *

Stand sideways against the wall, with the left heel and left hip touching it. Then, raise the right leg off the ground. As a matter of fact, it can't be done.

* * * * * * *

Hold your hands across your chest, straight out, with the tips of the forefingers pressed together. Defy anyone to hold you by your arms and pull your fingers apart.

PARTY GAMES FOR ALL

FORFEITS

At the conclusion of one or a series of party games, it is great fun to exact a penalty from those players who have failed to perform what is required of them. The performance of these penalties provides a good deal of amusement, not only for the onlookers, but for the victims themselves. Here is a capital collection of forfeits :

1. Place a poker on the ground so that you cannot jump over it. (It should lean against the wall.)
2. Bite an inch off a poker. (Hold the poker an inch from your mouth and bite.)
3. Lap up a small quantity of milk, water, etc., from a saucer dog fashion.
4. Sing a verse of a song.
5. Recite.
6. Put your right hand where your left cannot touch it. (Place it on the left elbow.)
7. Kiss the girl or boy you like best in the room.
8. Sing in one corner, cry in another, laugh in another, and dance in another.
9. Dance a jig.
10. Kiss your shadow.
11. Kiss a book inside and out, without opening it. (Kiss a book inside the room, and then take it outside and kiss it.)
12. Place two chairs together. Take off your shoes and jump over them. (You put two chairs together, take off your shoes and jump over your shoes.)
13. Place a candle so that every one in the room but yourself can see it. (On your head.)
14. Say the alphabet backwards.
15. Hop round the room on one leg.
16. Repeat five times quickly, " The horn of the hunter was heard on the hill."
17. Touch thousands at the same time. (Place your hand on your head.)
18. Kiss yourself in the looking-glass.
19. Spell " Constantinople " backwards.
20. Put yourself through the keyhole. (Write " yourself " on a piece of paper and pass it through the keyhole.)
21. Jump over the moon. (Draw the moon on a piece of paper and jump over it.)

22. Kiss your hostess's hand.

23. Lie down on the floor, fold your arms, and get up again without unfolding them.

24. Sit upon the fire. (Write the words "the fire" on a paper, and sit on it.)

25. Leave the room with two legs and return with six. (Walk out of the room and return with a chair.)

26. Read some print, that is selected by the host, but you must look at it in a mirror.

27. Put a feather on your nose and, while keeping it there, walk round the room.

28. While blindfolded, repeat Nelson's famous signal, "England expects that every man this day will do his duty." Suitable only for ladies.

29. Imitate without laughing, four animals named by members of the party.

30. Dance with the left shoe on the right foot and right shoe on left foot.

31. Make a nosegay of any six letters, or those spelling your own name; thus for M. A. R. Y. you could choose Marigold, Anchusa, Rose and Yarrow.

32. Go round the room on one leg and one hand.

33. Someone will pretend to be selling a certain article, such as a box of matches, a postage-stamp, etc., and you have to guess what it is.

34. Walk round the room with a stiff leg, your arm in a sling and a bandage over one eye.

35. Read three or four lines from a book that is upside down.

36. Balance a box of matches on both ears and walk upstairs.

37. Peel an apple and preserve all the peel in one length.

38. Mention six things that can be bought in a chemist's shop.

39. Sit at a table and pretend to telephone to somebody about the party that is in progress.

40. Stand by a gramophone and act for one minute as though you were broadcasting for the B.B.C.

41. Take somebody upstairs and bring him down on a feather. (This is performed by fetching him a fluff of down, supported on a feather.)

42. Kiss the lady you love best without anyone knowing it; *i.e.*, kiss everybody.

PARTY GAMES FOR ALL

43. Blow a candle out blindfolded.
44. Compare somebody with something in the room. Do this cautiously, *i.e.*, Miss So-and So is like such-and-such a book because both are interesting; but she is not like the book because the book never speaks and she does.
45. Walk three times round the room with your coat turned inside out, a paper hat on your head, and a walking-stick on your shoulder to imitate a soldier.
46. Spell some long word, such as Constantinople or Deuteronomy, but omit all the vowels.
47. Answer "yes" or "no" to four questions of which you are ignorant. Questions and answers are then read aloud to the company.
48. Do the opposite to six things you are told to do.
49. Take a word set you and use every letter, first, as the initial letter of a good quality and then as the initial letter of a bad quality, thus:

Good.	Bad.
Amiable.	Avaricious.
Unselfish.	Ungainly.
Nice.	Naughty.
Thoughtful.	Tiresome.

50. Make your will without knowing what it is that you are leaving. All you do is to suggest the person who is to have the legacy. The things and recipients are then read out aloud.
51. Repeat the twice and three times table, one item of each alternately; thus, twice one are two, three ones are three, twice two are four, three twos are six, etc.
52. Say any verse of poetry, uttering the odd-numbered lines out aloud and acting the even ones in dumb-show.
53. While blindfolded, draw the face of a watch and put in the twelve figures.
54. Rub one hand up and down your coat or dress, and near the other hand across. Ten times each, but they are to be done simultaneously.
55. Revolve one hand in a circle, the other in a circle, so; but the two circles to be in opposite directions.
56. Walk round the room with three boxes or books on your head.
57. Roll up a piece of string or wool with one hand.
58. Make up a sentence so that the initial letters follow

in alphabetical order: thus, "A boy can disturb everybody frightfully . . ."

59. Make up a perfect woman from those present. Thus, you name one girl's nose, another's hair, and so on.

60. Stand against the wall, with your heels touching the skirting board, and try to touch your toes with your fingers, by bending at the waist, not at the knees.

61. Select anyone in the room and make them laugh within one minute, by facial contortions.

62. While blindfolded, guess who it is holding your hand. The person must answer your questions; but in an assumed voice, if they like.

FUN AT THE DESSERT TABLE

What a lot of things can be made out of the good fare provided at the dessert table! There is no doubt that, with a little ingenuity, you will be able to amuse your friends to quite an amazing extent. Look at the pictures here. They are all things that you will be able to put together with no great amount of trouble.

No 1 is a litter of little pigs. The bodies are bananas. Choose those with nice curved sides so that the creatures may appear to have round backs. The ears are shavings cut out of almonds, while the curly tails are little twisted bits of apple. The eyes are slits in the skin with tiny pieces of dark apple peel fitted into them. The straw is apple, shredded.

No. 2 is a bunny's head. Select a pear of suitable shape for this model. Provide the ears by curling up two thin slices of apple. Make a hole in which to force them, by using the prong of a fork. The eyes are two tiny sweets, embedded in the pear. Cut out a strip of the skin to form the mouth The body-part is half an orange, with a piece cut out to allow the pear to rest on it.

No. 3 is a ship. Really, it is half a walnut. The mast are straight stalks of Muscatel raisins, and the sails are thi slices of apple. Waves, if required, may be formed by cuttir wavy strips of apple.

No. 4 is a boat, such as the Romans used. It is nothin more than a suitable banana skin, with dead matches thread through holes, to serve as oars.

No. 5 is a grotesque boy. His body is formed by cutti

the ends from a banana, while his head is a grape. Select one fixed to a stalk. Ram the stalk into the pulp of the banana. The hands are cut out of almonds, and the round buttons are shaped from some of the pieces left over. The scarf is twisted apple shavings, and the boots are bits of orange peel.

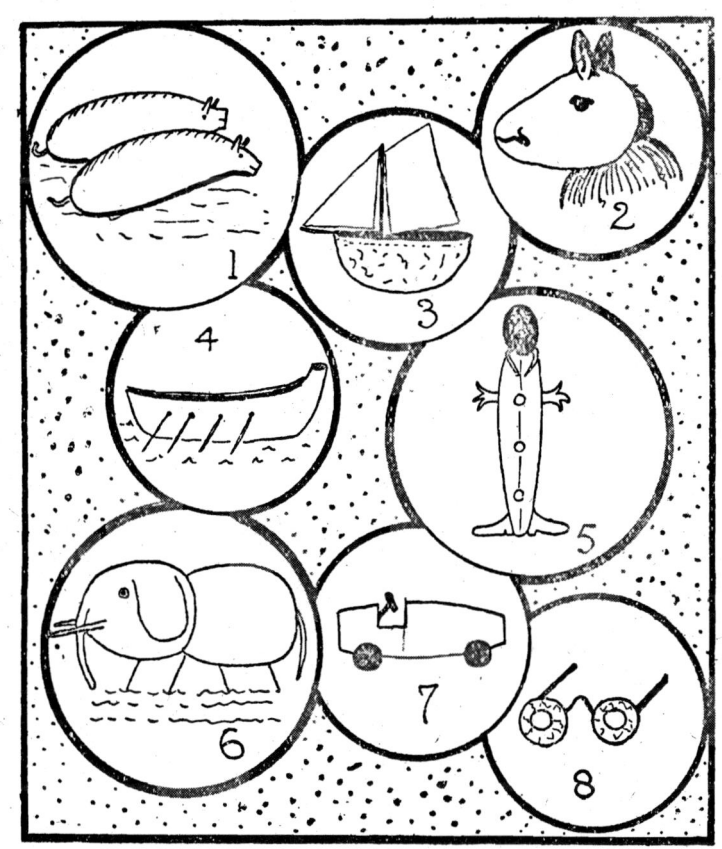

No. 6 is an elephant of sorts. The head and body are two oranges, fixed by introducing two dead matches into the skins. Lift up a piece of skin to make each ear. The tusks are pointed almonds, and the trunk is a curly piece of apple peel. The eyes are small sweets. Stand this creature on banana legs.

No. 7 is a racing car. The body is a banana with the ends cut off. Slice thin pieces off the unwanted ends and use them for wheels. Cut out a place for the driver, and shape the driving wheel out of a slice of banana and a match.

No. 8 is a pair of goggles, made from two half walnut shells, pierced with a nut-pick. The frame is made of thin strips of tough paper.

Additional shapes and things, we leave to your own ingenuity.

CONUNDRUMS WORTH ASKING

There is a laugh in each of these conundrums. Read them over yourself first of all, and then try them on your friends.

When were there only two vowels?
In the time of Noah (no A), which was before U and I were known.
Why is a waiter like a racehorse?
Because he runs for cups, plates and steaks (stakes).
Why doesn't it matter if a beggar wears a very short coat?
Because it will be long enough before he gets another.
Why is coal a tricky thing to buy?
Because when bought, it generally goes to the cellar.
What is most like a horse's shoe?
His other shoes.
Why are tall people more lazy than short ones?
Because they are always longer in bed.
Why is it absurd to ask a pretty girl to be candid?
Because she cannot be plain.
Why are washerwomen great travellers?
They are continually "crossing the line" and going from pole to pole.
What is the difference between a rejected lover and a devoted husband?
One misses the kisses and the other kisses the missus.
Why are seeds, planted in the soil, like a gate-post?
They both propagate.
What is the difference between a riddle and a lot of children sitting on a bun?
One is a conundrum and the other is a bun under 'em.
Why is there nothing so modest as a watch?
Because it is always running down its own works.
Why does the collector, at the railway station, punch a hole in your ticket?
To let you pass through.

Why is it bed-time immediately after tea?
Because when T (tea) is gone, night is nigh.
Why is the first chicken of a brood like the mainmast of a ship?
Because it is a little in front of the main hatch.
What is the difference between a bottle of medicine and a hearthrug?
One is shaken up and taken, and the other is taken up and shaken.
What is the best way to keep a woman's love?
Not to return it.
Why is a policeman like a rainbow?
Because he appears after the storm is over.
Why is the sun cruel?
Because it tans so many women.
When is a ten-shilling note of no value?
When compared with a pound note, because it is worth-less.
Why has a horse six legs?
Because it has fore legs in front and two behind.
On which side of a jug is the handle?
On the outside.
Why is a dog warmer in summer than in winter?
Because in winter, it has a coat, and in the summer it has the same coat and pants.
What is the difference between a camera and the measles?
One makes fac-similes and the other makes sick families.
What key is the hardest to turn?
A donkey.
Why is the alphabet like a philosopher?
They both end off with a YZ.
Why is Dartmoor like a person with a good memory?
Because it has great powers of retention.
Why is a sculptor's death a most terrible one?
Because he makes faces and busts.
Why is a dog's tail like the inside of a tree?
Because it a farthest from the bark.
Why is a fishmonger greedy?
Because his business makes him sell-fish.
Why does a baby boy always receive a splendid welcome?
Because he never comes a-miss.
What is the difference between sixteen ounces of tea and a girl using a typewriter?
One weighs a pound and the other pounds away.

CONUNDRUMS WORTH ASKING

Why is a horse cleverer than a mouse?
Because it can run away when in a trap.
If 32 degrees is freezing point, what is squeezing point?
Two in the shade.
Why is the word " kiss " spelt with two s's?
Because it takes two to complete the spell.
What is the difference between one yard and two yards?
A fence.
What is it that, when you knock out one eye, has only the nose left?
Noise.
How many peas are there in a pint?
One.
Who always finds things dull?
The knife grinder.
Why is a benevolent man like a cart horse?
He always stops at the sound of woe.
Which is the right side of a wedding cake?
The side that has been eaten because the other is left.
What were the first words Adam said to Eve?
No one can tell.
What beats a good wife?
A bad husband.
Which travels faster, heat or cold?
Heat, because you frequently catch cold.
Which is the cleanest letter in the alphabet?
H, because it is always in the midst of " washing."
Who may marry and yet live single all his life?
A clergyman.
Why is it impossible for a butcher to be honest?
Because he steels all the knives he uses.
What smells most in a chemist's shop?
The nose.
What is a kiss?
Nothing, divided by two.
How can we be certain that Eve was not the first woman?
Because Adam was the first made (maid).
Why is it so risky to get married?
Because the bride is generally miss-taken and miss-led.
When may a man be said to be older than he is?
When he is knocked into the middle of next week.
Which is the oldest wine you can get?
The Elder wine.

What is the difference between a cat and a document?
One has claws at the end of its paws; the other has pauses at the end of its clauses.
What is the difference between a bishop and a pickpocket?
The bishop watches the see and the pickpocket seizes the watch.
Why is the word " reference " like Ceylon?
They both contain many Cingalese (single E's).
Why are stone-deaf people like Dutch cheeses?
Because we cannot make them here.
Why is a pound, paid to you by a bookie, a guinea?
Because it is one pound won (one).
What is the difference between a tenant and the son of a widow?
The tenant has to pay rents and the son of a widow has not two parents.
Where does the Bible speak of the inside of a theatre?
Where it says that Joseph was taken from the family circle and put in the pit.
Why would a sparrow be angry if you called it a pheasant?
Because you would be making game of it.
What is the difference between a water pipe and a mad Dutchman?
One is a hollow cylinder and the other a silly Hollander.
Why is a cook more noisy than a squalling baby?
The youngster makes a din while the cook makes a dinner.
What part of a horse is like a new-born baby?
The tail, because it was never seen before.
What are the three degrees of comparison for a sharp lawyer?
First he gets on; then he gets honour; finally he gets honest.
Can you change a girl into a woman by adding three letters?
A.G.E.
What happened to the baby who swallowed a spoon?
It couldn't stir.
What is it that a blind man cannot feel but can see?
A good joke.
When did London begin with an L and end with an E?
They always have done so; " London " begins with an L and " End " with an E.
Why is a novelist a queer creature?
Because his tale (tail) comes out of his head.
What relation is a child to its father who is not its father's own son?
His daughter.

CONUNDRUMS WORTH ASKING

What animals grow on vines?
Gra(y) -apes.
When do you breakfast before you get up?
When you have a roll and a turn-over in bed.
What has four legs and flies?
Two birds.
Can you say how long girls should be loved?
The same as short girls.
What is worse than having a hole in your stocking?
Having one in each stocking.
Can February March?
No, but April May.
What is as bad as a hen stealing?
A cock robin.
How many days belong to a year?
325. The rest are Lent.
Why is the letter D like a wedding ring?
WE could not be WED without it.
Why is the letter G like matrimony?
Because it is the end of courting.
What does an artist like to draw best?
His salary, of course.
What is it we all often say we will do, and nobody has ever done yet?
Stop a minute.
Why may St. George be considered a careful driver?
He never appears without a drag-on.
What kind of tea makes one's head the lightest?
Insanity.
When does a Scotchman resemble a donkey?
When he stands on his banks and braes.
How did the whale that swallowed Jonah obey the divine law?
Jonah was a stranger and he took him in.
Why do you suppose that a glassblower can make the letter D gallop?
Because we know that he can make a D canter (decanter).
Why is a man who grumbles like an overbaked loaf?
They are both crusty.
What kind of portrait can be spelt with three letters?
Effigy (FEG).
Why are Algiers and Malta opposite?
There is a dey (day) in one and a knight (night) in the other.

What river in the north of England reminds you of naughty
  girls?
Tees (tease).
Why is a theological student like a very keen merchant?
They both study the profits (prophets).
If the alphabet were invited out, when ought U, V, W, X, Y
  and Z to go?
After T.
Why are birds in spring like a banking establishment?
*They issue promissory notes and rejoice when the branches are
  flourishing.*
Why is the water of a fountain like the Prince of Wales?
One is thrown into the air, the other is heir to the throne.
What most effectually checks a fast man?
A bridal.
Why is picking a pocket like painting?
It is a work of art requiring design and delicacy of touch.
Why is part of Buckinghamshire like an ox-goad?
It goes to Oxon and Herts. (oxen and hurts).
What requires more philosophy than taking things as they
  come?
Parting with things as they go.
Why are Government clerks like the fountains in Trafalgar
  Square?
Because they generally play from ten till four.
Why is a cow's tail like a swan's breast?
It grows down.
Why is there never such a thing as one whole day?
Because every day begins by breaking.
What reason is there to believe that Othello was really a
  lawyer?
Because he was a tawny general (attorney general) of Venice.
Why is a pretty girl like a muffin?
She is often toasted.
Why are good women like ivy?
The greater the ruin the closer they cling.
Why is an alligator a most deceitful animal?
He takes you in with an open countenance.
What is the difference between a very wet day and a lion distracted with toothache?
One is pouring with rain and the other roaring with pain.
Why is a bar of Margate rock like a racehorse?
Because the more you lick it the faster it goes.

CONUNDRUMS WORTH ASKING

Why does a duck go under water, and why does it come out again?
It goes under for DIVER'S *reasons and comes out again for sun-dry (sundry) purposes.*

What is the difference between a man going upstairs and one looking up the stairs?
The first is stepping up the stairs and the second is staring up the steps.

What is the difference between a lighted candle in a cave and a dance in an inn?
The first is a taper in a cavern and the second is a caper in a tavern.

Why is a plum cake like the sea?
Because they both contain a lot of currents (currants).

Why is it legally wrong to condemn a deaf man?
Because the law does not allow a man to be convicted without a hearing.

What is the difference between an auction sale and being sea-sick?
One is the sale of effects and the other the effects of a sail.

Why is an assassin like a happy man?
They both take life cheerfully.

Why is a vote in Parliament like a cold?
Because either the eyes (ayes) have it or the nose (noes).

If a man split his sides with laughter, what ought he to do?
Run till he got a stitch in his side.

Why is a good actor like a good architect?
Because they both draw good houses.

When is an original idea like a clock?
When it strikes one.

What is the difference between a blacksmith and a reliable horse?
One is a horse-shoer and the other a sure horse.

Why are policemen and postmen like the days of man?
Because they are numbered.

When is a silver cup most likely to run away?
When it is chased.

Why is the cashier at a bank a well-informed man?
Because he is constantly taking notes.

Why was Adam a good runner?
Because he was the first in the human race.

If a chicken could talk, why would it always swear?
Because it could only use fowl language.

Why is it wrong to use bad language in a cornfield?
Because there are so many ears there that will certainly be shocked.
What was it that Adam planted first in the Garden of Eden?
His foot.
What is the medicine which a man takes when he has to scold his wife?
He takes an elixir (he takes and he licks her).
What is taken from you before you get it?
Your portrait.
Why is a vain young lady like a drunkard?
They are both too fond of a glass.
What was it that Adam never saw, never had, yet provided two for each of his children?
Parents.
How long did Cain hate his brother?
As long as he was able.
Why would you be justified in picking the pockets of a dealer in engravings?
Because he has pictures (picked yours).
What disease is likely to affect reapers on a hot day?
A drop-sickle affection.
Why is a pulled-out tooth like a thing forgotten?
Because it is out of the head.
Why is the letter A like a sweet-smelling flower?
A bee (B) comes after it.
Why is a gooseberry pie like a George I penny?
Neither of them is current (currant).
Why are most conundrums like things brought to us from Australia?
Because they are far-fetched.
What trade does the sun follow in the summer time?
That of a tanner.
Why are pretty girls like fireworks?
Because they soon go off.
When is a bill like a rifle?
When it is presented and discharged.
Which is the favourite word with women?
The last one.
When does a dog become larger and smaller?
When let out at night and taken in in the morning.
What kind of bridge causes the most anxiety?
A suspension bridge.

CONUNDRUMS WORTH ASKING

Why is a sentinel going his rounds like a drunken Irishman?
They are both Pat-rolling.
When are roads like corpses?
When they are mended (men dead).
What part of a fish is like the end of a book?
The fin-is.
What fish is most valued by a married lady?
Her-ring.
What is the difference between a tree and an aeroplane?
One sheds its leaves and the other leaves its sheds.
What is the difference between a cow and a rickety chair?
The cow gives milk and the chair gives way (whey).
Why is the letter G like the sun?
Because it is the centre of light.
What is the difference between a sailor in gaol and a blind man?
The one cannot go to sea and the other cannot see to go.
Why are sheep of obviously bad character?
They gamble, they spend most of their time on the turf and the best of them are black legs. In mitigation, it may be said however, that they are fleeced every year.
Why is a pig like the letter N?
Because it makes a sty nasty.
When do your teeth do what your tongue is intended for?
When they chatter.
Why is the sun like a man about town?
Because they both turn night into day.
Why is St. Paul's Cathedral like a bird's nest?
Because it was built by a Wren.
What business never progresses?
The stationery business.
Why is a horse a very amiable animal?
Because it can stand a lot of chaff.
Why is a newspaper boy never cold?
Because selling papers maintains the circulation.
Why does a puss purr?
For an obvious pur-puss.
Why were Lord Lytton and Charles Dickens the two most industrious people that ever lived?
Lytton wrote " Night and Morning " and Dickens edited " All the Year Round."
Why is the Prince of Wales like thundery weather?
He is sure to rain (reign).

Why is a man who is being hanged better off than a tramp?
He has visible means of support which the tramp hasn't.
Why are cats like unskilful surgeons?
Because they mew till late (mutilate) and destroy patience (patients).
Why cannot flies see in the winter time?
Because they leave their " specs " behind them in the summer.
Why is twice ten the same as twice eleven?
Because twice ten is twenty and twice eleven is twenty-two. (twenty, too).
What kind of tables do we cook and eat?
Vegetables.
Why is the end of G never short?
Because it always ends " long."
What is the difference between weather when it is slightly foggy and a gentleman?
One is a mist and the other a mister.
What is that which occurs once in every minute, twice in a moment, but not once in a year?
The letter M.
When does a caterpillar grow good?
When it turns over a new leaf.
What is the difference between a frightened child and a shipwrecked sailor?
One clings to his ma and the other to his spar (his pa).
Why is a lady's jumper like a piece of orange peel?
Because they are both easy to slip on.
Why is a policeman like an aeroplane?
They both take people up.
Why is the letter F like a banana skin?
Because they both make all fall.
Why is a pig a curious creature?
Because you can't cure it before it is killed.
When is a rock not a rock?
When it is shamrock.
What key is best for unlocking the tongue?
Whisky.
What is that which you must keep after you have given it to somebody?
Your word.
What did Adam and Eve do when they were turned out of the Garden of Eden?
They raised Cain.

CONUNDRUMS WORTH ASKING

When a black man dies, what do his relations do?
Go a black burying.
Why is it wrong to speak of the number 288?
Because it is too (two) gross.
Why is the letter W like a scandalmonger?
Because it makes ill-will.
Why is a caterpillar like a greedy boy?
Because they both make the butter fly.
How may book-keeping be learnt quickly?
By remembering the maxim, " Never lend books."
What is the worst kind of fare for people to live on?
Warfare.
Why are old maids like volunteers?
They are always ready but seldom wanted.
What men are most above-board in their movements?
Chessmen.
Why is it that when you hunt for something mislaid, you always find it in the last place you look?
Because you do not go on looking when it is found.
What is the principal part of a horse?
The mane part.
What letter would be of great use to a deaf woman?
The letter A, because it would make " her " " hear."
Why is the letter S like a person who is always cheeky?
Because it begins and ends in sauciness.
Where is it that all pretty girls are equally pretty?
In the dark.
What two " beaux " does every girl have near at hand?
Elbows.
When is a beautiful girl like a post-office van?
When transporting the males.
What is it that we often return but never borrow?
Thanks.
What is the first thing you do when you fall into the sea?
Get wet.
Why is a horse like the letter O?
Because gee (G) makes it go.
Why is a king like a book?
Because he has pages.
What is as wonderful as a horse that can count?
A spelling bee.
At what age should a man marry?
Somewhere round the parsonage.

If I were in the sun and you were out of it, what would the sun be?
Sin.
Why is a 'varsity man like a thermometer?
Because he is graduated and marked by degrees.
What did the whale obtain by his little business with Jonah?
It got all the prophet (profit).
When is a ship sentimental?
When it hugs the shore.
What most frequently becomes a woman?
A girl.
Why is an egg like a colt?
It is no use until broken in.
Why is an empty purse a symbol of constancy?
Because there is no change in it.
What goes from London to Brighton without moving?
The railway line.
When is a soldier generous?
When he presents alms.
What makes the Pilgrim's Progress painful?
A Bunion.
Why will there be no men with beards in Heaven?
Because men will only get into Heaven by a close shave.
When do wives think their husbands are like Hercules?
When they constantly use their clubs.
What most resembles half a cheese?
The other half.
Why is a trouser button like an event that is constantly happening?
They are both continually coming off.
When is a smack like a hat?
When it's felt.
How many foreigners make a man bad mannered?
Forty poles make one rood.
Why is a young spendthrift like the letter Y?
He makes pa pay.
Why is an angry man like 59 minutes past 12?
He's going to strike one.
What tree is never beautiful?
The plane tree.
What is the difference between a bankrupt and a feather bed?
One is hard-up and the other soft down.

Why is a miser like a man with a bad memory?
He is always for getting.
What are the most unsociable things in the world?
Milestones. You never see two together.
Why should hungry people go to the Sahara?
Because of the sand which is (sandwiches) there.
When is a penny like a hermit?
When it is a loan.
Why should Ireland soon be rich?
Because its capital is Dublin.
When should you lose your temper?
When it is a bad temper.

PUZZLES

THE LABELS ON THE TRUNK

A dear old lady travelled about a good deal and her trunk became plastered with luggage labels bearing the names of the stations at which she had stopped. The labels, in course of time, became torn. Some were damaged on the left-hand end, some on the right, and some at both ends. When she looked at them from one to the other, the pieces read as follows: " Old Aunt came bang over the hatstand." What places had she visited?

Oldham, Taunton, Camelford, Bangor, Andover, Thetford and Whatstandwell.

THE NINE BOTTLES IN A ROW

Once upon a time, a man had a dishonest servant who used to help herself to the wine. The bottles went with uncanny regularity and, at last, the man determined to set a trap. He had at that particular moment twenty-eight bottles in a certain store and, so that he could tell at once if any were taken, he arranged them as shown in the diagram.

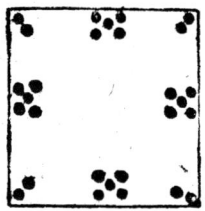

He laid special stress on the fact that there were nine bottles along each side of the bin. Apparently, the servant perceived his plans; so when she helped herself to four bottles she re-arranged the remainder so that there were still nine bottles along each side. Not only that, a little later she took four more bottles and again arranged the remainder so that there were nine bottles along each row. How did she place the remainder on the two occasions?

The first diagram shows how the servant arranged the bottles when there were 24 left and the second when there

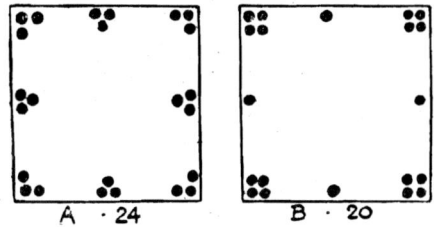

were 20. Note that there were, on both occasions, nine bottles along each side.

THE SIGNPOST

This little problem might come in handy some day when you are out motoring or walking in the country.

A man was going along a quiet road where nobody was about. After a while he came to a cross road and did not know which direction to take. He looked about and found that a signpost was lying on the ground; it had been knocked over by a careless motorist. As it no longer pointed in any direction, it did not help him much. Suddenly, a bright idea came to him. He looked at the post and muttered to himself, " I see," and then set off along the road which took him to his destination. How did he select the right road?

He knew where he had come from and that place was marked on the capsized sign-post. So, in his mind, he stood up the post with that place pointing to the way he had come. He could then tell to which roads the other arms pointed.

THE WATER BUTT

Two farm labourers were having an altercation about a water butt. One said that it was not nearly half full and the other claimed that it was more than half full. The argument got so heated that the matter had to be settled one way or the other. There were no other vessels at hand to help in measuring the water, so they turned to the farmer who came along at that moment and asked his opinion. " Can't tell, off-hand," said the farmer, " but I can soon find out," and he did. How did he do it?

The farmer tilted the butt until the water just came up to the top edge without any running over. As the level of the water did not reach the point X, the butt was not

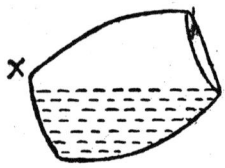

half full. If it had just reached X, it would have been exactly half full, but if the point X had been submerged by the water, the butt would have been more than half full.

THE BROKEN CLOCK-FACE

Somebody dropped an unfortunate clock on the floor and broke the face, shown here, into four pieces. When the bits were picked up, it was noticed that the numbers on all the separate pieces added up to the same amount. What was the amount and, on the accompanying illustration, show how the broken pieces were shaped.

Each piece of the clock face had figures adding up to twenty.

Piece No. 1 had printed on it X and X of XI.

Piece No. 2 had printed on it the I of XI, then XII, I, II, III and the first I of IIII.

Piece No. 3 had printed on it the last three ones of IIII, then V, VI, and VI of VII.

Piece No. 4 had printed on it the last I of VII, VIII and IX, the latter when read upside down being XI.

THE WIRELESS CABINET

A boy was making a wireless cabinet and he wanted a square piece of wood to finish the job. He looked about and found that he had run short of material. All he could find was a piece of board like that shown in the diagram.

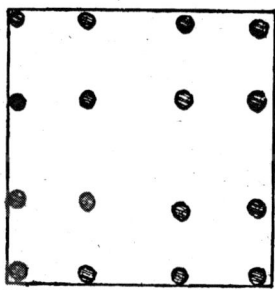

It was just four times as big as the piece he needed for the cabinet, but, unfortunately, it had been drilled with a number of holes. Now, how could he cut the piece he wanted out of this damaged square of wood? Naturally, he had to avoid all the holes.

He cut a square "diamond" out of the centre, thus:

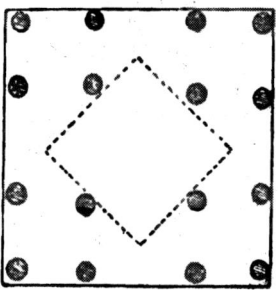

THE BOOK WORM

You know how books are placed side by side on a bookshelf. A friend of ours has an encyclopædia which is in three volumes. The other day he took them down from the shelf and found that one of those little creatures which infest books had eaten its way through the volumes. It had made a tunnel from the first page of the first volume to the last page of the last volume. What we want to know is exactly how far it had travelled. The covers of the books are a quarter of an inch thick and the pages in each book together make another inch.

Before reading the detailed working, it will be well to look at the diagram. Note that page 1 of volume 1 is on

the right of the book and that the last page of the last volume is on the left of the book. Therefore, the tunnel did not affect the pages of either of these volumes. It went through four covers, measuring an inch, and through the pages of Volume 2, measuring another inch, two inches in all.

WHAT THEY MAKE

Here is a little juggling with figures which will amuse your friends for a few moments. Ask them to write down four fives so that they make 100. Of course, the solution will be fairly obvious; it is $(5+5) \times (5+5)$. Then, try them with this one. How can four eights be written so as to make 100? The solution is $\dfrac{8}{\cdot 8} \times \dfrac{8}{\cdot 8}$

Point eight is, of course, eight-tenths and then the rest of the working will be obvious to any schoolboy. Lastly ask your friends to write down four nines so as to equal 100.

Here is the solution $99 \dfrac{9}{9}$

HOW DID THEY DO IT?

Two French workmen were clearing out some vats in a factory where wine was made, and they came across a full eight-gallon cask that for some reason or other had not been sold. Just at that moment the proprietor came along and, being a bit of a sportsman, he said to the workmen. " You can have that cask of wine for yourselves if you can share it equally between you, using only these two measures." and he handed them a three-gallon and a five-gallon measure. They were a little puzzled at first, but they managed the job all right and halved the wine. How did they do it?

This is the solution. The steps show how they poured the wine from one measure to the other.

8 gall.	3 gall.	5 gall.
8	0	0
3	0	5
3	3	2
6	2	0
1	2	5
1	3	4
4	0	4

One workman had his half of the wine in the eight-gallon cask and the other in the five-gallon measure.

THE FARMER'S HORSES

A farmer died and left behind him three sons and nineteen horses. In his will, the worthy man gave directions that the eldest son was to inherit half the horses; the next son was to have a quarter of the nineteen horses; and the youngest son was to have a fifth of the nineteen horses. But—and this was laid down very emphatically—none of the horses was to be slain in order to help in the division. Of course, it is not easy to divide 19 into two, four or even five parts without a remainder. Nevertheless, it was done in a few moments by a neighbouring farmer who happened to ride up just as the brothers were at their wits' end. How did he do it?

The farmer rode up, jumped off his own horse and put it with the nineteen, making twenty. Then he gave half the horses (10) to the eldest brother, a quarter (5) to the second brother and a fifth (4) to the youngest brother. The

10, 5 and 4 horses made 19. The twentieth horse was his own, upon which he remounted and departed. Now, the question is: How was it possible for him to add his own horse to the others, do the dividing exactly as required by the will, and have his own horse returned to him at the end? Simply because a half, a quarter, and a fifth do not add up to unity.

THE FIELD WITH A FENCE

The following problem baffles a good many people because the answer seems to be so obvious. It is just this. A mile of wire fencing exactly encloses a field of 40 acres. What size field will be enclosed by two miles of wire fencing?

As often as not, the answer is given as 80 acres. But this is wrong. Draw a plan of the field and you will see that the two miles of fencing will enclose four times as much space as the one mile. Therefore the answer is 160 acres.

THE ROLL OF CLOTH

Here is another problem of much the same character as the last. A man has ninety yards of cloth in a single roll. He wants to divide it up into ninety lengths of one yard each. He finds that he takes three seconds to cut each length. How long does he take to cut all the ninety pieces?

A favourite answer is ninety times three, or two hundred and seventy seconds. This, of course, is incorrect, because the ninety pieces are obtained by eighty-nine cuts, just as a length of two yards requires only one cut. Thus eighty-nine multiplied by three gives 267 seconds, which is the correct answer.

CUPS AND SAUCERS

The other day, we came across two cups and a saucer in the kitchen. Just for something to do we weighed each of the three pieces. On noting their various weights, we found that they possessed this peculiarity: Altogether they came to 12 ounces, but the larger cup with the saucer weighed just double the smaller cup, while the smaller cup with the saucer weighed exactly the same as the larger cup. What was the weight of each?

The larger cup weighed 6 ounces, the smaller cup 4 ounces and the saucer 2 ounces.

A CURIOUS FIGURE

Here is a curious figure. Although there are so many lines on it, it can be drawn from start to finish without lifting the pencil from the paper and without going over any part twice.

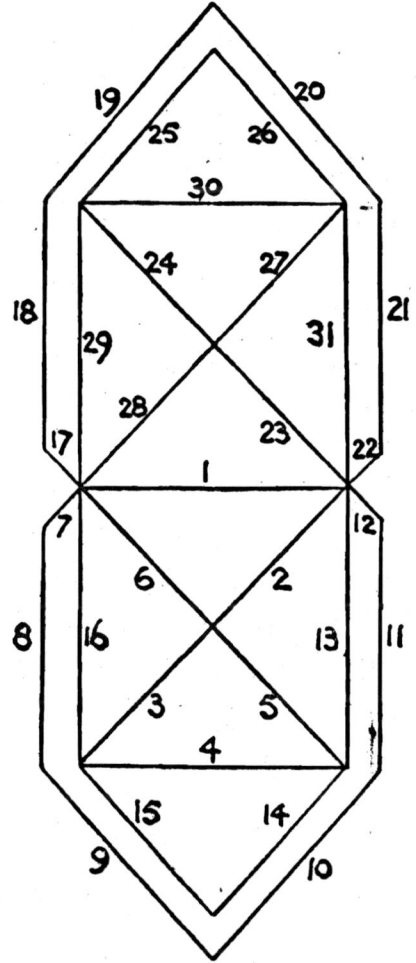

See if you can draw it yourself without looking at the numbers. Only look at them when you have had several tries and failed. After that, make up one or two involved figures on the same lines. It is quite good fun.

WHAT DID THEY COST?

This is a teaser but it can be worked out quite simply, once you stumble on the right lines.

A man buys a turkey, two ducks and three fowls for £4. The price of two ducks and three fowls is the same as three turkeys; and three fowls cost as much as two ducks. What did each creature cost?

We are told that two ducks and three fowls cost as much as three turkeys; it is obvious, therefore, that the £4 represents the price of four turkeys, or 20s. each. This leaves a balance of £3. But if three fowls cost as much as two ducks, each lot must cost 30s.—one half of the £3. Therefore each duck costs 15s. and each fowl 10s. Quite simple isn't it?—no elaborate calculations needed.

THE WILL OF THE OLD LADY

An old lady died and, when her will was read, it was found that she left £333 to be divided equally between two fathers and their two sons. She also mentioned that each was to receive £111. The lawyer was puzzled and concluded that a mistake had been made. The old lady was not so silly after all. Her arithmetic was quite correct. What is the explanation?

There were only three people. There were two fathers and two sons, it is true. But one of the sons was also a father, *i.e.*, they were son, father, and grandfather.

THE FIFTEEN GAME

Though apparently quite simple, this puzzle is really very

9	11	3	7
8	14	10	15
6	12	13	2
5	1	4	

1	2	3	4
5	6	7	8
9	10	11	12
13	14	15	

difficult of solution. Fifteen cubes of wood, severally marked from 1 to 15, are placed indifferently in a box made to hold sixteen, as shown in the diagrams.

PUZZLES

The puzzle consists in sliding the cubes from square to square, without lifting them or removing them from the box, until they are arranged in their natural order. It is easy enough to move the squares up to 12; but to get the last three into order is often a puzzle.

Note that at the outset, the squares should be placed in any order.

Although this game is properly played with a box containing the cubes of wood, the same results are obtained by cutting up a postcard into fifteen squares with one-inch sides,—then numbering them and placing them on a sheet of paper marked out and numbered as in the right half of the diagram.

THE THIRTY-SIX COINS

If you are thinking of trying this amusing puzzle on your friends, be provided with three shillings' worth of pennies, or you may perhaps have some counters at hand to serve instead. We have performed it with thirty-six cards out of a pack of playing cards. You first set out the coins or cards in a square, six in a row, six rows deep, and then ask if any member of the company can take away six coins or cards so that the rows that are left all contain an even number whether reckoned vertically, horizontally, or diagonally. There will be many who will attempt the problem but few, if any, will succeed correctly.

The solution is as follows, reckoning horizontally:
1. Do not alter rows 1, 2, and 3.
2. Remove coins 5 and 6 in row 4.
3. Remove coins 4 and 5 in row 5.
4. Remove coins 4 and 6 in row 6.

You will then have removed six coins and every row, as it now stands, whether taken horizontally, vertically, or diagonally, contains an even number of pieces. [Do not forget to count your money after the problem has been performed.]

TO DISCOVER A PERSON'S AGE

Let a person put down the number of the month in which he was born, thus: January 1, February 2, March 3, April 4, May 5, etc. Double this number. Add 5. Multiply by 50.

Add age last birthday. Subtract 365. Add 115. He must then tell you the figures that are left as a result of the operation. If there are two figures, the last will be the age and the first will be the month in which he was born. If there are three figures, the last two will be his age and the first will be the month. If there are four figures, the last two will be his age and the first two will be the month.

Example :

Born in July	7th month
Multiply by 2	14
Add 5	19
Multiply by 50	950
Add age, 16	966
Subtract 365	601
Add 115	716

Result : July (7), aged 16.

A MULTIPLICATION SUM

Great interest is being taken in puzzles of this character of late. All you have to do is to find the appropriate figures which are replaced by stars.

```
    *1*
    2*5
    ───
   1*7*
   2*0*
   *3*
   ─────
   8*6*5
```

The answer is ı

```
    315
    275
    ────
   1575
   2205
   630
   ─────
  86625
```

A DIVISION SUM

This is like the above in so much as you are required to find the missing figures.

```
        *1*)86*2*(*7*
            6*0
            ---
            **6*
            2**5
            ---
            *57*
            1***
            ---
            ....
```

The answer is:
```
        315)86625(275
            630
            ---
            2362
            2205
            ---
            1575
            1575
            ---
            ....
```

ANOTHER DIVISION SUM

Here is a division sum, not quite like the ordinary ones. Just find out what figures are represented by the letters. Note that the same letter is always represented by the same figure.

```
        AB)CDEF(JBG
           GC
           --
           HE
           BE
           --
           AFF
           EA
           ---
           E
           ---
```

To decipher this division sum, it is best to begin at the end. In the last process of substraction, in the hundreds column, we have "nothing from A leaves nothing." That shows that A can only be one or nothing. It cannot be nothing because, in the units column A from F leaves E. Were it nothing, we should have A from F leaves F. Therefore the first letter is fixed. A=1. Now run your eye up to the middle process of subtraction. In the units column, it says E from E leaves F. Therefore F=nothing. Go back to the last process of subtraction where EA from AFF leaves E. AFF is now known to be 100 and EA is something ending with one. It is clear now that E must be nine. Again revert to the middle process of subtraction, BE from HE leaves ten. H, therefore, must be one point higher than B. We know that J times AB equals GC, and that B times AB equals BE—as E is nine, B must be three, since B times B equals nine (E). H, therefore, must be four. Now we know that B=three, the divisor reveals itself to be 13. The remainder of the sum then is clear. It is 1

13)8290(637
78
—

49
39
—

100
91
—

9
—

THOSE DOZENS

Which would you prefer, in bank notes: half a dozen dozen, or six dozen dozen?

Half a dozen dozen is seventy-two; and six dozen dozen is 864. So presumably, you would prefer the latter.

A PUZZLER

Robinson is 36 years of age. Moreover, he is twice as old as Smith was when he, Robinson, was as old as Smith is now. How old was Smith a year ago?
Answer: 26 years old.

THE SAME FIGURES

Use the same three figures, in any manner you like, so as to make thirty. Do this in three different ways.

The answer—Six multiplied by six, with six subtracted from the answer equals thirty.

Five multiplied by five, with five added to the answer makes thirty.

Three cubed with three added to the answer gives thirty.

A STRIKING CLOCK

The clock in my hall strikes the hours only. How many times does the striker hit the gong in the course of a complete day?

Answer: 156 times. (Do not forget that it goes from one to twelve, twice.)

AN IDEA FOR JIGSAW PUZZLES

Of course, you will occasionally make jigsaw puzzles if you possess a fretwork outfit. Next time you set out to cut one, do it on these novel lines. Paste the picture on to the thin wood, then turn it over and draw, in pencil, on the back, all sorts of attractive shapes, such as that of a fish, a horse's

head, a peg-top, Cinderella's slipper, a Christmas cracker, a kite, a pair of specs, and so on. Then when you cut the puzzle follow the outline of these shapes. The pieces will be far more interesting than the ordinary odd sections, and when your friends make up the puzzles they will find the task much more enjoyable. Of course you will have to cut the pieces, coming between the shapes, in the usual manner.

A PUZZLE MADE WITH GIRLS' NAMES

Here are two large squares, and, before we get any further, please put a sheet of paper over the second one, so that you will not be tempted to look at it.

RY	J	O	GG	Y	B
A	M	YC	E	TY	ET
A	NA	E	P	ED	N
DI	E	N	I	DA	A
E	H	JA	S	T	VI
L	T	E	Y	LE	O

Just examine this first square. You will see that it is made up of thirty-six small squares, each containing one or two letters of the alphabet. The letters look as though

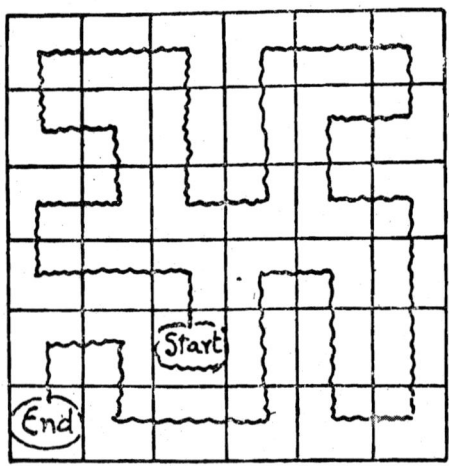

they are in a hopeless muddle—RY, J, O, GG, and so on. Nevertheless they are quite all right, but the puzzle is to read them. We are prepared to tell you this much: when read in their proper order they spell a number of girls' names—probably the names of friends of yours.

The best plan will be to make a large copy of the full square on a sheet of paper and then try to read the names. Start at any small square you think fit and then travel to any adjacent square, and continue in this way until all the squares have been visited. You may not go from one square to another unless they are adjoining, and you must not go to a square twice. If you have selected the correct starting square and have followed the correct route, the letters met on the way spell the names of a number of girls.
The second square, indicates the proper route.

THE PAPER SHAPE OF FIVE SQUARES

This is a good puzzle that will exercise your ingenuity. Draw six equal squares on a piece of stout paper, placing them in three rows of twos. Then cut them out in one piece,

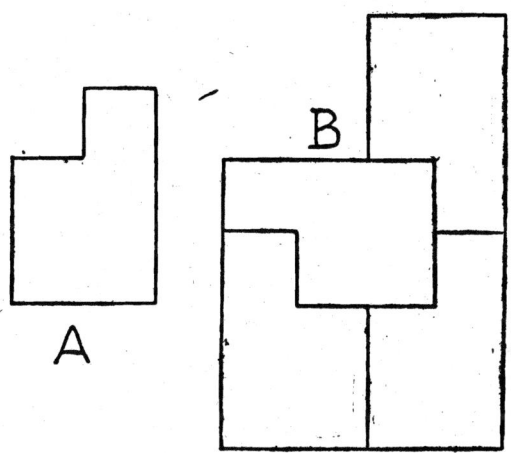

but omit to include the uppermost left-hand square. The shape will be like that shown in Diagram A. It is not a very attractive-looking piece of paper, it is true, but that hardly matters. Now what you have to do is to cut out three more of them, making four in all.

The puzzle consists in taking the four pieces and placing them together, so that the new figure, so formed, is the same shape as each piece, but considerably larger.
Diagram B shows how to do it.

A TEASING PAPER PUZZLE

Cut a square out of a stiff piece of paper and, for convenience, let each side be four inches long. Next divide all the sides into two portions, the left-hand portion being, say, one and a half inches and the right-hand portion two and a half inches. Join the marks on the opposite sides and you have a tilted cross.

Now cut along the cross lines and your square is divided into four pieces of equal size. Shuffle the pieces and get your friends to re-form the square. It is not at all an easy matter, and some of them will take a long while to coax the pieces back into a square. You will, of course, know how to do it because you did the cutting.

When they have made the square, ask them to form another and larger square with a square opening in the middle. It is done in this way: You will note that each piece has four corners, two of which are right angles. In making the original square one right angle of each of the pieces went in the corner of it. Now the other right angle of each of the pieces must be twisted so that it comes into the corner of the new square. Then you will have a larger square with a square opening in the middle.

AMUSING CARD GAMES

There are too many card games for them all to be given in a section of this book. Here we have selected about a dozen round games and a dozen patience games, which we know will provide enjoyable entertainment.

Should this selection produce a desire for more, we would recommend two very helpful books in *Foulsham's Home Library*. The first is "Card Games Up to Date," and the second, "More Card Games Up to Date." Each volume is 2s. net, and is bound in cloth.

HEARTS

Hearts is rather an ingenious game which may not inaccurately be described as "Whist upside-down." The play resembles Whist except for two important details, viz.:—

(1) There are no trumps; but hearts are the opposite thing to trumps, being the cards you hate to get and which you discard at every opportunity.

(2) In play, you aim to avoid taking any trick which contains a Heart.

Players must follow suit; and the penalty for a revoke, if revoker loses, is that he must pay up for the other losers; and if he wins, he must put his winnings into the pool.

There are usually no partners, play being each against the rest.

At the end of each hand, the players show the Hearts which are in the tricks they have taken. He with none, or the lowest number, receives from each of the others one stake for every Heart card that he (the loser) holds, together with the pool, if any.

Another method of staking is for each player to put one stake into the pool every time he takes a Heart.

If two or more players hold an equal number of Hearts at the end of the hand, they divide the winnings received from players with a higher number. Any odd stake is left in the pool for the next hand.

The game is sometimes played by partners, and in this variation there is considerable scope for good play. Whist principles, *inverted*, crop up in many ways. For instance, instead of leading a suit for your partner to trump you lead it for him to discard his Hearts upon. Again, the stronger you and your partner are in Hearts the greater is the necessity to avoid a lead of hearts.

" Hearts " well repays a little practice and study, and is by no means a child's game.

FAN TAN

There are several varieties of Fan Tan, one of which is a gambling game of evil reputation. The kind described here is quite a good round game, suitable for playing at parties and whenever it is desired to turn to cards without being over serious.

Before describing the play, it must be said that a full pack is required, that aces rank lowest and kings highest, that every player must be provided with an equal number of counters, say twenty, that five, six or seven players constitutes the best number for providing the greatest amount of fun, and that the object of each player is to get rid of his cards as quickly as he can.

When the play is about to begin, each player puts a certain number of counters in the pool. Any number may be decided on; but two will serve very well when there are more than five participants; three, if there are less.

Somebody is chosen for dealer; this may be done by popular election or by cutting the pack, the lowest taking the deal.

The dealer shuffles and the person on his right cuts. He then commences to deal, beginning with the person on his left. In some cases, the cards will not permit of being shared out equally: nevertheless, the full pack is dealt out in rotation and those who are saddled with an extra card must abide by their slight misfortune.

Play is opened by the person on the dealer's left. His duty is to put the seven of any suit, face upwards, in the centre of the table. If he does not possess a seven, he pays a forfeit of one counter to the pool. It is now the turn of the person to the left of the defective player. He must oblige with a seven, and, should he be similarly placed, he, also, must pay the forfeit. So the game goes on until somebody lays a seven.

Now let us turn to the first player. If he lays a seven as he should, the next player on his left must lay either a six or an eight of the same suit or any other seven. If he puts down a six, it goes to one side of the original seven; if he plays an eight, it goes the other side; and if it is a seven of some other suit, it goes below the first seven. Unless he can play one of these cards, he must place the same forfeit in the pool.

Should the player number two play, a second seven, the person on his left must follow with a six or an eight of either of the two suits led—or another seven.

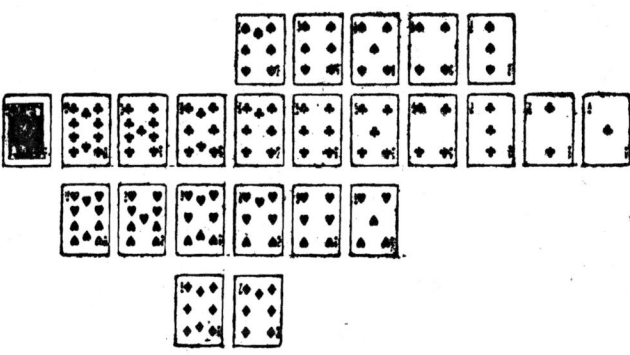

Fan Tan in progress

From this, it is clear that the duty of each player is to lay down a card that helps to build up the rows in sequence, without leaving a gap, or, failing that, to pay the forfeit.

The player, who first disposes of all his cards, takes the contents of the pool and, from all the players, a counter for each card they still possess. Then the game recommences. Each time, the new dealer becomes the person sitting at the left of the previous dealer.

There are one or two heavy penalties which must be mentioned. Anybody who passes, and it is afterwards found that he could have played, is fined three counters. Should it have been a seven that he might have put down, he must pay five counters, in addition, to those who hold the six and eight of the suit to which his seven belongs.

The art lies in "holding up" your opponents. It should be said that if you hold a card in sequence, or a seven, you *must* play it: but you frequently have a choice—and an unwise choice is easy to make.

"Middle" cards in sequence are the best to hold: thus if you hold six, seven, eight, and nine of a suit you can have two "free goes," as they are called, viz., the seven and eight.

The playing of these does not "let out" any other cards, and if you can manage to play others and hold on to the six and nine till towards the end of the game you will probably win.

The other players who hold the cards of the same suit above nine and below six can do nothing but pass in that suit until you lay one of them.

ALL FOURS

An interesting card game that is not generally known is All Fours. It is suitable for two players or two pairs of players.

You shuffle an ordinary pack of fifty-two cards, deal six cards each, one at a time, and turn up the next card to indicate trumps. If this is a knave, the Dealer scores one point which is in addition to the normal score.

The Elder Hand, or player on the Dealer's left, looks at his cards, and decides whether he will hold his own hand or "beg." If he decides to beg, the Dealer gives three more cards to each player, one by one as before. He also turns up a fresh card for Trumps. It is, however, a rule that this new Trump must be a different suit; so, if it is the same suit as before, he must deal three more cards to each player and turn up a new Trump, and repeat until this new Trump is of a fresh suit. If the pack is exhausted before such a change takes place, that hand is finished, and the deal passes to the next player.

As soon as this point is settled satisfactorily, the Elder Hand can play any card he chooses, bearing in mind that the highest card wins the trick, irrespective of suit. You need not follow suit, and Trumps do not score during the play of the cards.

When six tricks have been played, you score your points according to the following rules:—

One point for High.—This is the highest Trump actually played during the six tricks, and the *original holder* of this card scores the point.

One point for Low.—This is the lowest Trump actually played; the point goes to the *original holder* of the card, irrespective of who holds it at the finish.

NOTE.—As the full pack is not used, the *same card* is often both High and Low, in which case both points are awarded to the original holder.

One point for Jack.—This is the Jack of Trumps, if in play, and the point goes to the *winner* of the card—that is, the *final holder*.

One point for Game.—This point does not depend upon the Tricks made—they do not matter. You score certain points for certain cards, and the player whose score is the highest scores the Game point.

The game points are as follows :—

 4 for each Ace.
 3 for each King.
 2 for each Queen.
 1 for each Jack.
 10 for each Ten.

As none of the other cards have any value for the determination of the game point, and as frequently only six cards for each player need be dealt, it follows that in many rounds, no game point can be awarded, as no player may have any of the twenty cards that count. But in the case of *equal points,* then the game point is awarded to the non-dealer, or if more than two are playing, then to the Elder Hand. The Elder Hand, it may be added, is the term used to denote the first player.

MONTE BANK

This is a game of chance, in which skill plays no part at all. Any number of people may join in, one of whom takes on the rôle of banker. The pack consists of forty cards, it being robbed of the four eights, nines and tens.

How to play.—The banker shuffles the cards and, following this, any one or more of the players cuts. At this stage, the banker announces the sum he intends to put in the bank: this may be either money or counters.

Next, he holds the pack, face downwards, and takes the two bottom cards, likewise the two top cards, and spreads them on the table, face upwards in two rows. These four cards constitute the "lay out."

When this is done, the banker turns up the pack and shows the bottom card, which is known as the "gate."

If the gate belongs to the same suit as either of the two top cards, the banker pays out to those who staked on the top cards, and he pays out, in a similar way, to those who staked on the two bottom cards, if one of them is the same suit as the "gate." If no card in either the top or bottom "lay out" is the same suit as the "gate," the banker takes the stakes.

Payment consists in giving a sum equal to that which a player wagered.

When the round is finished, all the used cards are put aside, four more cards are turned up to make a new "lay out" and the card below them constitutes the new "gate."

PELMANISM

Pelmanism is named after the inimitable "Pelman Institute," and, as may be guessed, is a "memory" game.

An ordinary full pack is spread out by single cards, backs uppermost, on the table, not two regularly arranged.

The players, of whom there may be any reasonable number, take it in turn to lift any two of the cards, show them, and replace them in the same positions. If, however, the cards are a pair (*i.e.*, of the same denomination, such as two sixes, two knaves, and so on), the player removes them to a heap in front of him, and they count as a trick in his favour.

The essence of the game lies in remembering where particular cards are, so that when you raise your first card you may know where to go for its fellow, and thus secure a trick.

At the beginning, it is fairly easy to remember where three or four cards are, but as the game proceeds one is apt to get a little mixed.

The player securing most pairs or tricks is the winner.

It is a good game for young and old, but children can usually beat their elders at it.

I DOUBT IT

This is a good noisy game for any number of players; but, preferably, four or five. The pack of fifty-two cards is dealt out in the ordinary way; but all players receive an equal number of cards and as many as possible. If any are left over, they are put on one side, not being wanted.

Each player scans his cards and holds them in a fan; then, the person on the dealer's left commences. He draws a card from the fan, places it, face down, in the centre of the table and says "one." The person next to him, on his left, draws a card from his hand and says "two." This continues round and round the table by players laying cards, one over the other, face down, the cards having an ascending order. Jack, queen and king follow after ten as eleven, twelve and thirteen. When the king is laid, it is followed by the ace, or one, and the sequence is gone through again.

But this is where the fun comes in. The cards are not seen and it is open to a player to put down anything he pleases and call it one, two or three, or whatever the sequence happens to demand. Now should A put down a card, calling it, say, a five, and B, watching him, has his doubts about it, B challenges A by saying "I doubt it." Then, A must turn over his card and if it is what it purports to be, B has to take all the cards forming the built-up pack. On the other hand, if it is not what was claimed for it, then A has to take the cards.

The object of the game is to be the first to have parted with all his cards. Such a winner takes one point and ten points make a full game.

"I Doubt It" is a more scientific game than might be imagined. Take the case of a player with one or two cards, struggling to get out, first. Naturally, the fewer cards he holds, the more restricted is his choice of values and the more likely he will be to call incorrectly when his turn comes to put down a card. That is the time to challenge him, and if the built-up pack has been allowed to grow, his downfall will be complete.

MATRIMONY

We are not going to claim that Matrimony is a game suitable for shrewd players; but it certainly is a rollicking pastime for any number of people, from five to fourteen, who are anxious to enjoy plenty of fun with as much ease as possible.

The " lay out " for Matrimony consists of a fair sized sheet of paper, spread out on the table and marked with five divisions, named as follows : (1) Matrimony, (2) Intrigue, (3) Confederacy, (4) Pair and (5) Best.

When all the players are arranged around the table they cut for the deal and the lowest takes it. The dealer, then, shuffles the pack and the person on his right cuts. Before any cards are dealt out, the stakes must be laid. These, usually consist of counters. First, the dealer places, at least, two counters on each of the five divisions, mentioned above ; but, though he must put two on every division, he may lay more. How many he actually puts, depends on his own fancies ; but, of course, there is no sense in staking an inordinate number and, though there is no rule on the point, it will be unwise to put down more than five counters on any one section.

The dealer adds up the total number of his stakes and each player lays the same number, minus one. There is no law as to where the other players are to place their stakes, and apparently, they may all go in one division, if those who lay them are so minded.

How to Play.—The stakes being made, the cards are dealt out in the following manner : Each player is given a card, in turn, face downwards ; then another card is dealt to each, also face downwards. Following this, a third card is dealt to each, but these are given face upwards.

After this, the first thing to do is to examine each individual's face card. If anyone holds the ace of diamonds, he takes all the stakes laid on the five divisions and that round is completed. Fresh stakes are laid and another round is commenced, exactly as before, except that the person sitting on the left of the original dealer takes on those duties.

But, to return to the original round. If the ace of diamonds is not among the face cards, the players turn up their " down " cards in the order in which they sit. It is important that nobody should be allowed to look at the cards he holds before his turn comes, as this has the effect of spoiling the game.

As the down cards are exposed, they are carefully examined. The first to turn over a king and queen takes the stakes laid on the "Matrimony" division. The stakes on "Intrigue" go to the possessor of a queen and a jack; those on "Confederacy" to a king and a jack; and the first pair of any two cards takes the stakes on "Pair." The ace of diamonds, it should be noted, has no special value and can only gain stake money by being one of a pair, unless it is one of the original face cards. Note, also, that should two players hold any of the combinations, just mentioned, the stakes go to the one who has the right to expose his cards first.

When all the cards have been examined, the next round is commenced, and any stakes that have not been won, go to swell those of the following round.

NEWMARKET

This is a remarkably simple game, yet it is full of exciting possibilities. Any number of players may take part; but we think that three to five is the most suitable number.

Before play commences, each participant is given an equal number of counters, and the stakes are agreed upon as being four, eight or twelve counters at a time. Then, from a spare pack, the ace of spades, the king of hearts, the queen of clubs and the knave of diamonds are taken and placed in square formation in the middle of the table.

Next, a dealer is agreed upon for the first round and subsequent rounds are dealt by the player seated to the left of the previous dealer.

Before the cards have been shuffled and dealt, each player lays his stakes. For this an ordinary player uses four, eight or twelve counters, according to the agreed number; but the dealer lays twice as many as anybody else. The counters are placed on any of the four cards, above mentioned. An equal share may be put on each of the cards, several on some and few on others, or all on one, just as fancy dictates. In making the stakes, no skill is involved and this part of the game is purely a matter of whim.

The stakes being laid, the full pack of cards is dealt out, the first card going to the person on the left of the dealer, while a dummy hand is dealt to the centre of the table. Sometimes, the cards of this hand are placed face upwards; but it adds to the skill, if they are not seen.

Having arranged all the preliminaries, the player on the left of the dealer lays the lowest card he has of any suit he chooses. The player to his left is, then, given the opportunity of following with the next higher card of the same suit and so the game continues until somebody cannot go because the card necessary to follow on is in the dummy hand. This condition is called a " stop."

When a " stop " occurs, the person who played the " stop," leads afresh from any suit he chooses and play is resumed until, at last, somebody has no more cards. Such person is the winner of the game and the other players must pay him one counter for every card they still hold.

As every card is laid, it must be audibly named ; and note that the ace is the lowest card.

Perhaps it may be thought that Newmarket is a game fit only for small children ; but there is a great deal in playing it well. The first essential is to remember what is played and, unless this can be done, a success will never be made. To illustrate this point, let us suppose that someone commences with a five of diamonds and the run continues with a six, seven, eight, nine and then a " stop " comes. Also, let us suppose that the four of diamonds is in your hand. See how important it is to remember that your four is a " stop " card. At any time, when you happen to have the lead, the four may be played alone and you can lead again.

Naturally the " stops " increase in number as the game proceeds and more and more concentration is needed to remember them all.

The best cards to hold are sequences of runs, especially those terminating with a king, since this is the highest card of a suit and must, necessarily, be a " stop." The value of a sequence lies in the fact that it enables a player to get rid of several cards at a time. Next to a sequence, it is best to hold cards that run alternately, because, here again, there is a chance of parting with them rapidly.

So far, we have not explained the reason for the four " lay-out " cards and the stakes put to them. They are used in this way : As soon as a player lays one of these cards from his hand, he is entitled to all the stakes put to it. It should be, perhaps, recalled that the " lay-out " cards are not taken from the playing pack but are " spares " from another.

One thing remains. Suppose that the dummy hand contains one or more of the four " lay-out " cards. When this occurs, nobody can claim the stakes put to these particular cards, and they are left to accumulate during the next and possibly subsequent rounds, until claimed. To dispose of such stakes at the end of a game, the usual plan is to shuffle the full pack and for the last dealer to deal out the cards again, face upwards, omitting the dummy hand. Whoever happens to receive a card, on which there is unclaimed stake-money, takes it.

FOUR JACKS

This is a very simple game to learn; but, none the less, it is highly entertaining and full of possibilities. For any number of players, from four to seven, it is ideal.

The first thing is to make the pack by discarding all the sixes, fives, fours, threes and twos. This leaves a total of thirty-two cards, of which the ace carries the highest value. Such an arrangement is suitable for four players. When there are five or six, it is usual to discard the two black sevens and, in cases when seven people play, the dealer does not share in the cards.

How to Play.—After shuffling and cutting, the dealer hands out the cards to the players in turn. In some circles, a very intricate method of dealing is adopted; but the same end is gained by handing out one card at a time and it is, certainly, less involved.

The game consists in playing for tricks in much the same way as is recognized for Whist; but there are these differences: There is no point in gaining tricks, since they are not counted. What counts is the number of jacks that a player picks up in the tricks he wins and, note very carefully, it counts *against* him. Therefore, the aim is to lose a trick containing a jack, whenever possible.

The highest card of the suit that is led wins the trick and the winner of a trick leads the next round. It is necessary to follow suit, should this be possible; but, beyond that, it might be said that the tactics are the exact opposite of those of Whist, since to lose every trick would be a sure way to win at Four Jacks.

Although it is unnecessary to enter deeply into the science of the game, it may be pointed out, for the benefit of beginners, that the best way to get rid of a jack in hand is to throw it away, as quickly as possible, on a suit which cannot be followed.

At the end of every round, the jacks are counted up. Each player, possessing one, loses a point, or two points in the case of the jack of spades. The first to lose ten points is required to pay each of the other players according to the number of points they are short of ten.

RUMMY OR COON-CAN

This is an excellent game for any number of players up to six. Two ordinary packs of fifty-two cards are used, plus one joker, shuffled well together.

The players cut for deal, the highest dealing. Aces count low in the cut and the joker lowest. Ten cards are dealt one by one to each player, and when the deal is complete, a card is turned face upwards beside the remainder of the pack, which is laid face down in the centre of the table.

The object of each player is to get rid of all his cards by laying out on the table pair-royals or running flushes of three cards. A pair-royal is the cards of the same rank, e.g., three sixes; a running flush is three cards of the same suit in numerical order, e.g., four, five and six of Hearts.

The player on the dealer's left plays first. He picks up either the faced-up card, or the unexposed card from the top of the pack—whichever he pleases. Having done this, he may lay out any pair-royals or running flushes he now holds. If he cannot, or does not wish to do this, he must throw out one of his cards to replace the card he has drawn, placing it face upwards beside the pack.

The next player in the usual rotation now draws a card, and lays out or discards as the case may be; and so on for all the other players.

When once some cards have been laid out by a player, those that follow him may, between drawing and discarding, add any cards from their hands to the combinations on the table, no matter who laid them out.

Thus if there are three fours on the table, and you have a four, you may add it to those. Or if there is a sequence of, say, nine, ten, Jack, and you have seven and eight of the same suit, you may add both of them.

The Joker of course may be made to represent any card. If it is laid out at the end of a sequence (*e.g.*, six, seven, Joker—representing six, seven, and eight) a player wishing to add to that sequence may move it to the other end if it suits him. For instance, in the case mentioned a player holding three and four (of same suit) would move the Joker, so that the new sequence would be three, four, Joker, six, seven. The Joker can only be moved once, however: and if it is originally placed in the *middle* of a sequence it cannot be moved at all. Once moved, it is usually placed, as in Illustration, to indicate that it is " fixed."

A Fixed Joker at Rummy

Aces may count high or low, *i.e.*, in a running-flush of one-two-three or Queen-King-Ace. Note that King-one-two is *not* a " run."

As soon as a player gets rid of all his cards the hand is at an end. The others show the cards they still hold and pay him one stake for each "pip." The Joker counts fifteen, the Aces eleven, court cards all as ten, and other cards by face value.

If no player gets "out" before the pack is exhausted the drawing must then all be done from the top of the discard pile: and the players *must* discard a *different* card every time. (Previously they were at liberty to discard the same card.)

Certain simple principles should be borne in mind when playing. If you cannot secure cards to make the desired combinations, you can at least reduce the "count" of your hand by discarding your high cards. The Joker is to some extent a dangerous card to hold since it counts fifteen against you, but it can generally be used pretty soon—so should be held for a while.

You may, by observing what your opponents draw, be able to "baulk" one or more of them. If you see a player joyously grabbing a King from the discard pile, and you have a King, then you may keep him "looking" for a while by not discarding it until absolutely necessary.

Similarly, you should watch all the discards: it is of no use holding on to two Kings if all the other Kings have been thrown away, and are, therefore, somewhere amongst the discards where you have practically no hope of ever reaching them.

But the chief opportunity for the display of skill is in choosing the moment at which to "lay out." It is obvious that the sooner you lay out the sooner you give you opponents the opportunity of "adding" to the cards put down. Hence it is wise to hold your complete combinations in your hand for a while : but not too long—or somebody may suddenly lay out his whole hand and call upon you for stakes according to the "count" of your cards.

PONTOON OR VINGT-UN

Pontoon, as it is commonly called in this country, is the best known of a very large family of games of chance which have for the central idea the objective of getting nearer to a given number (by means of card values added together) than one player who is for the time being the "banker."

As the name indicates, twenty-one is the number aimed at. An ordinary pack is used and any number may play.

The dealer is the banker, and is chosen by any of the usual methods.

Having decided upon the dealer, the maximum stakes are agreed upon. Play begins as follows : The dealer gives one card to each player, and finally one to himself, face down. Each player may look at his card, including the dealer. Stakes are placed alongside the cards by each punter. The object of the game is to get cards which count twenty-one, or as near it as possible, *but not over it*. All court cards count ten, the Ace counts eleven or one, as desired by the holder. A player, or the dealer, therefore, holding an Ace and a tenth card is said to have a "natural." Stakes are, however, "made" on the first card dealt. The dealer, if he receives a good card, may say to the players, "I double you." This entitles the dealer to receive from each player double the amount of the stake in each case where the dealer wins; he also undertakes to pay out to the successful punters double the amount of their stake. The dealer wins on " evens " and on lower card combinations than his own, except in the case of a " natural " of two cards, which is provided for by cancellation.

A "Natural" at Vingt-un

After stakes have been made, and doubled or not, as the dealer decides, a second card is given to each in turn, the dealer getting his own last, still face downwards. Each player, including the dealer, inspects his cards. If the dealer finds that his two cards make a natural, he turns them up and declares this fact, and receives from each player *double* the amount of the stake (or four times its value if it has been doubled). If, however, one of the punters has also a " natural," he declares this and the two cancel each other.

But if the dealer, on inspecting his two cards, finds that he has not a " natural," it is his duty to offer a card, or cards as may be required, to each player in turn. If either of them has a " natural " he declares it, and receives from the dealer twice his stake (or four times its value if it has been doubled). The third and subsequent cards to each player will be dealt face upwards. The dealer's turn comes last. The players need not take a card, nor need the dealer. For, although the game is almost purely one of chance, there are certain principles which will materially assist a player if he knows and uses them consistently.

If, for example, a punter found that he had a court card dealt for his first, and an eight or a nine for his second, he would " stand "—or decline a third. If a player accepts cards which make his total over twenty-one he is " over," and must pay up his stake and throw his cards to the centre of the table. With cards counting as above eighteen or nineteen, the chances are that a further card accepted would make him "over," as there are many more cards of value above three or four than below. It is prudent, in fact, to "stand" at seventeen or even sixteen. The dealer is similarly guided.

When each player is satisfied to "stand," including the dealer, the latter "declares" his hand and receives from all players who are "even" or "under" his hand. To those over he pays the amount of their stakes. Should the dealer with his third card make twenty-one he receives from all the players. After the stakes have been paid or received, the deal is continued for another round from the remaining cards, which are dealt with the exception of the last, which is always thrown face upwards on the table. The cards which have been used are gathered, shuffled, and cut, and handed to the dealer by another player when wanted to complete the deal. The deal passes to another player, or to each in succession, as may be arranged, either by a time limit, termination of the pack, or on the dealer being beaten all round by the punters.

A player drawing two Aces may decide to draw extra cards for each, announcing to the dealer, "I go on both."

There is a variation of the game wherein the deal passes only when a player gets a "natural," which is turned up at once and is paid for at three times the stake. Twenty-one is paid double, and the "run," *i.e.*, five cards drawn without "bursting," is paid double. A player drawing two similar cards can go on both, and two Aces (the lowest hand in two cards) is paid *four* times the stake, but deal does not pass. If two players obtain a "natural," the first on the dealer's left only gets paid three times the stakes and gets the deal: the other gets paid double simply as twenty-one. If the dealer and player obtain "naturals," the dealer is paid single stakes from that player and he keeps the deal. He gets, of course, three times the stake from the other players. The dealer cannot go for five cards without "breaking"; that is, the hand only counts its normal value with him. If a player gets two Aces and the dealer a "natural," the player gets single stakes.

The dealer has, it should be observed, much the best position. He has the advantage of winning when there is a tie, and is also able to "double" when he likes. He does this when

(1) he had a good card, and (2) when the punters generally speaking do not seem to have good cards—judging from their small stakes. Good players assert that with an Ace or " ten " card as his first, he should always double and, on anything above a seven, he should also double, provided the stakes do not indicate many good cards amongst the punters.

AUCTION PITCH

Auction Pitch is a great favourite in the States and it is well worth a better acquaintance in this country. It is a capital game for four, five, six or seven players, though we consider four or five the best numbers. Each player acts for himself and there are no partnerships.

The full pack of fifty-two cards is used and the ace ranks highest; the two, lowest.

How to play.—The cards are shuffled and cut in the ordinary way and, then, the dealer hands out six to each individual, three at a time, beginning with the person seated on his left. The aim of each player is to hold the highest and lowest trumps in play, and to take those tricks which contain certain cards, as mentioned later.

An important part of the game is the bidding, which commences when the player on the dealer's left offers to sell his privilege of naming the trumps. The person sitting on his left has the right to bid first. After that, the right to bid continues round the table, always moving to the left. Nobody is allowed to bid more than once and each subsequent offer must be higher than any previous ones. A player who does not feel disposed to go higher may pass. No bid may be large enough to put the seller out and cause him to win straight away. Yet another rule is that the one who has the right to sell the privilege of naming trumps must make at least four points, if he does not offer to sell, or if he accepts none of the bids. If he does sell, he adds the points that are bid to his score.

As soon as the bidding is settled, the one who has secured the privilege plays the first card and that card constitutes trumps. Subsequent leaders may commence with any card they choose. Every player must play a trump, when trumps are led,—that is, if they have one—and, in the case of other suits they may trump although they have, perhaps, a card of the led-suit in their hand. The highest card wins the trick, as in Whist.

In the scoring, the points are high, low, jack and game.

(a) *High* is won by the player to whom is dealt the highest trump in play. It counts one point.

(b) *Low* is won by the player to whom is dealt the lowest trump in play. It counts one point.

(c) *Jack* counts one point to the player who wins the trick in which the jack of trumps is played.

(d) *Game.*—This counts one point for the player who gathers in the most valuable cards in the tricks which he wins. The cards which earn points and their values are: (a) tens, worth 10 points each; (b) aces, 4 points each; (c) kings, 3 points each; (d) queens, 2 points each and (e) jacks, 1 point each.

Note particularly, that these points are not put to the total score. They are merely added together to find out who has gained the greatest number and the individual who has secured the most takes the game point and adds one to his total score.

The winner is the player who first obtains from seven to ten points, whichever number is previously agreed upon. In the case of two players obtaining the necessary points in the same deal and one of them was the player who selected the trumps, the trump maker is adjudged the winner. If neither made the trumps, the score is reckoned up in the order set out above— *i.e.*, high, low, jack and game and the points are taken in that sequence.

Note.—That if there are two players who score the highest total for the game point, neither counts it.

GERMAN WHIST

This is an extremely good game for three players.

The ordinary pack of fifty-two cards is used; each player receives seventeen cards, while the last card is turned face upwards on the table, to indicate the trump suit. The ace is the highest card; every player must follow suit, if possible, otherwise he or she is free to trump or play an indifferent card, just as in ordinary four-player Whist. Every trick won, over four in number, counts one point, while each honour held in the tricks won also counts one point—note that it is not the original holder that scores, but the player who possesses at the end of the seventeenth trick.

Fifteen points forms a good game, but ten or twenty can be arranged if preferred, while two games wins the rubber. As soon as the player reaches ten points, in a fifteen point game, seven in a ten point, or fifteen in the twenty point variety, he is allowed to add to his score, during play, one point for each trick won over four; this is done in order to avoid a clash by two players claiming game at the end of a round. If no player has a score higher than nine at the commencement of a fresh deal, then Tricks count before Honours. If A and B start at nine, and at the count it is found that A scores five points for the tricks and one for honours, while B scores three points for tricks and three for honours, then the game is awared to A.

On the other hand, if C started at eight, while A and B were nine each, and C won nine tricks, with two honours, while A took the remaining eight tricks, and also had two honours, then C is the winner, though he had the lower original score at the beginning of that round.

NAP OR NAPOLEON

NAP is a good, fast game, for three or more players up to seven. Five makes the best number, as then the cards which are being used make about half the pack, five cards being dealt, singly, to each player. It is usually played for so much a trick, a penny, or less or more, as may be agreed amongst the players. Counters or "chips" may be conveniently used, bought from time to time from one player acting as banker, and "cashed" with him at the end of the game.

With five cards dealt in turn, one at a time to each player, it is seen that the most tricks than can be made by any player is five. To make five tricks is something of an achievement. This is called making "Nap," or "getting the lot." Because it is difficult to do, the player is allowed odds of two to one. That is, if he makes "Nap" (all five tricks) he is paid, by each player, twice the stake for each trick. Making five counts ten. Generally it is agreed to count "Nap" as twelve. Thus, if the stakes are a penny a trick, the player who makes "Nap" gets a shilling from each of the others. If he loses he pays out sixpence each. This is the essence of the game of "Nap": each player, for each hand either "pays out" or "receives." The player who tries to make the tricks is the caller. All the others combine to beat him.

To determine the "call" is the first procedure. The dealer calls last, the player to his left calls first. The call then goes round the board. If the first player does not want to call, if he thinks he cannot with his five cards, playing against all the other players, make two, or more tricks, he says "pass." It is then the next player's turn to call. We will suppose that he holds cards that he thinks will make three tricks—he calls "three."

The next player, unless he can make a higher call, must say "pass." We will suppose he does so, but that the dealer, whose turn now comes, calls "four." As the highest caller, he is entitled to lead. The lead in Nap is doubly advantageous, because the *first card led always indicates the trump suit.*

Now we will assume that there are five players in this instance. Twenty-five cards will have been dealt. There are then twenty-seven, to make up the fifty-two, left in the pack. It is, therefore, just a little more than an even chance that any given card will be left in the pack and not actually dealt out. If our dealer, who has called "four," for example, has in his hand the king, queen, ten and five of diamonds and the ace of clubs, it is about an even chance that the ace of diamonds will be in the pack and not dealt. As it is his own lead he plays the king of diamonds. Diamonds then become trumps. The ace has been dealt out, and the next player to the dealer puts it on the caller's king. The first trick then goes against the caller. He has to make all the others—he is "top-weight." Each player lays down his card in front of him, the winning card being turned over. The winner of the first trick now plays a heart. As the caller has no hearts he may trump. He is now the last player, and if the trick comes in to him without being trumped previously he can take it with his five of diamonds. He then plays again, this time the queen of diamonds; the queen draws, on this second lead of trumps, the jack of diamonds. The caller has now made two tricks. His ten of trumps is bound "to make" for his third trick. He has now one more trick to make, and he leads the ace of clubs. This card can only be beaten by a trump, but as no trumps were played to the ten which he led, he knows that he is safe. The caller has made "four," and each of the other players pays him four stakes. If there had been a small trump left in one of the hands to beat the caller's ace of clubs he would have "gone down," and would have had to pay each of the other players four stakes.

An absolutely sure hand at Nap is ace, king, queen, jack, ten, as these are the highest cards in order. But Nap is often called, and made, on hands of much less value. It depends largely upon the number of players. If only three are playing there will be fifteen cards dealt, with thirty-seven remaining in the pack. It is now just about two and a half to one that a given card will be in the pack, and not dealt. On the law of averages this means that in seven hands the trump ace or king will be in the pack five times, whilst it is only twice dealt out. *The smaller the number of players the greater will be the value of the cards that are held.* With seven players considerably more than half the cards will be dealt. It is then evident that the odds are in favour of the particular card being dealt. It would be foolish to risk a Nap, with seven playing, if the king was the best card in the hand.

But when there are a number of players the caller has the advantage in the splitting up of the trumps. Let us take five players again. There are twenty-five cards dealt, rather less than one-half; there will also be, on the average, about one-half the trump suit dealt, say six or seven at most— thirteen cards to the suit. If the caller has three trumps this leaves four amongst the other four players. If two are without trumps this means two each to the others. If, then, the caller can win the two first tricks, any trump will make a third trick. If the caller still has the lead an ace is as good as a trump. From this it will be seen that a good "three" hand is ace and king of trumps, and an ace of another suit, or a small trump.

One kind of "four" hand has been illustrated. Another would be, say, an ace and four small trumps. The ace being led would make. The second, the smallest trump, would be beaten, but it would draw the remaining trumps from the other players' hands, and the caller would make his three last tricks. It must not be taken from this that there are never three trumps out against a hand, with five players; there are sometimes even four trumps. But generally one can reckon on two trumps against the caller only in any particular hand. Any four small trumps will usually make two tricks for this reason. Two leads of trumps are given and lost to the caller and the others " make." Now, as we usually only expect to get two, or at most three, trumps against a call, an ace, king, ten, one other small trump and another ace will usually make Nap. The jack and queen of trumps, if dealt to other hands, will perhaps fall to the first two tricks, and if there be a third trump against the caller it is beaten by the ten on the third round. If the first three rounds are trumps, an ace and a king of another suit will complete a Nap. An ace and queen make a good run for the double stakes, and even an ace and jack are always worth a run with five players.

It should not be forgotten that small cards may be made trumps, by a first lead, and big ones of other suits used to take tricks. Thus, a hand may consist of the five, seven and nine of clubs, and two other aces, or an ace-king. This is a " three " hand by making the clubs trumps. The first club is led and lost. The next lead is up to one of the aces. This makes. Another trump is led and lost; this clears all the trumps, leaving two winning cards in the caller's hand. If the ace or king he holds is " led to " he wins with it and plays his trump. If anything else is led, he trumps it and plays his winning card for three.

A " two " call is ace and deuce of trumps and another ace. The best play is ace, which wins, then the second trump, which loses, and wait for the right lead. Some players think otherwise, and lead the second ace. If this is trumped, which very often happens, there is little hope for the small trump making. In playing against the call care should be used to allow as many players as possible to play after the caller. Thus, if the caller plays a small card, let this be beaten, if possible, by the player last after the caller. When he leads again the caller perhaps has to trump, and if there are three to play after him one or other of them may be able to over-trump. If the caller has only one more trick to make, lead trumps. It is then the " table " against his trump. If the caller has only a small trump left there may, by chance, be another left a little larger, which will beat it. In these circumstances, if a trick is already beaten and you hold a trump yourself, take the trick with a higher *suit* card, if you hold it, and lead the trump.

In most games of Nap it is the custom to allow a player the choice of the top card if he goes Nap. It may be that he will

AMUSING CARD GAMES

pick up a small trump, and can then exchange a doubtful fifth card for it. If a player looks at the top card he *must* go Nap. Each player is entitled to a call, so if Nap is called before it comes to the turn of the dealer or other player, it is usual to allow Double Nap. Generally the stakes are doubled for that round. Nap, then, if the stakes are a penny a trick, is two shillings from each player, if won; and a shilling paid out to each player if the caller " goes down." In the case of a " pass " all round it is usual to double the stakes for the next hand or until a call is won. A call of two, three, or four, is therefore doubled if made after a complete pass. A pool, or " kitty," is made by each successful player paying into a pool the agreed stake, a penny, twopence, or threepence which is allowed to accumulate for the first Nap which is made. Then the " kitty " starts again. It is often worth while to risk a Nap, which one would not otherwise call if the " kitty " is a big one. There are variations of the game in which conditional calls, of Wellington at double stakes, and Sir Garnet, for treble stakes, are allowed. In the latter case it is usual to deal another five cards and allow a hand to be made up from the ten for the call—the loser pays in full in this case.

A call is sometimes played of " misère," over a " three," but under a " four," in which all the tricks have to be *lost*. It is paid for as a " three."

This variation is becoming increasingly popular, and allows the use and development of considerable skill.

Sometimes trumps are still recognised when " misère " is called—sometimes the hand is played without trumps. This point should be agreed in advance. If trumps are recognised, the caller should of course lead a suit of which he has but a single card.

Generally speaking, low cards are essential to a " misère " call. But one, or even two, quite high cards need not always deter the player.

Thus, a hand consisting of two of spades, two and ace of diamonds, three and four of hearts might be played as follows : lead two of spades ; this trick is practically bound to be taken by another player. The trick winner—we will suppose—leads clubs. Having none of these, the caller can " throw away " the dangerous ace, and feel reasonably certain of losing the rest of the tricks in view of his very low cards.

. If by chance the first trick winner leads diamonds, the two can be played to lose the trick, whilst the ace may be thrown away later. For if you have none of a particular suit, it is likely that one of your opponents will have rather more than usual of them. Hence you are fairly sure of having opportunities to throw away dangerous cards.

When playing against a " misère " call, remember that the caller's weakness, if he has any, will be in his holding two cards or more of the same suit—one perhaps fairly high. Therefore do not change the lead if you can help it. Try him again with the suit wherein he has just successfully lost a trick.

Another variation is called " Purchase " Nap. This is an extremely good game and well worth trying. After the dealer has dealt, and before anybody starts calling, the dealer goes round again in turn, and serves out fresh cards from the pack in exchange for as many cards as the players may wish to throw away from their original hands. For every fresh card so exchanged the player has to pay one penny (or more, according to the stakes) into the pool. He must not exchange cards more than once in each round, but he can " purchase " any quantity up to five. The cards thrown away are not shown, nor used again till the next deal. The dealer must sell to each player in turn, and to himself last, after which the calls start from his left in the usual way. In view of the extra number of cards brought into the game, Purchase Nap should be confined to a table of not more than four players, and for the same reason the calls should be made on much stronger hands than at ordinary Nap.

BRAG AND POKER

BRAG is a simple form of poker, and serves well as an introduction to the latter. Both games are essentially different to the " trick-taking," like whist.

The play consists of betting that your hand is better than your opponents', and if none of them is willing to take your bet, the cards are not shown at all ! This of course rarely happens ; there will almost always be someone to take a sporting chance.

The values of various hands are reckoned according to the comparative frequency with which certain combinations of cards are met with when dealt round in the usual way from a shuffled pack.

AMUSING CARD GAMES

It will be appreciated that in a hand of five cards four aces are very rarely found. This being so, four aces is an extremely valuable hand in Poker. Other combinations are valued according to their rarity or otherwise.

Let us take Brag first as being the simpler game. Three cards make a "hand" at Brag. It is agreed beforehand whether three cards only shall be dealt to each player, or whether each shall have five dealt, two of which are discarded before play commences. The latter method makes the best game.

The hands rank in the following order of value :—

1. *Three of a kind,* sometimes called "pair royal" or "triplet." Three aces of course beats three kings; and so on.

2. *Running Flush, i.e.,* three cards of the same suit in numerical order. Ace, king, queen, beats king, queen, jack; and so on.

3. *A Run, i.e.,* three cards of any suit in numerical order. Four, five, six, beats three, four, five; and so on.

4. *A Flush, i.e.,* three cards of the same suit, in any order. The highest card of a flush determines its value compared with other flushes. Thus, a flush containing an ace beats one containing lower cards. If the highest cards in two flushes are of the same value the next highest card is referred to.

5. *A Pair, i.e.,* two cards of a kind, as two queens, two fives, of any suits. A pair of tens beats a pair of nines, and so on.

Note that all hands coming into one of the groups numbered above beat all hands coming into a lower group; *e.g.,* the smallest run will beat the biggest of flushes.

Having learnt these values we will commence play.

The player on the dealer's left has first bet. He bets whatever he likes (or nothing at all—in which case he says, "I drop out") that his hand is better than anyone else's. If it is a valuable hand he will bet fairly high. But not *too* high, or he may get no takers. Let us suppose he bets threepence. The next player may "come in" if he thinks his hand is as good as the first player's. The first player having placed his stake in the pool, those that "come in" must each place a like amount.

But the third player may be confident that he holds the better hand; if so, he may "raise" the stakes, saying "I raise it to sixpence."

If he does so, all those who "come in" after him must stake an equal amount.

The "raising" will probably cause the fourth or fifth player, who perhaps has a weak hand, to say, "I drop out." The turn thus comes round to the original caller again. If he is still confident that he holds the highest hand he may say, "I raise another threepence"—paying *sixpence* into the pool. If, on the other hand, he is not so sure, he may pay threepence to make his stake equivalent to the third player's. If this happens the hand is at an end. Those that have "come in," and remained in, will show their hands, he who has the highest taking the pool.

But the call may go round several times if someone "raises" during each round. Those wishing to remain in the game must make their stakes equivalent to the raiser's—or else make a further raise. Often all players but two drop out—and the hand ends by one player making his stake up to that of the raiser in order "to see" the "show-down" as it is called.

At first sight it may seem that success is a matter of pure chance. Not so; a good player will keep in mind the probabilities as to whether his hand is likely to have a serious rival—according as there may be few or many players. As explained in the section devoted to "Nap," and as all "Nap" players well know, if only half the pack is in use then it will be, roughly speaking, about even chances as to whether a given card is in play or not.

Further, the good player will save, and on occasion make, money by careful study of his opponents. There are many people who cannot conceal the fact that they have good cards, or *vice versa*. Their behaviour will vary of course in different individual cases. But by watching them certain useful indications will make themselves apparent.

On the other hand, a skilful player will cultivate methods of misleading his opponents, who, it must be remembered, are watching him for "signs" as to the *real* value of the hand on which he is betting.

POKER probably possesses more variations than any other game. So much so, that before commencing play it is a necessary and usual thing first to discuss exactly how the game shall be played. " Draw Poker " is the most commonly played variation, followed probably by what is known as " Whiskey Poker." But even these variations may be played in different ways—so that no player need consider that the variation with which he is familiar is " correct " or necessarily the best way of playing.

In Poker the hands are valued in the same manner as at Brag. But as a " hand " is five cards there are more possible combinations, and they run in slightly different order of value. The hands are :—

1. *Straight Flush*, *i.e.*, running flush of five cards.
2. *Fours*, *i.e.*, four of a kind, as four aces, which make the highest " four."
3. *Full House*, *i.e.*, a pair royal (three of a kind) *and a pair*. The value of the pair royal decides the winner as between two " full houses."
4. *A Flush*. Five cards of the same suit. The highest card or cards decide between two flushes.
5. *A Straight*. Five cards in numerical order, of any suits. Ace may be counted as high *or* low, *i.e.*, as a " one " or as an ace.
6. *Threes*. A pair royal, as three sixes.
7. *Two Pairs*. The highest pair decides between two or more hands of this type.
8. *A Pair*. Two cards of same value; a high pair beating a low pair.

If two or more hands should be equal as regards the main cards, as for instance two hands of two pairs, sixes and sevens, then the odd card becomes the deciding factor. This principle applies throughout. If two hands are exactly equal, the pool is divided. Some players give value to the suits (1st Hearts, 2nd Diamonds, 3rd Clubs, 4th Spades), and in this method no two hands can be equal.

The joker may be used if desired. Expert players consider that it does not improve the game, as it brings in too great an element of chance. If used, it may be counted as *any card in the whole pack* by the player fortunate enough to receive it. The highest hand when the joker is in use is five aces.

DRAW POKER is usually played as follows :—

Five cards are dealt to each player. Five players make

the best game, but from three to seven may play. It is an old-established rule that if a card falls face upward in the deal, it must be accepted. After the deal—for the privilege of which the dealer usually contributes one stake (called the "ante") to the pool—each player in turn is allowed, on payment of a stake into the pool, to receive additional cards up to five in number, discarding before he takes them from the dealer a like number from his original hand.

The dealer gives himself his own "draw" cards, but he must announce how many he is taking, so that all players can hear.

It will be seen that hands may be vastly improved by "drawing." If on the first deal you receive a pair and three indifferent cards, you will, of course, discard the latter and draw three more in the hope of turning the "pair" into a "three."

But the "draw" is more useful than this. By watching how many cards each player takes, you may receive a fair indication of what he commenced his hand with. It is, for example, tolerably certain that a player who draws three cards already holds a pair. His subsequent mien may indicate whether he has "improved" or not. Again, a player who draws one card may have either "fours" or the "makings" of a "flush," a "straight," even possibly a "straight flush"; or he may have two pairs—which are the "makings" of a "full house."

Hence—beware of the player who draws one card, and observe him closely. He either has a very good hand, or one that is worthless or nearly so. If he bets cautiously, he probably has obtained the card he wanted and wants as many players as possible to "come in." If he bets fiercely, he is perhaps "bluffing"—trying to make you think he "has them" by a display of confidence.

After all players have "drawn" (and you have duly noted each one), the player on the dealer's left may bet or "open," as it is called. If he does not desire to do so, the privilege passes to the next; and so on. Betting is usually as described for "Brag"—but there are many variations—some of which are rather complicated. The method should be agreed before play commences.

The reader will have gathered that "bluffing" is a great part of the game. It is done in many ways other than the naïve scheme of plunging heavily on a hand worth nothing.

You may bluff your opponents by drawing only one card when you hold say a "three." They will think you hold "two pairs" or a "broken" straight or flush. In these circumstances you stand a chance of a brisk contest with an individual who holds two high pairs, who has decided that you did not "improve" and that his pairs will beat yours anyway.

Your "threes" will, of course, cause him to lose heavily if he is a *very* positive sort of person.

Even if you attempt a bluff, on nothing, and get found out, it is not all dead loss. A little later on, when you really have a good hand, you will find perhaps that a larger number than usual of your opponents will "pay to see" your hand, because they think you may be bluffing again ! Conversely, if you have had a succession of really good hands and have won several "pots"—then a "bluff" in the nature of a good hearty bet will often scare all the others "out"—and you scoop the pool.

It may be noted here that unless someone "pays to see" your hand, he has no right to see it, and you should not show it.

A few hints on general play will serve to conclude :—

Always pay your stake and "draw," so long as you have a "pair" or higher in the original deal.

Do not pay to draw if your hand is merely mixed worthless cards. Above all, don't waste money on drawing five cards, or four "to an ace." The odds are enormously against your success. Avoid betting on "two pairs"; to new players, especially if the pairs are "picture cards," the hand looks good. It is practically worthless unless there are only say three players.

Remember always to watch what your opponents draw—and their subsequent behaviour. It is on this that success largely depends.

Do not get into habits, *e.g.*, of bluffing when you are winning lots of money, or when you have lost a lot. It will soon be noticed, and you will suffer.

On the other hand, watch for such habits on the part of other players; you may be able to profit by it.

It should perhaps be mentioned that a common variation of Draw Poker is "Jack Pots." In this no player can open unless he has at least a pair of jacks. If no one can open the hand is "passed," and stakes are doubled for the next.

WHISKEY POKER is a simple form of the game suitable for a low number of players. Each player puts in the pool an agreed amount by way of "ante." Five cards are then dealt to each player, with an extra hand, known as "the widow." The first player may either play his own hand, pass, or take the widow. If he adopts either of the former alternatives, the next player has a similar option, and so on till someone elects to "take the widow." He takes the spare hand, and lays his own on the table face upwards. The next in order is entitled to take in either of the exposed cards, discarding in its place one of his own, which is added to the remaining four on the table. The next player has a like choice, and so on round and round, till some player is content with his hand, which he signifies by a knock on the table. Each of the other players may still make one more exchange, after which the hands are exposed, and the best hand takes the pool.

Should any player knock before the widow is taken, the five cards are turned up, and each player (other than the one who knocked) has one draw from them. Should the round of the table have been made without anyone taking the "widow," the five cards are turned up, and the players draw from them in rotation until someone expresses himself content.

There is no "raising" or betting on the hands, the stakes consisting solely of the amount originally placed in the pool.

PATIENCE GAMES

In playing games of patience, it is highly necessary that the cards should be thoroughly shuffled between each attempt. To neglect this rule will mean that a variety of obstacles are unnecessarily encountered.

The following explanations will be much more easily remembered if they are read in conjunction with actual play.

"DEMON" PATIENCE (one pack)

This is a very popular but rather difficult game to conclude successfully.

A packet of thirteen cards is first dealt and placed face upwards (the top card only showing) on the table. The next four cards are dealt face upwards in a row clear of this packet (which is called the "stock" or "talon"). A further card is dealt and forms the first of a row of "foundations" above these rows. Other cards of the same value are placed beside it when they appear.

The remainder of the pack is kept in hand, and cards are turned up from it *in threes* on to a waste-heap.

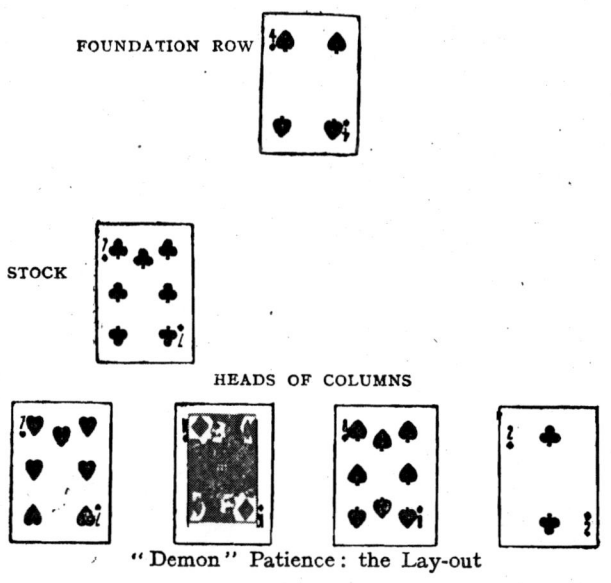

"Demon" Patience: the Lay-out

The object is to build on the foundations in ascending sequence of suit. In the play the first four single cards laid out from the heads of columns to be "packed" upon in *descending* sequence in *alternate colours*. The top card of the stock and of the waste-heap is always available for building, and any sequence or bottom part of a sequence may be moved from one column to another. The exposed (bottom) cards of columns are of course available for building the main sequences.

The Illustrations show the lay-out and the game in progress wherein the four of Diamonds may be moved to the foundation row. On this the top card of stock can be placed, followed by top card of waste-heap. Part of the auxiliary sequence in the right-hand column can be moved to the left-hand column, thus releasing six of Clubs for the main sequence.

When no exposed card or auxiliary sequence can be moved

with advantage three more cards are turned up on to the waste-heap from the cards in hand. When all these have been so turned up, the waste-heap is turned over (once only)

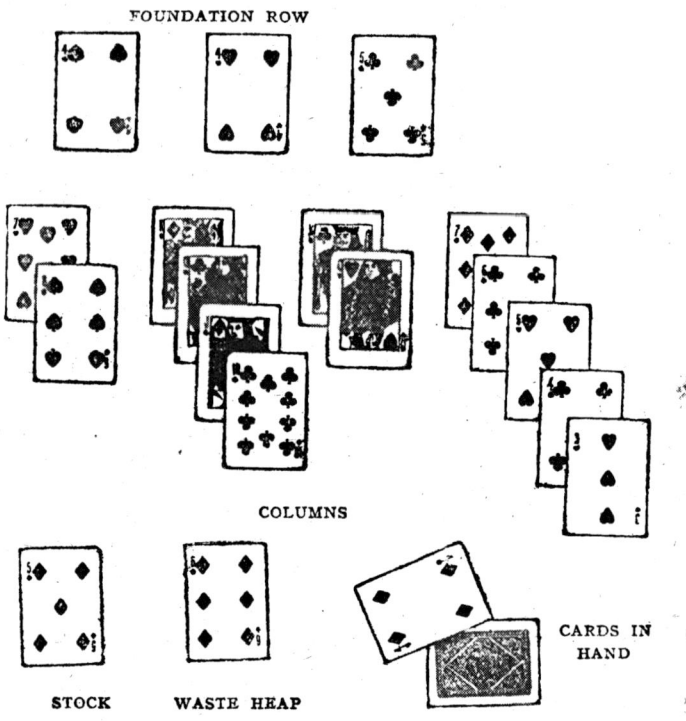

"Demon" Patience in progress

and dealt in three, as before. If the game is blocked, you are allowed one "grace," viz., to move *one* card from the foundation packet (main sequence) to the head or foot of a column, if it will fit. If this does not get you "out," the game is lost.

"ROLL-CALL" PATIENCE (one pack)

This is a most simple game; it is an excellent way of teaching children names of the cards and of keeping them occupied for a while.

An ordinary pack is dealt one at a time face upwards on to the waste-heap, the player meanwhile calling the names of the cards in rotation, thus "Ace, two, three, four, five,"

and so on, up to King and on to "Ace, two, three," etc.,
again. When a card "answers its name" (*i.e.*, comes at
the same time) it is thrown out. The game continues until
all are thrown out, or until they "won't answer." It is
purely chance which decides.

"TOWER OF HANOY" PATIENCE (one pack)

This, by way of a change, is a game of pure skill, and is
more in the nature of a mathematical puzzle than real
Patience. It is, in fact, an adaptation of an old puzzle.

Only nine cards are used: they should be of one suit,
from the two to the ten inclusive. They are laid out in three
rows of three, as shown in the Illustration.

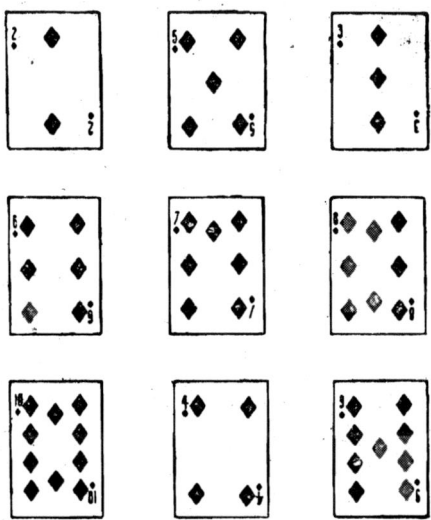

"Tower of Hanoy" Patience

The object is to get them into a single column in descending
sequence by moving according to the following rules:—

One card only may be moved at a time.
It must be a card from the foot of a column.
It can only be placed at the foot of another column and
below a higher card.
When a "vacancy" occurs (*i.e.*, when all in one column
have been moved) the bottom card of either of the remaining
columns may be used to fill the vacancy.

E

In the example illustrated, it will be seen that the ten cannot be moved at all, at first. It must be got into the top row as soon as possible. Here are the moves :—

> 4 under 10, 7 under 9, 5 under 7, 4 under 5 ; then 10 into vacancy.

The next process is to get the nine under the ten, which is not so easy.

The game is an excellent pastime, and generally a little more thought will solve the most hopeless looking " block."

MAGIC AND TRICKERY

THINGS YOU CAN DO WITHOUT BEING A MAGICIAN

MAGIC does not exist, and the mysteries of this world are all too few. Nevertheless, that need not prevent you and me from standing before an audience, and deluding the onlookers into thinking that we possess supernatural gifts.

Of course, people are very sceptical in these enlightened days, but, even so, they are still easily misled, and, probably it will not be long before you have sufficient skill to mystify a whole roomful of people. It is then that the conjurer finds his work interesting. He has just put over one of his favourite turns, we will say. It has gone with a bound from start to finish. He bows eloquently, and there is a stilly silence throughout the hall, broken suddenly by a timid clapping which develops immediately into a burst of applause. He bows a second time, and, all the while, he is stifling his chuckles, because he knows how remarkably simple the whole thing has been.

Yes, conjuring is great fun when you feel at home in front of an audience, and it is marvellous how quickly you do feel at home on the stage, when you have something good up your sleeve—in more senses than one.

In this book, I am going to take you behind the scenes and let you into many secrets. But there is one thing I ask. When you have learnt to work the tricks described in these pages, go out and perform them to all and sundry, but do not divulge the methods you have employed. When a mystery is known to everybody, it is no longer a mystery.

As I have already said, conjuring is great fun, but that does not mean that it entails no laborious practice. As a matter of fact, any trick worth doing is worth doing well, and you may have to try it over a hundred times before you get it to go sufficiently well to delude the audience.

Never appear in public with an unpolished performance. If your actions fall just short of the mark, somebody may see through the trick, and, as a rule, such a person finds it difficult to keep silent. An unfortunate word from him or her, and confusion is assured.

Every show that you give should be well mapped out beforehand. You should make up your mind how you will open, how you will end, while every turn coming between should be planned before starting. Even the sequence of the items is important, since there must be a natural flow from one turn to another. For instance, never find yourself in the position of having to say, "What shall I do now?"

A good conjurer is always cheerful, genial and happy. He adopts this manner because he knows that these qualities are infectious, and, if he is in a good mood himself, his audience will develop the same spirit. Sometimes, he pretends to be puzzled and mystified. Here, again, he does it in order to impart the same impression to his onlookers. They, too, quickly become mystified. To get flurried or worried is, of course, fatal. If something goes wrong, just laugh and exclaim, "That missed the mark, didn't it?" Your audience, then, will laugh with you, rather than at you.

Every trick has a weak point in it somewhere. While performing it, you will readily perceive where the weakness lies. On no account hesitate at this point, but turn to the next step quickly. You may be tempted to linger there; but, if you do, you will afford the audience time to unfathom the secret. Pass on like a flash, and they are denied such an opportunity.

Now let us turn to the real things. I am not going to describe any trick that you ought not to be able to master with a little thought and practice. No involved mechanism will be necessary, but, as I think that small gadgets often take the place of acquired skill, I have introduced the use of these, when necessary.

VANISHING GLOVES

It is half the battle won if you can make a good beginning in your magical entertainment. I am old-fashioned enough to think that the gloves which go where they are told make a very suitable and impressive introduction. Moreover, the trick can be made at home, with a pair of gloves which you are in the habit of wearing—or the whole thing can be purchased at any magical depôt for less than a florin. The effect is as follows: The performer appears wearing white evening gloves, which he proceeds to remove, whilst making his introductory speech. As he takes his gloves off, however, they at once disappear—in a most bewildering manner. To begin with, the gloves should be of white cotton, and fit easily. To the middle of the front portion, nearest the wrist, sew a piece of thin elastic (this should be one foot in length and covered with silk thread), at the free end of which make a loop, and pass it over a strong safety-pin, which fix securely to the inside of your coat sleeve, in such a manner that when the gloves have vanished the tips of the fingers of the gloves are at least two or three inches up the coat sleeve, and therefore well out of sight.

WHERE DID THE CIGARETTE COME FROM?

Here is a trick that may be performed on the stage, in the drawing-room, or even when walking along the road with friends. If done without any bungling, it is particularly neat.

You appear to want a cigarette, and, naturally, you pull out your cigarette case. With a good deal of show, you make it quite clear that the case is empty, and you return it to your pocket with a certain amount of disappointment.

Of course, somebody immediately offers you a smoke from their own packet, or, if they do not oblige, you make some remark about having to depend on your own resources, as your friends are so backward in coming forward.

Anyhow, you don't take a cigarette from a friend, but you produce a box of matches, take out a match, strike it on the rough side, and, with the box still in your fingers, you put your hands together as though shielding the flame from the wind, and you light—a real cigarette. From where did it come—that is the mystery. It all happened so quickly that your friends or your audience are amazed.

The secret may be said to lie in the fact that a box of Swan Vestas is just the right length to take a cigarette—which is something very few people have noticed. Well, beforehand, you cut a neat round hole in the edge of the tray of the box, just large enough to enable the end of a cigarette to pass through. A cigarette is put in the box, so that one end projects through the hole about an eighth of an inch; then matches are fitted into the box, in the ordinary manner.

When you struck the match and were shielding the flame, you were really hiding the fact that you were pulling the cigarette out with your lips. The secret is now clear.

When the cigarette is alight, put the box of matches into your pocket immediately. Somebody may ask to examine it, but there will be a moment's hesitation before they do. Have a second box of vestas in the same pocket, and, if there is any request to see the box, bring out the duplicate without any demur.

TO PASS A PENNY THROUGH A GLASS OF WATER

In long conjuring programmes it is perfectly useless to expect every item to be of equal standard, and there must obviously be some tricks which are not quite " 22 carat "—these are more or less resorted to as time-killers. The one about to be described is not exactly " hall-marked," but at the same time many people have not seen it worked—and, provided the manipulation is good, there is no reason why the deception should not appeal to a certain number of spectators. A twelfth part of a shilling is borrowed, and marked (with a pin or penknife, so as to be easily recognized again); covered by a handkerchief (which may also be borrowed), and held over a glass of Adam's ale. At a given signal, the coin is permitted to drop into the glass of water; the aqua is poured away and the " copper " ultimately found in the most unlikely or impossible place. The glass sold by magic merchants for the performance of this apparent miracle is, as a rule, coloured, and has a perfectly flat bottom. A disc of glass the exact size of a penny is also sold with the tumbler. This circle of glass fits the bottom of the tumbler perfectly, and will adhere thereto when moistened by water. Having borrowed the necessary coin, the exponent of modern magic adroitly exchanges it (under cover of pocket-handkerchief) for the already palmed piece of glass, and palms the penny instead, in his left hand—at the same time holding a glass of water with that hand. The disc, now under cover of the 'kerchief, is held over the tumbler of water by a member of the company, who naturally supposes that he holds a penny, and, indeed, there is no reason why he should think otherwise, for has not the magical expert given his word of honour that "he wouldn't deceive them for the world!" At the given sign the helper lets go of the would-be coin, which immediately falls into the glass of liquid, where it is naturally expected to be found; but, to the bewilderment of the uninitiated it has miraculously vanished. The reason why has already been fully explained, and it is not difficult to see how the original coin (which the entertainer has had palmed in his left hand the whole time) can now be made to appear from the assistant's nose or hair.

THE USEFUL BOWLER

A bowler hat should form part of every conjurer's kit, since it can be used in several ways. Take the following instance.

Present a pack of cards to your audience and ask for five cards to be selected. When this has been done, tell your friends to stack the selected cards, so that you cannot see what they are, and then hold out your bowler for somebody to put them into it.

You now hold the bowler just above your eye-level, and, so that your view shall be masked, you lift up the inside lining. This makes an additional screen, which effectively prevents you from seeing over the top of the brim.

At this point you say, "I will now give you the three of diamonds," or some other card in the hat, and you pick out the three of diamonds. You repeat this until all the five cards have been correctly named and drawn out of the hat.

It looks very astonishing. How is it done?

A peep hole has been cut through the bowler at a point which is normally hidden by the leather lining, on the inside, and by the silk ribbon, on the outside. You lift up the leather lining, ostensibly to screen your view, and, unseen

FUN BOOK

by the audience, you push the ribbon out of the way while holding the hat. Thus, the peep hole becomes effective, and you look through that and see what the bowler contains.

SWEETS FROM A HANDKERCHIEF

This is the very trick to work at a party of young people; for children invariably appreciate really high-class confectionery. Moreover, there is nothing in the world which will more quickly bring a conjurer into favour with his audience than a neatly executed *distribution* trick.

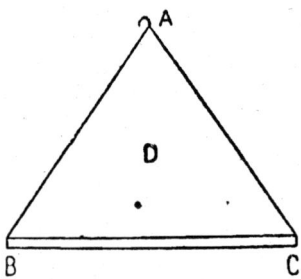

The handkerchief from which the sweets are produced is a borrowed one, and is freely shown (both sides) before and after the deception. The diagram is not intended to illustrate a dunce's cap, nor a proposition in Euclid—it is nothing more than the fake which is necessary for the performance of this illusion. It is made of white linen, at the apex of which (A) is a curved pin. At the base of the triangle (BC) are two pieces of thin flat wire or whalebone, such as I am told are worn by ladies in their corsets. D is fitted with "sugar and spice and all things nice," which cannot escape from the mouth of the triangular bag, owing to the presence of the wires either side of same. Thus loaded, the bag is put upon a servante at the back of magician's table; and the pin A is attached to the back edge of the table-cloth. Having borrowed a good-sized white handkerchief, place it on the table in such a way that the middle of it comes immediately over the bent pin A; then, in picking up the handkerchief again, possession is also gained of the sweets, which latter (as previously stated) will not fall out until pressure is brought to bear upon the sides of the bag (AB and AC). When this is done, however, a shower of good things takes place—to the delight of those present.

THE BALANCING CIGARETTE

Entertainers frequently have to stand by and wait while some part of their performance is progressing, and, more often than not, they light a cigarette and smoke it, to show how unconcerned they are.

Certainly, the cigarette helps to give the impression after which they are seeking, and I often light one myself. Occasionally, I take out a stunt cigarette which provides a turn of its own.

My favourite stunt cigarette contains a small, but heavy, piece of sheet lead, bent to form half a cylinder, which is fitted just inside the paper covering, close to the mouthpiece. Its shape and position do not prevent the cigarette being smoked in the ordinary way, a condition which is very useful.

When smoking one of these manipulated cigarettes, I suddenly take it from my mouth and place it on the edge of the table, but with about nine-tenths of its length overhanging. "That's a funny cigarette!" I exclaim, and then I balance it on a finger. Here, again, it stands level, although most of its length is to one side. It is put on several other things, and every time it appears as though it ought to fall, but it remains balanced. Of course, it is the lead weight which does the trick.

THE MAGIC WHISTLE

This is one of those silly things that cause a good deal of consternation.

You stand up before your audience, holding in your hand a wand, which you are careful to explain has magic properties. At the end of the wand is tied a piece of string, and at the end of the string is a very ordinary whistle. In order to show that there is absolutely no deception, you pass round the wand and the whistle for examination.

Then, when these preliminaries have been settled, you ask somebody to put a question, the answer of which is known to everybody. The answer must take the form of "yes" or "no." For instance, the question may be, "At this moment are we in Timbuctoo?" or "Is an elephant bigger than a cockroach?"

Before proceeding further, you explain that, when the

answer is "no," the magic wand will cause the whistle to blow once, but when it is "yes," the whistle will act twice.

Someone puts the question, "Do shrimps sing in their sleep?" and the whistle gives one shrill blast. This is followed by "Ought caterpillars to be kind to their young?" Two blasts are heard. In this way, the answers to five or six questions are given correctly, much to the enjoyment of the company.

The secret?

The whistle at the end of the string is not the one that makes the sounds. In your left hand, you hold a rubber bulb which is joined to a length of tubing that travels up

Why does the whistle blow?

your arm and goes into one of the pockets of your waistcoat. Here, it is fixed to the tip of a second whistle. By squeezing the bulb, the whistle sounds. Be very careful to smother the air hole of the whistle as little as possible, or a muffled blast will be given, and this will cause suspicion. Always stand a few paces away from the nearest spectator, so that the distance between the two whistles cannot be appreciated.

THE PALM TREE

For this you will require a long strip of paper, the longer the better. If using newspaper, take a complete sheet,

MAGIC AND TRICKERY

four pages in all. Fold it across the columns, so that you make three equal widths; tear twice and use only one of the pieces.

Again, place the paper behind you and roll it up, not too tightly. When this is done, and while the paper is still out of sight, tear down the roll four or five times from one end almost to the middle. The tears may be straight or crinkled, whichever you prefer.

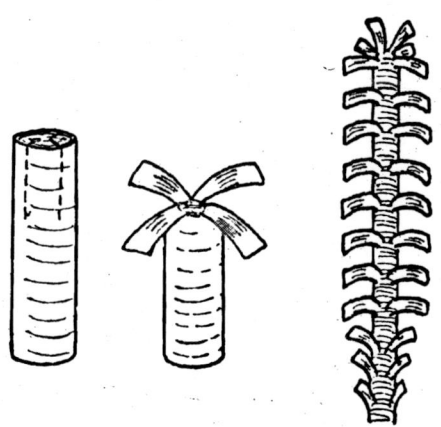

Three Stages in the Evolution of the Palm Tree

Now, show the roll to the audience, and, gripping the untorn end with the left hand, pull one of the innermost torn sections. As it comes up, it forms a column, which is the tree trunk, with numerous flaps of paper on all sides. These are the branches or leaves.

Although a botanist might not consider your model a reasonable facsimile of a tree, it is none the less a very picturesque affair, and the audience will, probably, appreciate your talent by applauding.

THE MAGIC CORKS

EFFECT.—A circular wooden box is shown, quite empty. Four pieces of cork are placed in it, the lid put on, passes made, and, behold! upon removing the lid it is found that the corks have multiplied to eight, in a most baffling manner. The lid is replaced once more, cabalistic sentences pronounced by the performer, and, upon taking off the lid, four corks only are now to be seen, as at the beginning.

SECRET.—The box (see diagram) has two lids, the bottom, in reality, being in the middle. Thus it will clearly be seen that if four corks are placed in the top half and eight corks in the

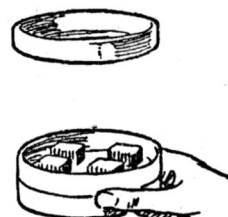

lower half, either of these quantities can be produced at any given moment, according to whichever lid is taken off; and in order to increase or diminish the number of corks, as the case may be, all that the performer need do is to simply turn his apparatus upside down, and the thing is done! No noise is heard, cork being silent in movement.

THE MYSTIC NAIL

EFFECT.—A box of ordinary household nails is given for examination, and then, after one has been selected by the audience for use, the conjurer passes it through his finger.

Upon withdrawal of nail, the said finger is found to be absolutely free from injury, and the nail may be passed round for further inspection.

SECRET.—The illustration below completely gives away the show. The box contains nails of one kind only (not mixed sizes), and they are of the same sort as the faked duplicate, which you hold in the palm of your right hand. As, however, you hold the box of nails in the same hand, the fake is not seen by anybody. A nail has been chosen, and you return to your table in order to place down the box. At this critical moment you have your chance, and you make use of it.

The previously palmed fake is adjusted to the finger, whilst the genuine nail is securely held under the cover of thumb, second, third, and fourth fingers, as indicated by the dotted lines. After making dreadful faces, and groaning, as if in great pain, you again turn towards your friendly table—ostensibly to pick up a small tray, but in reality to give opportunity for palming fake. Reproducing real nail, this is allowed to drop on to tray, and then once more handed round for minute inspection.

HANDKERCHIEFS THAT TIE AND UNTIE THEMSELVES

EFFECT.—Two coloured silk handkerchiefs are exhibited and may be handed round for close inspection. They are then

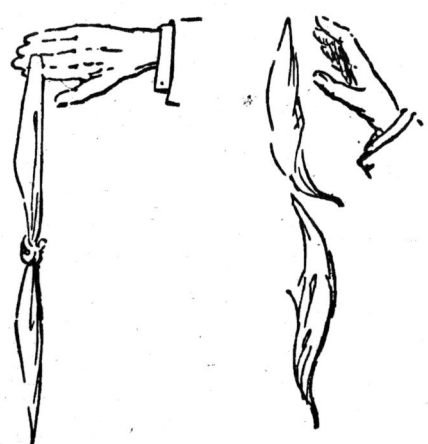

thrown up into the air and come down tied together. They are once more tossed into the air, and on descending it is noticed that they are single, no trace of a knot is to be seen.

SECRET.—Get a very small, thin indiarubber band, and place it over the thumb and first finger of the right hand, keeping the thumb and first finger as close together as possible. With your left hand pick up the two coloured pieces of silk, and hand them to one of the audience for scrutiny. In receiving the handkerchiefs back from the scrutineer, care should be taken to catch hold of one corner of each, and to promptly place them between the thumb and first finger of the right hand, immediately below the elastic band. Standing with your left side towards the audience, you then throw the handkerchiefs into the air. But before doing this, you drop your hand slightly, and in that moment the elastic band is allowed to slip from its previous position, and to encircle the handkerchiefs, which now appear to be tied together as they fall to the floor. You now gently pick up a corner of one silk, and the other is seen to be hanging therefrom, as if they were tied together. In throwing them a second time into the air, be careful to give the handkerchief which you are holding a sudden pull just as it leaves your hand. This will at once free the elastic band, and as the silks again descend the audience will notice that no knot (or sign of one) is to be found. Explain to the company that this is a very knotty problem! This deception is illustrated.

THE HANDCUFF PUZZLE

You tie the hands of two people together with two pieces of string, as shown in the diagram. You will see from the picture that the two lengths of string are looped at A, so that there is no possibility of the "prisoners," as we will call

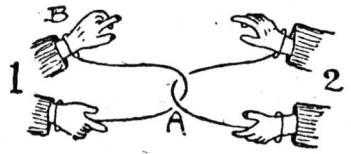

them, getting away from each other. At least, that is what appears to be the case. Now, what you challenge your friends to do is to separate the two people who are tied up. The solution is quite easy—much easier than it is to explain.

MAGIC AND TRICKERY

A loop is made in the string, bound to prisoner No. 2, and this is passed under the manacle of prisoner No. 1, so that it points towards No. 2. It is then slipped over both hands of No. 2. At this stage it is quite a simple matter to disengage the strings by noting how they are caught together.

THE HAUNTED UMBRELLA

The great charm about "the Haunted Umbrella" is that it requires no initial outlay.

EFFECT.—An ordinary umbrella is freely examined by the audience (or otherwise, according to taste). The conjurer seats himself upon a chair, and proceeds to make mystic passes over and around the umbrella; when, to the astonishment of everybody (the conjurer excepted), the umbrella stands at "attention," as shown in the illustration.

SECRET.—The mystic passes are of no consequence, one way or the other; they are merely introduced as a species of showmanship, on which account they should not be neglected. Prior to the commencement of this marvellous illusion, you must take the precaution to put on a black suit of clothes. To the left trousers leg, previously sew a strong piece of black thread, at the end of which you have made a loop. The loop-end must now be inserted into your left trousers pocket. The only other requirement is a fair-sized black pin, which must be placed in readiness behind the right knee. Whilst pattering freely upon umbrellas generally, and the one in question in particular, ample opportunity is afforded for transferring the piece of black thread from your left trousers pocket to behind your right knee, where the loop encircles the aforesaid black pin. The umbrella, of course, stands between the performer and the thread; so that when the knees are at a sufficient distance from one another to cause the thread not to sag, the poor old umbrella has no other alternative but *must* stand at " attention ! "

THE PAPER RINGS

We are not going to say that this is a particularly thrilling stunt. It is not. Nevertheless, it is very mystifying to those who do not know the secret, and it has the merit of pleasing those who do.

For this work, provide yourself with a coil of paper tape. It is an inch wide, gummed on one side, is very strong, and it is sold for sticking up light parcels. It can be had in a variety of colours. We have a partiality for red, which is certainly attractive.

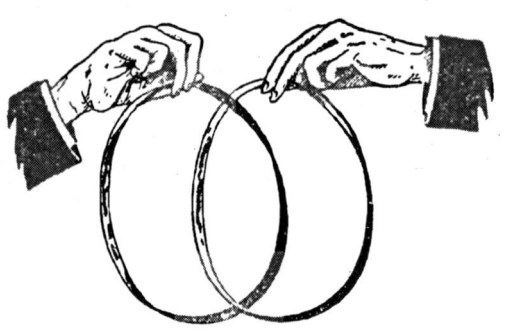

The Paper Rings

Cut off two lengths, each of thirty-six inches, for a performance. These lengths, you take to the footlights and ask if any member of the audience would care to inspect them. Naturally, there is always somebody who comes forward, and this inspection, to our mind, is usually the funniest part of the show. We have often wondered what these people expect to find when they come out and handle the tapes.

When the inspection is finished, proceed to join up the two ends of each length, and so make two separate paper hoops. It only takes a few moments for the gum to dry and then you can get on with the cutting.

In each case, cut the hoops, with a pair of scissors, so that the width of the tape is halved. There is no difficulty in doing this, except at the commencement of each cut; but this is no real trouble if a short piece of the hoop is folded and the scissors make their way into the paper.

Now, if you cut the two hoops in halves, throughout their entire length, it is reasonable to suppose that you will produce two results absolutely alike, but, curiously enough, in the first case you get two separate narrow hoops, and, in the second, two narrow hoops that are linked together.

That is the mystery. How does it happen?

In one case, you bring the ends of the tape together with the material perfectly free from any twist; but in the second, you give the tape a twist before joining it. Naturally the audience is not told this.

It is possible to make three, four, and even more hoops, in a similar way, but for this the tape has to be twisted several times, and, when the material is so treated, the wide-awake onlookers would be sure to guess what was happening. That is why you should stop short at two hoops.

THE ADHESIVE PENCIL

The following trick has deluded thousands of people, and will probably do the same to thousands more.

Hold up your left hand, palm facing the audience and clutching a pencil in a horizontal manner. Now, tell your hearers that, by straining the muscles very severely, you can exert a mysterious adhesive property. Once, you will add, you nearly dislocated your wrist, while performing this trick, so, to prevent a recurrence, you will grip the wrist tightly with the right hand.

This you do in such a way that the thumb is in front, as shown on left of the diagram.

Now, without apparently altering the grip on the wrist, you revolve the left hand, so that the back comes to view with the pencil protruding from either side. The fingers are clutching the pencil, but slowly you straighten them out and bring the left hand thumb round the front of the pencil so that it no longer supports the pencil. In fact, none of the fingers are supporting it, now that they are stretched out.

What is it that keeps the pencil from falling? Why, your adhesive properties, whatever that may mean.

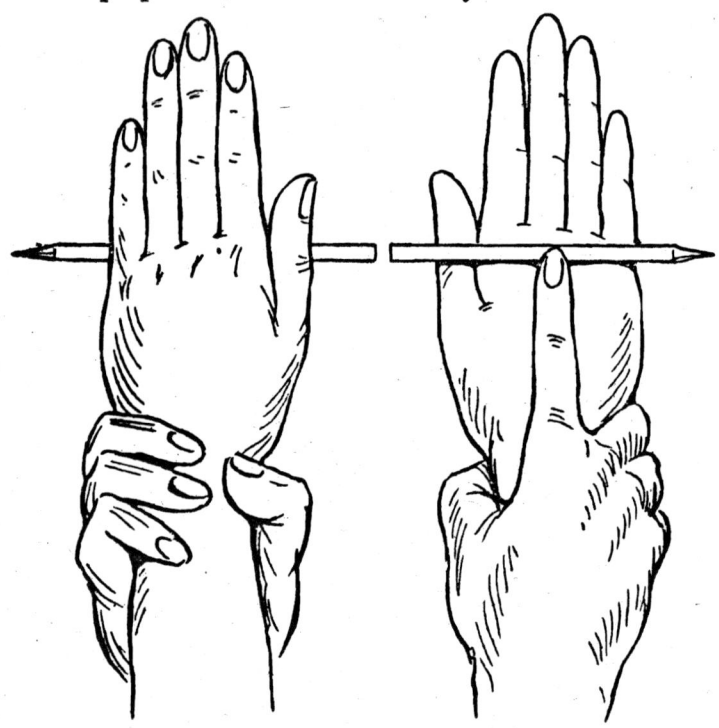

What the Audience sees   How the Pencil is supported

No, the explanation is that when you rotated your left hand within the right-hand grip, you quickly raised the index finger of the right hand, and, being turned away from the audience, it could not be seen. It is this index finger that supports the pencil.

You may think that the audience would at once notice how this trick is done. Practise it a few times in front of a mirror, and then try it before your friends. You will be surprised to find that the onlooker does not notice the absence of the index finger round your wrist.

BALANCING A WINE GLASS ON A PLAYING CARD

It is wonderful how some people can balance things. I once saw Cinquevalli put two billiard balls on the tip of a cue and walk round the stage with the cue on his forehead. But what I am going to describe is a little easier than that.

Take an ordinary playing card, hold it up for inspection; then go to your table and pour wine into a glass until it is three parts full. Stand the glass on the edge of the card and

How does the Wine Glass stand on the Card?
The small diagram gives the solution

hold it out at arm's length. Your performance will be sure to meet with applause.

You do it in this manner.

Show an ordinary card for inspection, then go to your table and replace it by a card of the same value that has been provided with a back strut, as shown in the small illustration. By opening the strut, you have not a two-way, but a three-way support, and the glass is easily balanced. Of course, the strut must be hidden from the audience.

You should suggest that it is the weight of the glass of wine that keeps the card from falling.

THE BIG BUTTONS AND THE LITTLE HOLE

This is a trick that never fails to amaze those who do not know it. Get a sheet of thick but pliable paper, about six by three inches in size, and cut in it, long ways, two parallel slits, three inches in length. Just below the end of the two slits make a circular hole, having a diameter equal to the distance between the slits. Now take a piece of fine twine, loop it through the slits, fold it through the circular hole, and tie a button to each end of the twine. The diagram will make

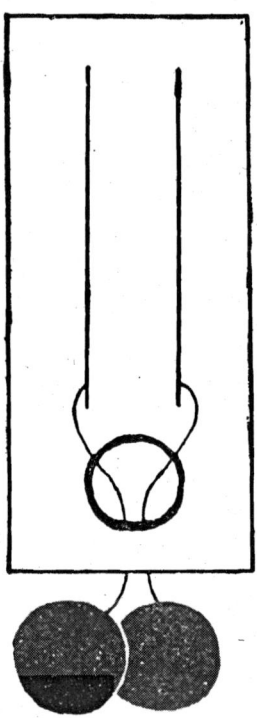

The Big Buttons and the Little Hole

the arrangement clear. The buttons, it will be seen, are too large to permit of them being pushed through the circular hole. Now, what you will require your friends to do is to separate the twine from the paper.

The puzzle is quite easy. Thread the strip of paper coming through the two long slits through the circular hole. This can be done by bending the sheet almost in two. When a good size loop of paper appears through the hole, the string and the buttons will drop away from the paper.

THE PLIABLE COPPER

The Penny trick which is here explained is a real eye-opener when you know how it is done. You are required to cut a hole in a sheet of notepaper, exactly the same size as a half-penny and then to pass a penny through the hole. Of course, you are not allowed to tear the paper in doing it. We have heard people say that it must be impossible to work the larger coin through the space of the smaller one; but try it and if you are not successful, the solution given will show you the way.

SOLUTION.—Fold the paper so that the crease runs across the circle that you have cut out, keeping the folded edge downwards. Put the penny inside the folded paper just over the hole and hold the two bottom ends of the paper, one in each hand. Draw the two hands slightly apart. The penny slips down a trifle through the hole. Draw the two hands a little further apart. The penny slips a trifle more through the hole. Continue to draw the two hands apart and, in a moment, the penny falls through the hole. What appears to be impossible is then accomplished.

THE JUMPING SIXPENCE

Here is a little trick that requires a slight knack but nothing more. Take an empty wine-glass, drop a sixpence into the well of it, and place a shilling on top. Ask your company if anybody can remove the smaller coin from the glass without touching either of the coins or the glass. Of course, your onlookers will not be able to. Bend down to the glass and blow with all your might on to the shilling, but a little to one side. The shilling will spin over and flick the sixpence into the air. We advise you to practise this trick beforehand, as it calls for some slight knowledge in estimating the correct amount of force required.

THE SIXPENCE THAT DOES AS IT IS TOLD

A good many people know this trick, so you must choose your audience carefully. Perhaps it is well to add the trick can only be performed when there is a smooth tablecloth on the table. It is, therefore, just the thing for performing after supper. Put separate shillings on the cloth just sufficiently far apart to allow the rim of an inverted tumbler to stand on them. Before inverting the tumbler place a sixpence midway between the two shillings. When all are in position, tell your friends that you can take away the sixpence without shifting the glass or the two larger coins. All you have to do is to scratch on the cloth with your finger nails and the sixpence will walk either towards you or away from you.

THE PENNY THAT STAYS

This is a simple little trick that every boy in the party will be performing for the rest of the evening after you have once shown him. Therefore, do not perform it too early in the proceedings. Hold up the middle finger of your left hand, balance on the top of it a cigarette-card, and place a penny on the top of that. See that the coin is " dead central " over your finger. What is required to be done is to take away the card without capsizing or even moving the penny. All sorts of futile attempts will be made and then you will show the method. With the thumb and middle finger of the right hand give the edge of the card a sharp flick. Away flies the card and the penny stays in position.

THE SUGAR HAT

This is an amusing trick that any child may perform with ease. The performer must first place a number of hats on a table and then ask for the sugar basin. He next selects a lump of sugar, and says that he will swallow it, and, by a magical power which he possesses, will guarantee that it shall be under one of the hats—whichever the company may select. Of course, they all think he will secure another piece of sugar and endeavour to place it under the hat chosen, and therefore a very sharp look out is kept on the sugar-basin. He swallows the sugar, asks which hat it is to be under, and on being told, places this on his own head—and, of course, fulfils the contract !

MAGIC AND TRICKERY

SOMETHING TO FEEL

This is something quite different. Ask a small boy in the company whether he can feel. He will naturally be surprised at your question, for it seems such a senseless one. "Well," you will add, "if I touch you with one or two things do you think you will know the difference?" "Why, of course," he will answer straight away. This is your opportunity, for everybody in the room will have by now grown interested. Sit the young gentleman on a chair, produce two pencils sharpened to a neat point and assure your victim that what you are going to do will not hurt. Hold the two pencils so that the points are level and just touch him on the soft part of the neck, immediately below the ear. It is absolutely impossible for him to tell whether one or two points are touching him on the spot, unless he can see what you are doing.

TRICKS WITH CARDS

THE TORN CARD TRICK

Take a card from an ordinary pack and offer the remainder to be shuffled. The card abstracted should be the same as a second pack that you possess. Whilst the shuffling is going on—or beforehand if you wish—you should tear a corner from the abstracted card, retaining the corner in your hand, and laying the mutilated card in some inconspicuous position on the table. Now take the pack from the person who has been shuffling, walk towards another person or your table, and substitute the second pack. Allow a card to be "chosen" from this. Request the chooser to tear it into pieces—say about sixteen (this precaution is necessary, or he may tear it into very minute fragments). Whilst the tearing is taking place, get rid of the second pack and lay the original ordinary pack on top of the card from which you have torn the corner. Now ask the spectator to hand you the fragments, with which you proceed to walk towards your table. Pausing, however, as if by after-thought, you say, "You had better keep one piece for identification," and you hand him the corner of the card *which you yourself have torn*. Then with great solemnity perform some business such as burning the fragments separately, or all in a heap in an ash tray. Or you may ask another onlooker to do this. Take the ashes and dispose of them in any manner you choose (if you wish to be very effective, pour them into the barrel of a small pistol, and then fire at the pack lying on the table). Pick up the pack, shuffle it a little to get the torn card into the middle, and then (after executing a "ruffle" if you have not made use of the pistol business) hand it round for the torn card to be discovered. Upon its discovery, request the person holding the torn-off corner to see if it fits; it will do so exactly, of course, much to the bewilderment of the audience.

THE BEST CARD TRICK

We look upon the following as the very best card trick. It may seem a little involved to follow in print, but run through it with a handful of actual cards and it becomes perfectly simple.

You stand on the stage before the audience, and hold out ten cards, fan-wise. "Would some lady or gentleman be good enough to come to my assistance?" you ask. Somebody offers.

"Now, what I want you to do is to remember one of the cards I have in my hand," you say, and, then, for the first time, you hold the ten cards still, so that they can be looked at properly. Until then, you were holding them out, but moving them about, in order that too much stock should not be taken of them.

The particular card being noted, you take the whole ten to a table, behind you, and stand them on end, against some support, so that they are never out of sight.

Next, give a pencil and a sheet of paper to the volunteer in the audience and ask him or her to write the name of the card upon it. When this is done, hold up the paper. "Our friend has picked out the two of diamonds," you proclaim, naming whatever card it was. "Now for the two of diamonds."

At this point you draw the attention of the audience to a large envelope displayed somewhere in the background of the stage. It is heavily sealed with wax. "Do you see that envelope? I'm going to walk three times round my table; then repeat those solemn words, Abracadabra, Antofogasta and Antimacassar; and when that is done, the card that is named on the paper will be no longer in the pack "—pointing to the cards, on end—" but in the envelope."

You walk round the table, chant the mystic words in a low dirge, then pick up the cards, and, with much show, count them. There are nine, and the two of diamonds is not among them. The tenth has disappeared! "So far, so good," you say, with a sigh of satisfaction. " Now for the second part."

You go to the envelope, walk with it to your table, break the seals and rip open the cover. Inside the large envelope you reveal a second envelope, and sometimes, a third, which is firmly stuck down. You carry this to your volunteer.

The Composite Card

" Open it please," you say. The volunteer opens it, and there, sure enough, is the two of diamonds! You mop your brow and utter the words: " Thank goodness! That was very hard work!" There is a burst of applause, and everybody is wondering how it happened.

Now for the secret.

Before commencing the trick, you take nineteen cards, all different, and peel the backs from the fronts. Next, make eight fresh cards by sticking sixteen fronts together. Also make one more card. On one side, it shows a face in the ordinary way, but, on the other there are two faces, overlapping as shown in the diagram.

Now, when the nine cards are looked at, there will appear

to be nine or ten cards according to which side is examined. This is secret number one.

When you hold out the ten cards in a fan, from which the volunteer is to make a selection, there are really only nine. The cards overlap by reason of their fan formation, and the fact that one card is merely two halves is not evident.

Also, when you deal out the cards, you have naturally, turned them over, and they appear to be nine cards. In addition, the two of diamonds is not among them, simply because the nineteen manipulated cards are all different.

Here let us make a digression. The ten cards forming the fan must not be the same as the nine dealt out later, for obvious reasons. This fact should not be noticed by the audience. Therefore, do not let them look at the fan too long. In addition, choose nondescript cards for both groups. Twos, threes, fours, sixes, are very difficult to memorise, and it will be practically impossible to do so if the reds and blacks are, in both cases, chosen in almost equal numbers. Therefore, no suspicion will be raised on that score.

At this point, it is evident that you must be able to withdraw from the big envelope any one of ten cards, *i.e.*, those that figured in the fan. This is not difficult. There are ten cards in the big envelope and each card is enclosed in a separate smaller envelope. Then, these ten envelopes are put, in pairs, in five larger envelopes and the five last mentioned envelopes are dealt with as follows: Four are put in pairs, in two still larger envelopes, and one is left by itself. All these are now sealed up in the biggest envelope of all. By breaking into the envelopes and noting the secret marks on them, you can memorise where you can find the particular card that is needed. That is how you are able to hand a sealed envelope, containing the two of diamonds, to the volunteer who elects to help you.

REVEALING A DISCOVERED CARD

1. Get the card on the top of the pack. Whilst talking, with the pack held between fingers and thumb by the shorter edges of the cards, gently push the top card (with the thumb of the other hand) a little way off the pack, so that its long edge projects about three-quarters of an inch from the other cards. This should be done in such a manner that the pro-

MAGIC AND TRICKERY

jecting edge is hidden under the palm of the hand which holds the pack.

Hold the cards about two feet above table or floor, and release your grip smartly, letting the whole pack fall. The rush of air, acting on the projecting edge of the top card, will cause it to turn over and lie face upwards on the top of the pack. Five minutes' practice will enable you to obtain the desired result every time.

2. Get your card, as before, on top of the pack. Previously moistening the fingers (not thumb), hold the pack towards the audience bottom card upwards, gripped between fingers and thumb by one corner, as illustrated; ask someone to knock the pack downwards out of your hand. All the cards will fall with the exception of the undermost, which remains between your moistened fingers and thumb, staring your temporary assistant in the face.

3. Take the "discovered" card, with seven others, and lay them face downwards on the table. Ask someone to indicate any four of them. Now remove those cards, *whether indicated or not*, which do *not* contain the card you are to "reveal." Repeat the process, getting someone to choose two of the remaining four cards, and removing the cards *you* do not want as before. With the last two cards go through the business again, returning the unwanted card to the pack. One card, face downwards, remains on the table; ask the original "chooser" of the card what his card was, and then turn it up.

This last is a very effective finish. You should "patter" to the effect that the audience *themselves* have chosen which cards you should return to the pack. Of course, they have not; but if you are lucky, the cards indicated may have contained on each occasion the card to be revealed; and even if you have been forced to remove the indicated cards in one instance, and in another to leave them on the table, there is little fear of this being noticed by an audience to which this simple deception is unknown. You should, of course, converse during the process, saying, " You choose those ? Very well, that leaves me these," or " Very good, then I will return these to the pack."

4. Having placed the card which is to be " revealed " on

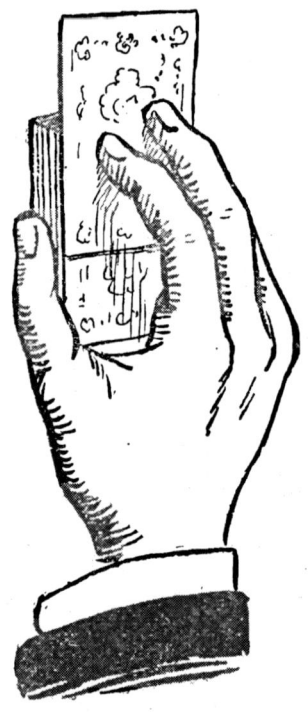

the top of the pack, you may cause it to rise up out of the pack apparently of its own accord in the following manner : Hold the pack so that the bottom card directly faces the audience. With the first and second fingers, as shown in the second illustration, push the card upwards with the fingers in alternate steps. When the top card is well up you can hold it in position with the first finger, and work up two or three more following cards, if so desired, with the second finger alone. To the audience each card appears to rise up out of the middle of the pack.

THE TWO CARDS SELECTED

This little trick is a puzzler to the audience, and it has the merit of always being a certainty. There is nothing to do in the way of sleight-of-hand and everything depends on memorizing a few facts. First of all, take any twenty cards out of the pack and put them in ten heaps of two. Allow your audience to do all this, if it will inspire their confidence. Next, ask someone to lift up the two cards of any heap and note what they are. Three or four people can select pairs, if they like. Tell your friends that you are quite prepared to go out of the room while they are making their choice, if it would give them any pleasure. When the pairs have been selected, pick up the twenty cards and do not shuffle them, as the pairs must remain together.

Now look at the following table; the words have no meaning but they will help you to memorize certain positions which will be explained:

```
M U T U S
D E D I T
N O M E N
C O C I S
```

You will see that every letter that appears in this table appears twice, and, remember, you are dealing with pairs of cards. Having begun to realize the connexion between the cards and letters, the rest will come to you easily. Take the twenty cards and set them out in four rows of five, but do it in this way. Let the first card take the position of the M in the first row and the second card the position of the M in the third row. The third card fills the position of the first U in the top line and the fourth card the position of the second U in the same line. In other words, the first pair represents the two M's, the second pair the two U's, the third pair the two T's, the fourth pair the two S's, the fifth pair the two D's, the sixth pair the two E's, the seventh pair the two I's, the eighth pair the two N's, the ninth pair the two O's, and the tenth pair the two C's.

When you have set out the full twenty cards, ask your friend in which row or rows his two cards figure. As an example, we will suppose that he says the second and third rows. You quickly think of the table and remember that E is the only letter that comes in both these rows, and you also remember that it comes second in the second row and fourth in the third row. You single out the two cards in these positions, and, sure enough, they are the two he looked at and noted at the commencement. Had he said the cards are both in the first row, your key letter is U, which tells you that the required cards are the second and fourth. Naturally, you will not divulge the letters to your onlookers, but you will keep them firmly in mind.

SPOTTING THE CHOSEN CARD

There is no easier card trick than this one, yet it is extremely mystifying, when you do not know how it is done. Before your friends arrive, sort out the whole pack into two heaps, placing all the odd numbered cards in one, and all the even-numbered in the other. Look upon the Jack and King as odd and the queen as even. Shuffle both heaps separately and reform the pack by putting one heap on the other.

When a friend arrives, tell him you can show him a wonderful trick. Place the pack on the table and get him to withdraw a card without you seeing its face. Watch him carefully and note whether his selection comes from the top or bottom half of the pack. When all this is done, you cut the pack and tell him to drop his card on top of what remains standing on the table. The main part of the trick lies on your cut. If his selected card came from the top half of the pack, you cut so that it is returned to the bottom half and *vice-versa*.

Now you take the whole pack and turn over the cards one by one. When you come to an odd card among a number of even cards, or an even one among the odd cards, you know you have reached his selection. " There is is," you say, triumphantly.

FINDING A CARD " THOUGHT OF "

Take twenty-five cards, and allow the audience to shuffle and cut them as they please. Then lay them out in five rows of five cards face upwards. Ask an onlooker to think of any of the cards thus exposed, and tell you in which row it is. On being told, note the card at the left-hand end of that row. Next, take up the cards in the following manner : begin at the last (or right-hand) card of the bottom row, placing it on the face of the card immediately above it in the next row. Place these two cards on the card immediately

MAGIC AND TRICKERY

above them in the next higher row, and so to the top. Repeat this in turn with each of the five vertical rows which your cards necessarily form if they are laid out neatly. The last card you pick up will be the left-hand card of the first or top horizontal row.

Now deal out the cards again in five horizontal rows as before. Ask the onlooker to tell you in which row his card appears this time. When he tells you, look along the top or bottom row for the card which you noted as being first in the row to which he pointed the first time. Above it or below it, vertically, in the row to which he now points, is the card of which he " thought."

ANOTHER METHOD

Take any odd number of playing cards which is a multiple of three (*e.g.*, nine, fifteen, twenty-one, twenty-seven). Deal them face upwards in three heaps, asking a spectator to note one card, and to tell you in which heap it is. Pick up the heaps, with the indicated heap between the other two, and repeat the process *twice*. When the spectator points to a heap for the third time, you may know that his chosen card is the middle one of the heap—that is, if each heap contains five cards it will be the third ; if seven, the fourth, and so on. If you do not know this little trick, try it and see why it should be so.

TELLING THE CARDS

This is a remarkably easy trick, yet it usually mystifies your audience.

You take a pack of cards and begin to shuffle them. Just as you are about to finish, you say, " Oh, I suppose it would be best if I asked a few friends to give the cards a shuffle," and, thereupon, you hand round the pack and various people do as requested. Naturally, it is quite impossible for you to know, now, where any particular card is placed.

At this point, you regain the pack, put the cards, without looking at them, in a box and shut down the lid.

With a majestic thump, you hit the top of the box, and say, " Ladies and Gentlemen, I have acquired a certain amount of skill in the art of divination, and, to prove to you what I say, I am going to tell you the top card of the pack. It is the five of hearts."

Thereupon, you open the box, pick up the top card, and, sure enough, it is the five of hearts.

You throw the card down on the table, and then pick up a handful of other cards from the top of the pack. The exact number does not matter, but you endeavour to take up five or six.

Spreading out these five or six cards, fan-wise, and face down, you say, "Let me show you the three of clubs, the queen of diamonds, and the ace of spades." Immediately, you draw three cards out of the fan, and everybody is surprised to find that you are absolutely correct.

The trick depends on putting the cards in a box with a dummy lid. Behind the dummy lid are a few cards, the names of which you have memorised. That majestic thump which you gave the box, brought down the dummy lid, and placed the prepared cards at the top of the pack, where they awaited your pleasure.

READING THE CARDS

There are dozens of ways of reading cards, and, though audiences know quite well that every one of them involves some trick, they still clamour for them and consider a show incomplete unless a pack of cards is produced and the faces are read to them.

The best method, for singling out the cards, is to hold the pack in the hand backs towards you and faces towards the audience. The cards should be held at arm's length, and a trifle higher than the eye level. This satisfies the audience that you cannot see the faces of the cards.

The cards have previously been shuffled, and, while getting things ready, you talk about the mysterious properties of paper and the magnetic effect it has on some people's eyes, notably your own. During this nonsense, you stick a tiny pellet of wax on the index finger of your left hand and press into it a tiny mirror, such as can be bought for a few pence.

Then you hold the pack in the same hand, and the index finger, carrying the mirror, is so poised, a little to the front, that it reflects to your eye the card which is facing the audience. Naturally you read out the card with the utmost ease. The right hand then shuffles the pack while your left arm is still at full length, and, in this way, some other card is brought into view. You read that one and continue in the same way half a dozen times before turning to an entirely different item.

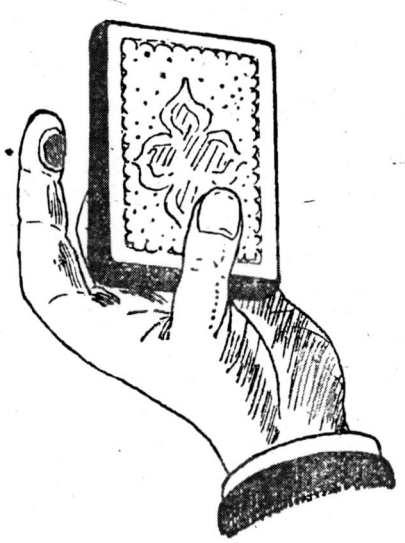

What Card is it ?
The tiny mirror on the finger tells you

Watch the audience all the time, and, if you see someone explaining to his neighbour how he thinks it is done, switch off to the next turn at once. Never give anybody time to reason out your methods.

TO CATCH A CARD (OR TWO CARDS) FROM A SHOWER OF CARDS

Place the card to be revealed at the top of the pack. If two cards, place one at each end of the pack. Draw the card or cards to be revealed a little way off the remainder. Hold the pack between fingers and thumb, having previously moistened the fingers (if one card) or fingers and thumb (if two cards); flick the pack upwards, causing all the cards, excepting those retained by the moistened fingers and thumb, to fly into the air in a shower. The eyes of your audience will be on the cards in the air; your hand, holding the retained card or cards, should be lowered momentarily behind the table or behind your leg. (You should stand " sideways " to the audience if you are not behind a table.) Then, as the cards are fluttering down, thrust your hand quickly amongst them; as they fall to the ground your hand remains holding up the card or cards to be revealed, and it will really look as though you had caught them in mid-air.

This somewhat spectacular effect cannot be obtained without some little practice, but it is not by any means difficult; you have only to experiment a few times to learn just how high and how widely to throw the "shower."

Finally, a word must be added with reference to "getting the card on the top of the pack." The reader ere this has perhaps said to himself: "Ah, there's the rub!" True, it is much easier to say than to do. But it is not half so difficult as might be expected, even for a complete novice. The previously suggested method of laying out the cards apparently haphazard and picking them up with every appearance of carelessness will rarely cause comment. The great thing is to keep the minds of the audience occupied whilst you are doing this sort of thing. For this nothing is so efficacious as a perfectly self-possessed and casual conversational manner. A stock of good stories should form part of your repertoire; no "patter" is successful that does not include several of these—fairly short ones, necessarily. You will find a good selection in the first section of this volume.

TO TELL WHICH OF FOUR CARDS HAVE BEEN TURNED ROUND DURING YOUR ABSENCE

If you examine an ordinary pack of cards closely you will find that on some of the cards the small "pips" or suit marks are not placed equidistantly from the edge of the paste-board; the "pip" at one corner in some cases is twice as far from the edge as the "pip" at the other corner. Select four cards where you can detect this fairly easily, but beware, of course, of choosing any cards where it is too obvious. Lay the cards on the table with all the close-to-the-edge "pips" at the top. If, when you return after a short absence, one or more of the cards has been turned round, you will be able to detect it at once.

This is very simple when you know the secret, but the audience generally takes some time to discover exactly what it is.

THOUGHT-READING AND SECOND-SIGHT

Unless your guests are very young there is little doubt that they will enjoy a brief séance of thought-reading or second-sight. With a little preparation there is much that you can do that is both mystifying and exciting, and we strongly recommend you to try a few " stunts " when most of your visitors are over the age of twelve.

The professional thought-reader often acts alone, but as you will only be disposed to spend a limited time in practising the art it will be much simpler if you work with a confederate. Your course of action may follow one of two very different plans. In the first your assistant will help you without the audience knowing that he is in any way connected with you. In the second he will appear openly in the rôle of your medium.

We will suppose, first of all, that you decide to keep the audience in ignorance of the fact that you have an assistant. You will then plan such mysterious items as the following; " Ladies and Gentlemen," you will say, " I have had a certain amount of dealings with the ancients who taught the laws of mystification. I cannot claim that divination is one of my strong points, but this much I do aspire to, and that is to expose the simple thought of my audience." This opening statement is, of course, merely an empty piece of verbiage to get your hearers into the proper frame of mind. " Now," you will continue, " I would like you all to agree on a number less than a hundred while I am out of the room, and I should like one of you to come with me to make quite sure that I am not listening outside the door." You then ask the audience to select anyone they choose to watch over you while outside. This offer on your part to submit to a guard inspires confidence, and it means absolutely nothing. Somebody is then chosen and you are led from the room. It might possibly happen, as bad luck will arise at times, that your confederate is chosen by the multitude to watch over you outside, when, of course, he must remain within at all costs. If he has not wit enough to suggest someone else without attracting attention, you will have to say, supposing you are of the male sex, " Well, that's rough luck, I was hoping that some lady would be deputed to come with me." And it is a thousand to one that a lady is chosen in the end.

While you are outside, the company jointly agrees on the number twenty-five, we will suppose. Loud cries from within herald the news that all is ready and you re-enter looking very thoughtful. "Ah, yes," you mutter in low tones, "the spirit of the unseen materialism is a little diffuse; but I think we can delve into its quandaries." You then go amongst your audience and, half apologetically, ask permission to place your hand on certain people's foreheads. If the people are few, do it to all, but if numerous select both prominent and unprominent guests. Say that some are not concentrating but others are very distinct. Linger over some and hurry over others. Whatever else you do, you must feel the forehead of your confederate and he will give you the clue. He will shut his teeth tightly and, without moving his face in the least will click his jaws twice, then pause slightly and give five clicks. This will tell you that the required number is twenty-five. The clicks can be felt quite plainly on the sides of the temples. Of course, you will not cry out "twenty-five" immediately after you have sounded him; you will discreetly go to two or three other people and then say, "Ah, it is now apparent. One quarter of one hundred" (or any other number) " comes to me from the depths of mystery."

Having performed this little fraud with satisfaction, turn to something else, as it is a good rule never to do exactly the same thing twice. Decide this time that you will divine any card out of a pack of playing cards, and, beforehand, agree with your confederate that one tap means hearts, two taps diamonds, etc., and that after a pause, one, two, three, etc., means one, two, three, etc., of the suit. You will not feel the foreheads this time, but hold the hands, one by one, of certain members present. You must be careful to hold your confederate's hand so that the tips of his fingers can lightly tap the palm of your hand, and he must be careful that he taps so lightly that no jerks are apparent. Of course, if you care to code your work a little more thoroughly, the signals may be shortened by agreeing that a tap with the third finger counts five and taps with the second count one. This will get over the trouble of having to give eleven, twelve, and thirteen signals for a jack, queen, and king respectively.

A less scientific form of thought-reading may be carried

MAGIC AND TRICKERY

out in this way. You ask your audience to decide on any animal it chooses, while you are out of the room, and when you return to read out a list of twelve animals containing the selected one and eleven others. The names must be read over slowly and deliberately, and everybody, you will stipulate, must think hard of the chosen creature. While the names are being gone over you naturally scan the sea of faces because you are reading the thoughts, and you look anxiously from one to the other. As a matter of fact, you really only look at the confederate, and, when the selected animal is mentioned, he just touches some part of his head—it may be to rub an eye, to flick an ear, or adjust his glasses. His act is done quite unassumingly and with every show of legitimacy. But it is sufficient for your purpose, and when the list has been read over you say, "Kangaroo," because it was when this name was mentioned that your assistant gave the agreed signal. It will add to the mystery if you stop the names being read out, say half-way through, offering the excuse that Miss So-and-So is not concentrating, and you are sorry to say the "aura will be spoiled if everybody is not doing his or her bit to complete its continuity."

Now, let us turn to work done openly with a confederate. You both come into the room, and, on being blindfolded by a selection made from the audience, you take a seat in a corner, your back to the room. Your assistant produces a pack of cards from his pocket and asks somebody to choose one at random. A card being decided on, your partner asks you which it is of the fifty-two possible cards, and is immediately told correctly.

Now this accurate divination of the card appears a little mysterious to the onlookers. You certainly could not see, and the card was not the choice of your confederate. How then did you tell? Well, the latter is quite easy to explain. It all rests on the fact that what the confederate said to you was coded.

Every thought-reader will naturally prefer to make his own code, but here is a simple specimen code :

(1) When the card is a diamond, the confederate speaks to the blindfolded partner, using a sentence beginning with the word "Now."

(2) When the card is a heart, the sentence begins with the word "Well."

(3) When the card is a spade, the sentence begins with the word "What."

(4) When the card is a club, the sentence begins with the word "Which."

From this it will be seen that the suit is easily divined. The actual card in the suit is told just as easily, for the confederate uses a sentence containing one word for each spot on the card. Thus:

"Well?" stands for the ace of hearts.
"Well, what?" stands for the two of hearts.
"Well, what card?" stands for the three of hearts.
"Well, what is it?" stands for the four of hearts.
"Well, what card is it?" stands for the five of hearts; and so on, jack, queen, and king being reckoned as eleven, twelve, and thirteen, respectively.

In order to mystify the audience still more it is a good plan to allow two people to select a card simultaneously and, by framing two sentences on the above lines, you can immediately tell which the two are.

It would, of course, be unwise to devote much of a séance to divining cards. After one example has been worked it will be well to turn to coins, because these the members of the audience can provide themselves. The coins that are likely to come up for scrutiny are the (1) farthing, (2) halfpenny, (3) penny, (4) threepenny bit, (5) sixpence, (6) shilling, (7) florin, and (8) half-crown.

(a) To be able to tell the *value* of a coin, select eight keywords to come at the beginning of the confederate's sentence. These eight words should fit in with the eight values mentioned above.

(b) To be able to tell the *date* of a coin, work as follows:

(1) If date commences with "eighteen" the confederate uses some hesitating expression as "Er," which is otherwise left out of all reckoning.

(2) If date commences with "nineteen," which will be most usual, no hesitating commencement.

(3) Two remarks are now made. The first will commence with the key-word (see above), and contain as many words as is indicated by the third figure of the date. The second remark will commence with any word, and contain as many words as is indicated by the fourth figure of the date.

MAGIC AND TRICKERY

(4) If a nought enters into the date, a slight cough suggests its presence.

Thus the value and the date of your coin are quickly told. By remembering that George V came to the throne in 1910, Edward VII in 1901, and Victoria in 1837, you may wisely tell the audience that the coin bears the head of such and such a sovereign before you divulge the date.

It is not a bad plan to have a simple code word to denote all foreign coins, since some member of the audience may easily have an odd mark or franc in his pocket. " Ah," you say, with a smile, as soon as you get the code word, " I am being offered a coin that cannot be spent in England; it is of no use in our country ; it is foreign."

Many other simple things besides cards and coins can be dealt with. The confederate should, for instance, ask if anybody present has a watch that has stopped, and by means of his code you tell when it stopped. If nobody has such a watch, perhaps somebody would care to write down any time he chooses on a piece of paper, suggests the confederate, and a member of the audience obliges with " Twelve twenty-five." The confederate then makes four rapid remarks, the first consisting of one word, the second with two, the third with two, and the fourth with five. A pause of slightly longer duration is made between the hours and minutes and a little cough or clearing of the throat denotes the presence of a nought.

When a number of tricks of this character have been performed, the " turn " is slightly varied. You remove your bandage and distribute a number of sheets of paper and ask the audience to write on them the name of a country, a noted person, a town, etc. When the writing is finished, the papers are carefully folded or sealed in envelopes so that the names are obscured. The papers are collected and set before you. " Ah," you say as you pick up one, " this bears the word ' Bombay.' " You open the paper and read " Bombay," and rapidly proceed to the next. " This one says—now let me see—Stockholm." You open the paper and read " Stockholm." " Which gentleman or lady, please, wrote Stockholm ? " Up goes a hand and everybody is satisfied. In the same way a good number of papers are first divined and then read, following which some member of the audience admits having written the name. The trick is this. The first paper did not say " Bombay " but

"Stockholm." "Bombay" was merely invented by you and you were quick to pass it over. The name you gave out as being on the second paper was really on the first, the one you gave out as being on the third paper was on the second, and so on. Thus you always read the name on a paper before you gave it out to the audience.

With this, we must draw to a close our remarks about thought-reading. Undoubtedly it is an art which offers very fine opportunities for those who will take the trouble to apply these hints to fresh themes. Five or six items will usually take up quite as much time as will be convenient for a party.

COMMUNITY SINGING

Most of us cannot sing well enough to stand up and perform by ourselves, and many more have not the pluck; but all of us derive considerable enjoyment from singing in company with others. Even if we only make a noise, it is satisfying. Therefore, do not overlook the social value of community singing, when you have friends gathered under your roof. And, if you want your guests to derive the maximum amount of fun out of their efforts, give each of them a paper hat. With such a hat on their heads, people are much more likely to let themselves go.

All the songs set out below are universal favourites, and everybody knows the tunes. It is the words which prove the stumbling block.

THERE IS A TAVERN IN THE TOWN

There is a tavern in the town, in the town,
And there my dear love sits him down, sits him down,
And drinks his wine 'mid laughter free,
And never, never thinks of me.

Chorus—
 Fare thee well, for I must leave thee,
 Do not let the parting grieve thee,
 And remember that the best of friends must part, must part.
 Adieu, kind friends, adieu, adieu, adieu.
 I can no longer stay with you, stay with you.
 I'll hang my harp on a weeping willow tree.
 And may the world go well with thee.

He left me for a damsel dark, damsel dark,
Each Friday night they used to spark, used to spark,
And now, my love, once true to me,
Takes that dark damsel on his knee.
 Chorus.

Oh! dig my grave both wide and deep, wide and deep,
Put tombstones at my head and feet, head and feet,
And on my breast carve a turtle dove,
To signify I died of love.
 Chorus.

ONE MORE RIVER

Old Noah once he built the ark,
 There's one more river to cross.
And patched it up with hickory bark.
 There's one more river to cross.
One more river, and that's the river of Jordan,
One more river,
There's one more river to cross.

He went to work to load his stock,
 There's one more river to cross.
He anchored the ark with a great big rock.
 There's one more river to cross, etc.

The animals went in one by one.
 There's one more river to cross.
The elephant chewing a caraway bun.
 There's one more river to cross, etc.

The animals went in two by two.
There's one more river to cross.
The rhinoceros and the kangaroo.
There's one more river to cross, etc.

The animals went in three by three.
There's one more river to cross.
The bear, the flea, and the bumble bee.
There's one more river to cross, etc.

The animals went in four by four.
There's one more river to cross.
Old Noah got mad and hollered for more.
There's one more river to cross, etc.

The animals went in five by five.
There's one more river to cross.
With Saratoga trunks they did arrive.
There's one more river to cross, etc.

The animals went in six by six.
There's one more river to cross.
The hyena laughed at the monkey's tricks.
There's one more river to cross, etc.

The animals went in seven by seven.
There's one more river to cross.
Said the ant to the elephant, "Who are you a-shovin'?"
There's one more river to cross, etc.

The animals went in eight by eight.
There's one more river to cross.
They came with a rush 'cause 'twas so late.
There's one more river to cross, etc.

The animals went in nine by nine.
There's one more river to cross.
Old Noah shouted, " Cut that line."
There's one more river to cross, etc.

The animals went in ten by ten.
There's one more river to cross.
The ark she blew her whistle then.
There's one more river to cross, etc.

And then the voyage did begin,
There's one more river to cross ;
Old Noah pulled the gang-plank in.
There's one more river to cross, etc.

They never knew where they were at.
There's one more river to cross ;
Till the old ark bumped on Ararat.
There's one more river to cross, etc.

The old ark landed high and dry,
There's one more river to cross ;
The cow kissed the baboon good-bye.
There's one more river to cross, etc.

Now please just look out for the text,
There's one more river to cross ;
To be continued in our next.
There's one more river to cross, etc.

I LOVE SIXPENCE

I love sixpence, I love sixpence,
 I love sixpence better than my life.
I spent a penny of it, I lent another,
 And I took fourpence home to my wife.

Oh, my fourpence, I love fourpence,
 I love fourpence better than my life.
I spent a penny of it, I spent another,
 And I took twopence home to my wife.

Oh, my twopence, I love twopence,
 I love twopence better than my life.
I spent a penny of it, I spent another,
 And I took nothing home to my wife.

Oh, my nothing, I love nothing,
 What will nothing buy for my wife ?
I have nothing, I spend nothing.
 I love nothing better than my wife !

BONNIE DOON

Ye banks and braes o' bonnie Doon,
 How can ye bloom sae fresh and fair?
How can ye chant, ye little birds,
 And I sae weary fu' o' care ?
Thou'lt break my heart thou warbling bird,
 That wantons through the flow'ry thorn ;
Thou minds me o' departed joys,
 Departed never to return.

Aft hae I rov'd by bonnie Doon,
 To see the rose and woodbine twine ;
And ilka bird sang o' its love,
 And fondly sae did I o' mine.
Wi' lightsome heart I pu'd a rose,
 Fu' sweet upon its thorny tree ;
And my fause lover stole my rose,
 But ah ! he left the thorn wi' me.

LITTLE BINGO

The farmer loved a pretty young lass,
And gave her a wedding ring-o;
There was R with an I, I with an N,
N with a G, G with an O,
There were R, I, N, G, O—
For he gave her a wedding ring-o.

Now is not this a nice little song—
I think it is, by Jingo;
There is J with an I, I with an N,
N with a G, G with an O—
There are J, I, N, G, O,
It's a nice little song, by Jingo!

O DEAR! WHAT CAN THE MATTER BE?

O dear! what can the matter be?
Dear, dear! what can the matter be?
O dear! what can the matter be?
Johnny's so long at the fair.

He promised to buy me a bunch of
  blue ribbons.
He promised to buy me a bunch of
  blue ribbons,
He promised to buy me a bunch of
  blue ribbons,
To tie up my bonny brown hair.
And it's O dear! etc.

He promised he's bring me a basket
  of posies,
A garland of lilies, a garland of roses,
A little straw hat, to set off the blue
  ribbons,
That tie up my bonnie brown hair.
And it's O dear! etc.

COME, LANDLORD, FILL THE FLOWING BOWL

Come landlord, fill the flowing bowl,
Until it doth run over.
Chorus—
  For to-night we'll merry merry be,
  For to-night we'll merry merry be,
  For to-night we'll merry merry be,
  To-morrow we'll be sober.

The man who drinketh small beer,
And goes to bed quite sober.
Chorus—
  Fades as the leaves do fade,
  Fades as the leaves do fade,
  Fades as the leaves do fade,
  That drop off in October.

The man who drinketh strong beer,
And goes to bed right mellow.
Chorus—
  Lives as he ought to live,
  Lives as he ought to live,
  Lives as he ought to live,
  And dies a jolly good fellow.

But he who drinks just what he likes,
And getteth half seas over.
Chorus—
  Will live until he die,
  Will live until he die,
  Will live until he die,
  And then lie down in clover.

The man who kisses a pretty girl,
And goes and tells his mother.
Chorus—
  Ought to have his lips cut off,
  Ought to have his lips cut off,
  Ought to have his lips cut off,
  And never kiss another.

COCK ROBIN

Who killed Cock Robin?
" I," said the sparrow,
" With my bow and arrow,
I killed Cock Robin."

Chorus—
All the birds in the air fell a-sighing
  and a-sobbing,
When they heard of the death of
  poor Cock Robin,
When they heard of the death of
  poor Cock Robin.
Johnny will you go, Johnny will you
  go, Johnny will you go with an
  F I O?
Johnny will you go, Johnny will you
  go, Johnny will you go-i-o?

Who saw him die?
" I," said the fly,
" With my little eye,
I saw him die."
            Chorus.

Who'll toll the bell?
" I," said the bull,
" Because I can pull,
I'll toll the bell."
            Chorus.

Who'll dig the grave?
" I," said the owl,
" With my little trowel,
I'll dig his grave."
            Chorus.

Who'll be the parson?
" I," said the rook,
" With my bell and book,
I'll be the parson."
            Chorus.

Who'll be chief mourner?
" I," said the dove,
" I mourn for my love,
I'll be chief mourner."
            Chorus.

IF ALL THE WORLD WERE PAPER

If there had been no heroes,
And none that did great wrongs;
If fiddlers should turn farmers all,
What should we do for songs?

If all things were eternal,
And nothing their end bringing—
If this should be, then how should we
Now make an end of singing!

HERE'S A HEALTH UNTO HIS MAJESTY

Here's a health unto his Majesty,
With a fa la la la la la la.
Confusion to his enemies,
With a fa la la la la la la.
And he that will not drink his health,
I wish him neither wit nor wealth,
Nor yet a rope to hang himself,
With a fa la la la la la la la la,
With a fa la la la la la la.

All Cavaliers will please combine,
With a fa la la la la la la.
To drink this loyal toast of wine,
With a fa la la la la la la.
If anyone should answer " No,"
I only wish that he may go
With Roundhead rogues to Jericho,
With a fa la la la la la la la la,
With a fa la la la la la la.

THE BRITISH GRENADIERS

Some talk of Alexander,
And some of Hercules,
Of Hector and Lysander,
And such great names as these;
But of all the world's brave heroes,
There's none that can compare,
With a tow row row row row row,
To the British Grenadiers.

COME, LASSES AND LADS

Come, lasses and lads, get leave of your dads,
And away to the Maypole, hie.
There ev'ry He has got him a She,
And the Fiddler's standing by ;
For Willy has got his Jill,
And Johnny has got his Joan,
To trip it, trip it, trip it, trip it,
Trip it up and down,
To trip it, trip it, trip it, trip it,
Trip it up and down.

" You're out," says Dick, " Not I," says Nick,
" 'Twas the fiddler played it wrong."
" 'Tis true," says Hugh, and so says Sue.
And so says ev'ry one.
The fiddler then began
To play the tune again,
And ev'ry girl did trip it, trip it,
Trip it to the men,
And ev'ry girl did trip it, trip it,
Trip it to the men.

" Good-night," says Harry, " Good-night," says Mary.
" Good-night," says Poll to John ;
" Good-night," says Sue to her sweetheart Hugh ;
" Good-night," says ev'ry one.
Some walked and some did run,
Some loiter'd on the way,
And bound themselves, by kisses twelve,
To meet the next holiday,
And bound themselves, by kisses twelve,
To meet the next holiday.

GOOD KING WENCESLAS

Good King Wenceslas look'd out
On the feast of Stephen,
When the snow lay round about ;
Deep and crisp and even ;
Brightly shone the moon that night,
Though the frost was cruel,
When a poor man came in sight
Gath'ring winter fuel.

" Hither page and stand by me,
If thou know'st it telling,
Yonder peasant, who is he ?
Where and what his dwelling ? "
" Sire, he lives a good league hence,
Underneath the mountain,
Right against the forest fence ;
By Saint Agnes' fountain."

" Bring me flesh and bring me wine,
Bring me pine logs hither ;
Thou and I will see him dine
When we bear them thither."
Page and Monarch, forth they went,
Forth they went together ;
Through the rude wind's wild lament
And the bitter weather.

" Sire, the night is darker now,
And the wind blows stronger ;
Fails my heart, I know not how,
I can go no longer."
" Mark my footsteps, good my page ;
Tread thou in them boldly ;
Thou shalt find the winter rage
Freeze thy blood less coldly."

In his master's steps he trod,
Where the snow lay dinted ;
Heat was in the very sod
Which the saint had printed.

Therefore, Christian men be sure,
　Wealth or rank possessing,
Ye who now will bless the poor,
　Shall yourselves find blessing.

HERE'S TO THE MAIDEN

Here's to the maiden of bashful fifteen;
　Here's to the widow of fifty;
Here's to the flaunting extravagant queen,
　And here's to the housewife that's thrifty.

Chorus—
　Let the toast pass, drink to the lass,
　　I'll warrant she'll prove an excuse for a glass.

Here's to the charmer whose dimples we prize;
　Now to the maid who has none, Sir;
Here's to the girl with a pair of blue eyes,
　And here's to the nymph with but one, Sir.
　　　Chorus.

Here's to the maid with a bosom of snow;
　Now to her that's as brown as a berry.
Here's to the wife with a full face of woe,
　And now to the girl that is merry.
　　　Chorus.

For let 'em be clumsy, or let 'em be slim,
　Young or ancient, I care not a feather;
So fill a pint bumper quite up to the brim,
　And let us e'en toast them together.
　　　Chorus.

I MARRIED A WIFE

I married a wife, O then! (O then!)
I married a wife, O then!
I married a wife, she's the plague of my life,
And I longed to be single again.
Chorus—
　Again and again, again, (again),
　Again and again, again,
　I married a wife, she's the plague of my life,
　And I longed to be single again.

My wife took a fever, O then! (O then!)
My wife took a fever, O then!
My wife took a fever, I hoped 'twouldn't leave her,
For I longed to be single again.
Chorus—
　Again and again, again (again,)
　Again and again, again,
　My wife took a fever, I hoped 'twouldn't leave her,
　For I longed to be single again.

My wife she died, O then! (O then!)
My wife she died, O then!
My wife she died, and I laughed till I cried:
I was glad to be single again.
Chorus—
　Again and again, again (again),
　Again and again, again,
　My wife she died, and I laughed till I cried:
　I was glad to be single again.

I went to the funeral then! (O then!)
I went to the funeral then!
The band it did play, and I danced all the way,
With joy to be single again.
Chorus—
　Again and again, again (again),
　Again and again, again,
　The band it did play, and I danced all the way,
　With joy to be single again.

But I married another, O then (O then!)
I married another, O then!
I married another far worser than t'other,
And I longed for the old one again.
Chorus—
　Again and again, again (again),
　Again and again, again,
　I married another far worser than t'other,
　And I longed for the old one again.

THE LASS THAT LOVES A SAILOR

The moon on the ocean was dimmed by a ripple,
Affording a chequered delight,
The gay jolly tars passed the word for the tipple,

And the toast, for 'twas Saturday night.
Some sweetheart or wife he loved as his life,
Each drank and wished he could hail her.

Chorus—
But the standing toast that pleased them most,
Was the wind that blows,
The ships that goes,
And the lass that loves a sailor.

Some drank the King and his brave ships,
And some our constitution,
Some " May our foes and all such rips
Own British resolution,"
Some sweetheart or wife that he loved as his life,
Each drank while he wished he could hail her.
Chorus.

Some drank our King and some our land,
Our glorious land of freedom !
Some that our tars might never stand
For heroes brave to lead 'em !
That beauty in distress might find
Such friends as ne'er could fail her.
Chorus.

DOWN AMONG THE DEAD MEN

Here's a health to the King, and a lasting peace,
To faction an end, to wealth increase,
Come, let's drink it while we have breath,
For there's no drinking after death.

Chorus—
And he who will this health deny,
Down among the dead men,
Down among the dead men,
Down, Down, Down, Down,
Down among the dead men, let him lie !

Let charming beauty's health go round
In whom celestial joys are found,
And may confusion still pursue,
The senseless woman-hating crew.
Chorus.

LOCH LOMOND

By yon bonnie banks, and by yon bonnie braes,
Where the sun shines bright on Loch Lomond,
Where me and my true love were ever wont to gae,
On the bonnie, bonnie banks o' Loch Lomond.

Chorus—
Oh ! ye'll tak' the high road and I'll tak' the low road,
And I'll be in Scotland afore ye,
But me an my true love will never meet again
On the bonnie, bonnie banks of Loch Lomond.

I mind where we parted in yon shady glen,
On the steep, steep side of Ben Lomond,
Where in deep purple hue the Heiland hills we view,
And the moon comin' out in the gloamin'.
Chorus.

The wee birdies sing, and the wild flowers spring,
And in sunshine the waters are sleeping,
But the broken heart will ken nae second spring again,
Thro' the waefu' may cease frae their greeting.
Chorus.

MY BONNIE

My Bonnie is over the ocean,
My Bonnie is over the sea,
My Bonnie is over the ocean,
O bring back my Bonnie to me.

Chorus—
Bring back, bring back,
Bring back my Bonnie to me, to me ;
Bring back, bring back,
O bring back my Bonnie to me !

O blow ye winds over the ocean,
O blow ye winds over the sea,
O blow ye winds over the ocean,
And bring back my Bonnie to me.
Chorus.

Last night as I lay on my pillow,
Last night as I lay on my bed,
Last night as I lay on my pillow,
I dreamed that my Bonnie was dead.
Chorus.

The winds have blown over the ocean,
The winds have blown over the sea,
The winds have blown over the ocean,
And brought back my Bonnie to me.
Chorus.

MARCHING THROUGH GEORGIA

Bring the good old bugle, boys, we'll sing another song,
Sing it with a spirit that will start the world along,
Sing it as we used to sing it fifty thousand strong,
While we were marching through Georgia.

Chorus—
  Hurrah, hurrah, we bring the Jubilee!
  Hurrah, hurrah, the flag that makes you free!
  So we sang the chorus from Atlanta to the sea,
  While we were marching through Georgia.

How the darkies shouted when they heard the joyful sound:
How the turkeys gobbled which our commissary found;
How the sweet potatoes even started from the ground,
While we were marching through Georgia.
Chorus.

Yes, and there were "Union" men, who wept with joyful tears,
When they saw the honoured flag they had not seen for years;
Hardly could they be restrained from breaking forth in cheers,
While we were marching through Georgia.
Chorus.

So we made a thoroughfare for Freedom and her train,
Sixty miles in latitude, three hundred to the main.

Treason fled before us, for resistance was in vain,
While we were marching through Georgia.
Chorus.

ONE MAN WENT TO MOW

One man went to mow, went to mow a meadow,
One man and his dog went to mow a meadow.

Two men went to mow, went to mow a meadow,
Two men, one man and his dog went to mow a meadow.

Three men went to mow, went to mow a meadow,
Three men, two men, one man and his dog went to mow a meadow.

Four men went to mow, went to mow a meadow,
Four men, three men, two men, one man and his dog, went to mow a meadow.

Five men went to mow, went to mow a meadow,
Five men, four men, three men, two men, one man and his dog went to mow a meadow.

Six men went to mow, went to mow a meadow,
Six men, five men, four men, three men, two men, one man and his dog went to mow a meadow.

Seven men went to mow, went to mow a meadow,
Seven men, six men, five men, four men, three men, two men, one man and his dog went to mow a meadow.

Eight men went to mow, went to mow a meadow,
Eight men, seven men, six men, five men, four men, three men, two men, one man and his dog went to mow a meadow.

Nine men went to mow, went to mow a meadow,

Nine men, eight men, seven men,
six men, five men, four men, three
men, two men, one man and his
dog went to mow a meadow.

Ten men went to mow, went to mow a
meadow,
Ten men, nine men, eight men, seven
men, six men, five men, four men,
three men, two men, one man and
his dog went to mow a meadow.

SO EARLY IN DE MORNING

South Carolina's a sultry clime,
We used to work in de summer-time
Massa 'neath de shade would lay,
While we poor niggers toiled all day.
Chorus—
So early in de morning,
So early in de morning,
So early in de morning,
Before de break of day.

When I was young I used to wait,
On massa's table, lay de plate ;
Pass de bottle when him dry,
Brush away de blue-tailed fly.
Chorus.

Now massa's dead an' gone to rest,
Of all the massa's he was best ;
I nebber see de like since I was born,
Miss him now he's dead and gone.
Chorus.

OLD KING COLE

Old King Cole was a merry old soul,
And a merry old soul was he,
He called for his pipe and he called
for his bowl,
And he called for his fiddlers three.
Now ev'ry fiddler had a fine fiddle,
And a very fine fiddle had he.
Chorus—
Then fiddle-diddle dee, fiddle dee
went the fiddlers,
Merry men are we,
For there's none so rare as can
compare,
With the sound of my harmony.

Old King Cole was a merry old soul,
And a merry old soul was he,
He called for his pipe and he called
for his bowl,
And he called for his pipers three.
Ev'ry piper he had a fine pipe,
And a very fine pipe had he.

Chorus—
Then fiddle-diddle dee, fiddle dee
went the fiddlers,
Tootle-tootle-too, tootle-too went
the pipers,
Merry men are we, etc.

Old King Cole was a merry old soul,
And a merry old soul was he,
He called for his pipe and he called
for his bowl,
And he called for his harpers three.
Ev'ry harper he had a fine harp.
And a very fine harp had he.
Chorus—
Then fiddle-diddle dee, fiddle dee
went the fiddlers,
Tootle-tootle-too, tootle-too went
the pipers,
Twang-a-twang-a-twang, twang-a-
twang went the harpers,
Merry men are we, etc.

DE OLD FOLKS AT HOME

Way down upon de Swanee ribber,
Far far away,
Dere's where my heart is turning ebber,
Dere's where de ole folks stay.
All up and down de whole creation
Sadly I roam,
Still longing for de ole plantation
And for de ole folks at home.
Chorus—
All de world am sad and dreary
Eb'rywhere I roam,
O darkeys, how my heart grows
weary,
Far from de ole folks at home.

All roun' de little farm I wandered,
When I was young ;
Den many happy days I squandered,
Many de songs I sung,
When I was playing wid my brudder,
Happy was I,
O take me to my kind ole mudder,
Dere let me lib and die.
Chorus.

One little hut among de bushes,
One dat I love,
Still sadly to my mem'ry rushes,
No matter where I rove.
When shall I see de bees a-humming
All roun' de comb ?
When shall I hear de banjo strumming,
Down in de good ole home ?
Chorus.

WIDDICOMBE FAIR

Tom Pearce, Tom Pearce, lend me your grey mare,
All along, down along, out along lee.
For I want for to go to Widdicombe Fair,
With Bill Brewer, Jan Stewer, Peter Gurney, Peter Davy, Dan'l Whiddon, Harry Hawke,
Old Uncle Tom Cobleigh and all,
Old Uncle Tom Cobleigh and all.

And when shall I see again my grey mare?
All along, down along, out along lee.
By Friday soon or Saturday noon,
With Bill Brewer, etc.

Then Friday came and Saturday noon,
All along, down along, out along lee.
But Tom Pearce's old mare hath not trotted home,
With Bill Brewer, etc.

So Tom Pearce he got to the top of the hill,
All along, down along, out along lee.
And he see'd his old mare down a-making her will,
With Bill Brewer, etc.

So Tom Pearce's old mare her took sick and died,
All along, down along, out along lee.
And Tom he sat down on a stone and he cried
With Bill Brewer, etc.

But this isn't the end o' this shocking affair,
All along, down along, out along lee.
Nor, tho' they be dead, of the horrid career
Of Bill Brewer, etc.

When the wind whistles cold on the moor of a night
All along, down along, out along lee.
Tom Pearce's old mare doth appear ghastly white
With Bill Brewer, etc.

And all the night long he heard skirling and groans
All along, down along, out along lee.
From Tom Pearce's old mare in her rattling bones
With Bill Brewer, etc.

EARLY ONE MORNING

Early one morning, just as the sun was rising,
I heard a maid sing in the valley below:
Chorus—
" O, don't deceive me! O never leave me!
How could you use a poor maiden so?"

" Oh, gay is the garland, and fresh are the roses,
I've cull'd from the garden to bind on thy brow."
Chorus.

" Remember the vows that you made to your Mary,
Remember the bow'r where you vow'd to be true."
Chorus.

Thus sang the poor maiden, her sorrows bewailing,
Thus sang the poor maid in the valley below.
Chorus.

POLLY-WOLLY-DOODLE

Oh, my Sal she am a maiden fair,
  Sing " Polly-wolly-doodle " all the day,
With laughing eyes and curly hair,
  Sing " Polly-wolly-doodle " all the day.
Chorus—
  Fare thee well, fare thee well,
  Farewell, my fairy fay,
Oh, I'm off to Louisiana for to see my Susy Anna,
  Singing " Polly-wolly-doodle " all the day.

Oh, I came to a river, and I couldn't get across,
  Sing " Polly-wolly-doodle " all the day,
And I jumped upon a nigger, for I thought he was a hoss,
  Sing " Polly-wolly-doodle " all the day.
Chorus.

Oh, a grasshopper sitting on a railroad track,
  Sing " Polly-wolly-doodle " all the day,

A pickin' his teef wid a carpet tack,
  Sing " Polly-wolly-doodle " all the
    day.
      Chorus.

Behind a barn, upon my knees,
  Sing " Polly-wolly-doodle " all the
    day,
I though I heard a chicken sneeze,
  Sing " Polly-wolly-doodle " all the
    day.
      Chorus.

He sneezed so hard wid de hoopin'-
    cough.
  Sing " Polly-wolly-doodle " all the
    day,
He sneezed his head and his tail right
    off,
  Sing " Polly-wolly-doodle " all the
    day.
      Chorus.

CLEMENTINE

In a cavern in a canyon,
  Excavating for a mine,
Dwelt a miner, forty-niner,
  And his daughter Clementine.
Chorus—
  Oh my darling, Oh my darling,
    Oh my darling Clementine,
  Thou art lost and gone for ever,
    Dreadful sorry, Clementine.

Light she was and like a fairy,
  And her shoes were number nine
Herring boxes, without topses,
  Sandals were for Clementine.
    Chorus.

Drove she ducklings to the water
  Every morning just at nine,
Hit her foot against a splinter,
  Fell into the foaming brine.
    Chorus.

Saw her lips above the water
  Blowing bubbles mighty fine;
But alas! I was no swimmer,
  So I lost my Clementine.
    Chorus.

Then the miner, forty-niner,
  Soon began to peak and pine;
Thought he oughter jine his daughter,
  Now he's with his Clementine.
    Chorus.

In my dreams she still doth haunt me,
  Robed in garments soaked in brine;
Though in life I used to hug her,
  Now she's dead I draw the line.
    Chorus.

How I missed her, how I missed her
  How I missed my Clementine,
But I kissed her little sister,
  And forgot my Clementine.
    Chorus.

CAMPTOWN RACES

De Camptown ladies sing dis song,
  Doodah, Doodah!
De Camptown race-track five miles
    long,
  Doodah, Doodah-day!
I come down dah wid my hat caved in,
  Doodah, Doodah!
I go back home wid a pocket full of tin.

Doodah, Doodah-day!
Gwine to run all night,
Gwine to run all day!
I'll bet my money on de bob-tail nag,
  Somebody bet on de bay.

De long tail filly, and de big black hoss,
  Doodah, Doodah!
Dey fly de track an' dey cut across,
  Doodah, Doodah-day!
De blind hoss stickin' in a big mud hole,
  Doodah, Doodah!
Can't touch de bottom with a ten-foot
    pole,
  Doodah, Doodah-day! etc.

Ole muley cow come on to de track,
  Doodah, Doodah!
De bob-tail fling her ober his back
  Doodah, Doodah-day!
Den fly along like de railroad car,
  Doodah, Doodah!
And run a race wid a shootin' star
  Doodah, Doodah-day! etc.

See dem flying on a ten-mile heat,
  Doodah, Doodah!
Roun' de race-track, den repeat,
  Doodah, Doodah-day!
I win my money on de bob-tail nag,
  Doodah, Doodah!
I keep my money in a ole tow bag,
  Doodah, Doodah-day! etc.

THE BAILIFF'S DAUGHTER OF ISLINGTON

There was a youth, and a well-beloved youth,
 And he was a squire's son,
He loved the bailiff's daughter dear,
 That lived in Islington.

But she was coy and never would,
 On him her heart bestow,
Till he was sent to London town,
 Because he loved her so.

When seven years had pass'd away,
 She put on neat attire,
And straight to London she would go,
 About him to enquire.

And as she went along the road,
 Through weather hot and dry,
She rested on a grassy load,
 And her love came riding by.

" Give me a penny, thou 'prentice good;
 Relieve a maid forlorn!"
" Before I give you a penny, sweetheart,
 Pray tell me where you were born."

" Oh I was born at Islington."
" Then tell me if you know
The bailiff's daughter of that place."
" She died, sir, long ago."

" If she be dead, then take my horse
 My saddle and bridle also,
For I will to some distant land
 Where no man shall me know."

" O stay, O stay, thou gentle youth,
 She standeth by thy side!
She's here, alive, she is not dead,
 But ready to be thy bride!"

THE MARCH OF THE MEN OF HARLECH

Hark! I hear the foe advancing,
 Barbed steeds are proudly prancing;
Helmets in the sunbeams glancing,
 Glitter through the trees.
Men of Harlech lie ye dreaming?
See ye not their falchions gleaming,
While their pennons gaily streaming
 Flutter in the breeze?

From the rocks rebounding
 Let the war-cry sounding
Summon all at Cambria's call,
 The haughty foe surrounding,
Men of Harlech, on to glory!
See, your banner famed in story,
Waves these burning words before ye,
 " Britain scorns to yield!"

'Mid the fray see dead and dying,
Friend and foe together lying;
All around the arrows flying
 Scatter sudden death!
Frightened steeds are wildly neighing,
Brazen trumpets hoarsely braying,
Wounded men for mercy praying
 With their parting breath!

See, they're in disorder!
Comrades, keep close order!
Ever they shall rue the day
 They ventured o'er the border!
Now the Saxon flees before us;
Victory's banner floateth o'er us!
Raise the loud, exalting chorus,
 " Britain wins the field!"

THE THREE CROWS

There were three crows sat on a tree,
 O Billy Magee Magar.
There were three crows sat on a tree,
 O Billy Magee Magar.
There were three crows sat on a tree,
And they were black as black could be.
 And they all flapped their wings and cried, CAW, CAW, CAW,
 Billy Magee Magar.
 And they all flapped their wings and cried,
 Billy Magee Magar.

Said one old crow unto his mate,
 O Billy Magee Magar.
Said one old crow unto his mate,
 O Billy Magee Magar.
Said one old crow unto his mate,
" What shall we do for our grub to ate?"
 And they all flapped their wings, etc.

There lies a horse on yonder plain,
 O Billy Magee Magar.
There lies a horse on yonder plain,
 O Billy Magee Magar.
There lies a horse on yonder plain,
Who's by some cruel butcher slain.
 And they all flapped their wings, etc.

The meat we'll eat before it's stale,
 O Billy Magee Magar,

The meat we'll eat before it's stale,
　O Billy Magee Magar.
The meat we'll eat before it's stale.
Till naught remains but bones and tail.
　And they all flapped their wings, etc.

HEART OF OAK

Come, cheer up, my lads! 'tis to glory
　we steer,
To add something more to this wonderful year,
To honour we call you, not press you
　like slaves,
For who are so free as the sons of the
　waves?

Chorus—
　Heart of oak are our ships,
　Heart of oak are our men;
　We always are ready;
　Steady, boys, steady;
　We'll fight and we'll conquer again
　　and again.

We ne'er see our foes but we wish 'em
　to stay,
They never see us but they wish us
　away;
If they run, why, we follow, and run
　'em ashore,
For if they won't fight us we cannot
　do more.
　　　　Chorus.

AULD LANG SYNE

Should auld acquaintance be forgot,
　And never brought to min'?
Should auld acquaintance be forgot,
　And days o' lang syne?
　　For auld lang syne, my dear,
　　　For auld lang syne,
　　We'll tak' a cup o' kindness yet
　　　For auld lang syne.

And here's a hand my trusty frien',
　And gie's a hand o' thine;
We'll tak' a right gude willy waught
　For auld lang syne.
　　For auld lang syne, my dear,
　　　For auld lang syne,
　　We'll tak' a cup o' kindness yet,
　　　For auld lang syne.

FORTUNE TELLING AND CHARACTER READING

THE TEACUP FORTUNE TELLING GAME

Everybody knows how soon an interesting Tea-party can tail off into commonplace remarks; yet how easily the whole function can be saved by arranging something unusual.

The art of Fortune Telling by Teacups is one that cannot fail to create intense interest. Keep this book handy by

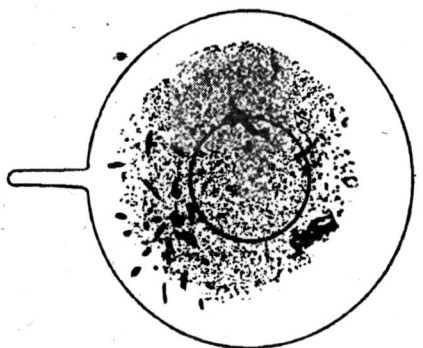

Key—New Undertaking
Explosion—Danger
Engine—Travelling

you, and as your guests drink their tea, offer to "tell their fortunes." Everyone will be keen. Take each cup in turn, follow the directions concerning the preparation of the cup, look for the different shapes and symbols which will be found at the bottom and on the sides of the cup and then read out the messages as printed in the alphabetical list.

In each cup you will find a number of shapes, all of which should be deciphered before you proceed with the next teacup reading. Any teacup can be used, though a wide and shallow cup is best.

About a teaspoonful of fluid tea should be left at the bottom of the cup which should be taken in the left hand, and turned three times, then carefully turned upside down into the saucer, and left there a minute or two so that all the moisture will be drained away.

The handle of the cup should be held nearest to you. Time can be foretold more or less by the position of the leaves. Close to the brim—immediate events. The left hand of the handle suggests past events; and the right side, the present and future.

Shapes and formations made by the tea-leaves give the following readings:

AIRCRAFT. New projects—elevation. If to the right of the handle—a journey will bring gain.

ANCHOR. A restful life. If surrounded by dots, a voyage bringing success and a secure position in the future.

ANGEL. This is a symbol of love and peace. At the bottom of the cup—protection.

APPLE. Good health. If at the bottom of the cup, it shows recovery from serious illness.

ARCH. This portends that your success will come in an unexpected manner.

BABY. An awakening—a birth, if dots are around, a new interest.

BASKET. A gift. In the clear and near the handle—an addition to the family. If a ring should be near—an offer of marriage.

BELL. Happy omen. News. Two bells—a marriage; at the bottom of the cup, bad news.

BIRDS. Happiness and joyful tidings. A single bird in flight means a telegram.

BOAT. Pleasure. Seen with clouds—troubles. At the top of the cup—pleasure and personal benefits.

BOOK. An open book denotes a revelation of importance. A closed book—unexpected research.

BROOM. Avoid rushing into an intimacy which you might later have cause to regret.

FORTUNE TELLING

BUTTERFLY. Frivolity. In the middle of the cup, inconstancy. At the top of the cup—sincere and natural pleasures.

CAGE. In the clear, and complete—an offer of marriage. In the middle, with dashes round—a marriage of convenience. At the bottom, disappointed love.

CAT. Deception; but if near the handle, at the top, and in a resting position, it shows domestic comfort.

CROSS. Hindrances—obstacles—suffering.

CROWN. Success and honours. If wavy lines are near—delays in the way of deserved honours.

DAGGER. Beware of being too hasty.

DOG. Protection, friends, money.

DRUM. A hazardous enterprise. Quarrels. An unfortunate publicity.

EAGLE. This symbol shows the coming of wealth and honour.

EAR. Scandal or abuse. Interesting news.

EGGS. New plans and change of place.

ELEPHANT. Obstacles and hindrances.

EYE. Caution, inspection. A warning that enquirer must carefully examine any new proposal or project that may be brought forward.

FACE. Friendship. Several faces denote a wedding.

FAIRY. A strange adventure of love or romance.

FAN. Flirtation and vexation. Indiscretions.

FEATHERS. Large feathers show prosperity, but small feathers are indicative of fears that are hard to overcome, but will later appear absurd and groundless.

FISH. Riches. Lucky speculations.

FLOWERS. These indicate appreciation, praise, love, honours and favours.

GATE. This shows some restriction, limitation or hindrance.

GUN. Discord and slander.

HAMMER. Irritating or irksome duties that must be done.

HAND. A parting.

HARP. Harmony, romance.

HEART. A wealthy partner. A marriage.

HORSEMAN. A mounted horseman shows the approach of a stranger, who will benefit the enquirer.

HUMAN FIGURE. The arrival of news.

KEY. Enlightenment. Guard against a robbery.

KITE. Beware of projects which are hazardous and fanciful.

KNIFE. A wedding is approaching.
LADDER. Advancement through industry and perseverance.
LAMP. Twice married. A legacy.
LEAVES. Happiness later in life.
LINES. Indicate journeys.
MAN. Expect a visitor of the opposite sex.
MOON. A crescent moon denotes fortune and romance.
MOTOR CAR. Short journeys, pleasure and success.
MOUNTAIN. Hindrances to prospects, and interferences.
MUG. A merry meeting between former lovers or very old friends.
NAIL. Physical pain. A visit to the dentist.
NECKLACE. If complete—conquest. If broken—the breaking of a bond.
OAR. A broken oar denotes recklessness.
OVAL. Lovers should be very cautious—jealousy might part them.
PADLOCK. An open padlock—a surprise. A closed padlock—caution.
PARASOL. A new lover from an unexpected quarter.
PIPE. Assurance of domestic happiness.
PISTOL. Warning of danger—violence.
RIDER. Hasty news. Lucky dealings.
RING. Marriage. If dots are around it—a wealthy marriage. Two rings—a hasty marriage.
ROSE. A token of fortune, joy and love.
SCALES. Justice—lawsuit. A speedy judgment.
SCEPTRE. An offer of a title.
SCISSORS. Friction—quarrels.
SNAKE. A sign of treachery, falsehood and enmity.
SPIDER. Someone is trying to undermine your efforts.
SPOONS. A christening. Luck. Two spoons in the clear—a flirtation.
SQUARES. Indicate letters or parcels.
STAR. Emblem of hope—destiny. Surrounded by dots—good fortune.
SUN. This promises health, happiness and success in love matters.
SWORD. Slander and dangerous gossip.
TEA POT. Committee meetings—consultations.
TELESCOPE. Discernment—adventure, travel and success in domestic affairs.
TREE. A lucky sign. Several trees—your wishes gratified.

TRIANGLES. A sign of both good luck and bad luck.
VASE. Sacrifice—reward. It denotes that steadfast service will bring its measure of reward.
WHEEL. A wheel at the top of the cup indicates that an inheritance is about to fall to you.
WHIP. To a woman—vexation. To a man—severe disappointment.
WINGS. Messages. Good and bad messages.
WOMAN. In the clear—fertility. Surrounded by dots—wealth and good children. Happiness. Several women—scandal.

FORTUNE TELLING BY CARDS

Remove from a pack of cards the twos, threes, fours, fives, and sixes and thoroughly shuffle the remainder. Place the pack on a table, and sit on a chair, with your back to the fireplace. Cut the pack with your left hand and raise the top card of the lower stack, with your right hand. This card is the one that speaks of your fortunes. What it portends may be found by consulting the following list.

ACE OF CLUBS. Signifies joy, great wealth, or good news.
KING OF CLUBS. A frank, liberal, affectionate, upright, and faithful person, fond of serving friends.
QUEEN OF CLUBS. An affectionate person, but quick tempered, rather amorous, one that will yield to a generous lover, happy and loving; will be married.
KNAVE OF CLUBS. A clever individual, generous and sincere.
TEN OF CLUBS. Great wealth, success, or grandeur.
NINE OF CLUBS. Unexpected gain, or a legacy.
EIGHT OF CLUBS. Signifies a dark person's affections, which, if returned, will be the cause of great prosperity.
SEVEN OF CLUBS. Promises a most brilliant fortune, or unexpectedly recovered debts.
ACE OF HEARTS. A love-letter, or some pleasant news.
KING OF HEARTS. A fair complexion; a liberal person.
QUEEN OF HEARTS. A mild, amiable character, of great personal charm.
KNAVE OF HEARTS. A gay, person, who dreams only of pleasure, fond of racing.

TEN OF HEARTS. Indicates happiness, triumph.
NINE OF HEARTS. Joy, satisfaction, success are your delight.
EIGHT OF HEARTS. A fair person's affections.
SEVEN OF HEARTS. Will be happily married, pleasant and tranquil.
ACE OF DIAMONDS. Shows a person fond of rural sports, also fond of gardening. It also signifies a letter soon to be received.
KING OF DIAMONDS. A fair person of fiery temper, both cunning and dangerous.
QUEEN OF DIAMONDS. An ill-bred, scandal-loving character, unsteady.
KNAVE OF DIAMONDS. A tale-bearing servant, or unfaithful friend.
TEN OF DIAMONDS. Indicates a husband and wife with great wealth, many children; a journey or change of residence.
NINE OF DIAMONDS. Annoyance, delay.
EIGHT OF DIAMONDS. Love-making.
SEVEN OF DIAMONDS. Declares that you will spend your happiest days in the country, and have uninterrupted happiness.
ACE OF SPADES. Pleasure.
KING OF SPADES. An envious person, an enemy, who is to be feared.
QUEEN OF SPADES. A loving, faithful person.
KNAVE OF SPADES. A dark ill-bred person.
TEN OF SPADES. A card of bad import. Tears. A prison.
NINE OF SPADES. Tidings of a death.
EIGHT OF SPADES. The most unlucky card in the pack. Approaching illness.
SEVEN OF SPADES. Slight annoyance. Loss of a friend.

FORTUNE TELLING BY DICE

This is a certain and innocent way of finding out common occurrences about to take place. Take three dice, shake them well in the box with your left hand, and then cast them out on a board or table, on which you have previously drawn a circle with chalk, a foot in diameter, but never throw on a Monday or Wednesday. Should the dice fall outside the circle, repeat the cast.

THREE. A pleasing surprise.
FOUR. A disagreeable surprise.
FIVE. A stranger, who will prove a friend.
SIX. Loss of property.
SEVEN. Undeserved scandal.
EIGHT. Merited reproach.
NINE. A wedding.
TEN. A christening, at which some important event will occur to you.
ELEVEN. A death that concerns you.
TWELVE. A letter, speedily.
THIRTEEN. Tears and sighs.
FOURTEEN. A new admirer.
FIFTEEN. Beware that you are not drawn into some trouble or plot.
SIXTEEN. A pleasant journey.
SEVENTEEN. You will either be on the water, or have dealings with those belonging to it, to your advantage.
EIGHTEEN. A great profit, rise in life, or some most desirable good will happen almost immediately; for the answers to the dice are usually fulfilled within nine days.

To show the same number twice at one trial, shows news from abroad, be the number what it may.

If the dice roll over the circle, the number thrown goes for nothing, but the occurrence shows sharp words; and if they fall on the floor, it is blows. In throwing out the dice, if one remains on the top of the other, it is a present, of which ladies should beware.

DOMINOES WILL TELL YOUR FORTUNE

Lay the dominoes with their faces on the table, and shuffle them; then draw one, and see the number.

DOUBLE-SIX. Receiving a handsome sum of money.
SIX-FIVE. Going to a public amusement.
SIX-FOUR. Law-suits.
SIX-THREE. Ride in a car.

Six-Two. Present of clothing.
Six-One. You will soon perform a friendly action.
Six-Blank. Guard against scandal, or you will suffer by your inattention.
Double-Five. A new abode to your advantage.
Five-Four. A fortunate speculation.
Five-Three. A visit from a superior.
Five-Two. A water party.
Five-One. A love intrigue.
Five-Blank. A funeral, but not of a relation.
Double-Four. Drinking liquor at a distance.
Four-Three. A false alarm at your house.
Four-Two. Beware of thieves or swindlers. Ladies, take notice of this; it means more than it says.
Four-One. Trouble from creditors.
Four-Blank. Will receive a letter from an angry friend.
Double-Three. Sudden warning, at which you will be vexed.
Three-Two. Buy no lottery-tickets, nor enter into any game of chance, or you will lose.
Three-One. A great discovery at hand.
Three-Blank. An unfortunate occurrence.
Double-Two. You will be plagued by a jealous partner.
Two-One. You will mortgage or pledge some property very soon, or borrow from the bank.
Double-One. You will soon find something to your advantage in the street.
Double-Blank. The worst presage in all the set of dominoes; you will soon meet trouble from a quarter from which you are quite unprepared. Look out and it may be avoided.

It is useless for enquirers to draw more than one domino at one time of trial, or in one and the same month, as they will only deceive themselves; shuffle the dominoes each time of choosing.

THE FORTUNE TELLING TABLET

As used by the Egyptian Magi

The person whose fortune is to be told closes his or her eyes and, then, pricks the tablet with a pin or other sharp instru-

FORTUNE TELLING

nent. On opening the eyes, the letter is noted, and, whatever is indicated, is consulted in the following list.

B				A	C			E
		F	X	L	N	A	D	
	P	N	O	C	D	L	Q	B
	Y	R	S	T	E	H	G	L
K	V	W	T	S	V	A	N	M	Z
U	C	D	P	O	R	B	W	X	J
B	I	X	F	G	S	B	H	L	K
	A	C	K	E	O	F	T	Y	
	L	M	D	H	K	G	I		
		J	S	B	A	K	R		
A				Q	C			D

WHAT THE ORACLE SAYS

A. If this letter is fixed upon by a man, it assures him, if single, a homely wife, but rich; if married, an access of riches, numerous children, and good old age. To a lady, the faithfulness of her lover, and a speedy marriage.

B. Very good fortune, sudden prosperity, great respect from high personages, and a letter bringing important news.

C. This letter, to a woman, is wonderful in showing, if single, a handsome, rich, and constant husband; and if married, a faithful partner, who is of a good family, as she has married above her condition. To a man, similar.

D. This is a general good sign, and your present expectations will be fulfilled.

E. If a married man or woman draws this, if under fifty, let them not despair of a young family. To the single, very sudden marriage.

F. A friend has crossed the sea, and will bring home some riches, by which the parties will be much benefited.

G. Shows the party success in all undertakings.

H. No doubt but the chooser is very poor, and thought insignificant, but let friends assist, as he or she is much favoured.

I. A very sudden journey, with a pleasant fellow-traveller, and the result of the journey will be generally beneficial to your family.

J. A sudden acquaintance with the opposite sex, which will be opposed; but the party should persevere, as it will be to his or her advantage.

K. A letter of importance will arrive, announcing the death of a relation for whom you have no very great respect, but who has left you a legacy.

L. Be very prudent in your conduct, as this letter is very precarious, and much depends on yourself; it is generally good.

The above are the fortunate letters. The others possess no useful significance.

YOUR HANDWRITING REVEALS YOUR CHARACTER

Here is a good pastime for your next party. If you care to delineate the characters of your friends, in exchange for a few lines of their hand-writing, it will cause a good deal of pleasant fun and amusement.

Invest the business with a show of apparent seriousness, in the following way. Arrange a little table with a chair beside it. On the table, place nothing but a small writing-pad, a pot of ink, a sheet of blotting paper and a few penholders. These should be provided with different kinds of nibs to suit various hands. Have another chair at the side, for yourself, and invite your friends one by one, to come and write a few lines, while everybody else stands around.

FORTUNE TELLING

Sincerely Yours, 1 Bertha 2

Mother sends her love 3

expecting to see you soon 4

George Washington 5 Margaret 6

Leybourne Lodge 7

when shall we come? 8

it serves the same purpose as that 9

Yours affectionately 10

Great happiness 12 Diana 11

Can you come to-day 13

Red Lion Court 14

Herbert Chatterton 15

although you can 16

Happy Thoughts 17

As each person completes his or her contribution, you tear the sheet from the pad and commence the analysis aloud.

Now, it takes weeks to become an expert in reading writing —one might even say years—but you want to learn quite a lot in a few moments. So what, we propose to do here is to pick out the main features of the science and leave the minor points alone. If you depend on them, you will not go far wrong.

Here are the tests to apply :—

(a) Large, clear writing shows an orderly mind that takes a broad view of life. As a rule, people who write in this way can be trusted. I would not say that they are necessarily brilliant, but they will get things done, and, accordingly, are reliant. (*See* **No. 1**).

(b) Large writing, such as **No. 3** and **No. 17,** still reveals the broad outlook on life and the trustful character : but there is not the same orderly mind. **No. 3** is an imaginative person, with a lovable and sympathetic nature ; while **No. 17** is a " sport " who would go to the end of the earth for the sake of a friend, but is careless and absent-minded.

(c) Small writing usually suggests a small mind ; one which worries about trifles that hardly matter. You have a typical example in **No. 15.**

(d) Untidy writing, such as **No. 2** and **No. 14** betoken an individual who would never hang a dress up in the wardrobe when it could be thrown over the back of the bed or on a chair. Such are untidy by nature and nothing will ever make them orderly. The rounded character of the letters in **No. 14** suggests a kind nature and, perhaps, the same may be claimed for **No. 2,** but to a less degree.

(e) Look at **No. 5.** The downstrokes are heavy and plump, compared with the upstrokes. There is too much variety indicated here. It is the writing of an individual who would never tolerate, in others, the faults he possesses himself.

(f) Very different is **No. 10.** Here all the strokes are heavy ; not only the downstrokes. This is a sign of determination. Such a person will get on or die in the attempt.

(g) **Nos. 6** and **7** are very much alike. They show the business instinct very much developed. By this, we do not mean that £ s. d. is their chief god ; but that they can organise

FORTUNE TELLING

and run large concerns. If parts of the writing suddenly run upwards and leave the horizontal, as **No. 6,** it shows that the individual might be a formidable rival if he or she ever came to blows with you.

(*h*) Now turn to **No. 9.** Clearly it is rapid, hurried writing, showing a desire to get it done. The writer does everything in haste and possesses the failing of leaving things to the last minute. Such people are late in keeping appointments and they often see the end coaches of trains.

(*i*) **No. 11** is the handwriting of an artistic individual. Neat and tidy in habits, and a very sane outlook on life.

(*j*) **No. 16** is much the same. Artistic and sane in outlook. Generous and happy, but not so tidy.

(*k*) **No. 4** is the writing of a person with a friendly and cheerful nature. Such can be interesting, but not the kind that would pass examinations easily.

(*l*) **No. 8** reveals a twofold character, one that blows hot and cold. When they find things are favourable, all is well : but wait until the wind changes! The angular disjointed letters show all this.

(*m*) Business qualities are revealed in **No. 13,** but this is the hand of one that is not going to consider details. Such an individual will think out the main scheme and go off to a dance, while somebody else is working out the ways and means.

(*n*) The last specimen is **No. 12.** Look for a temperament steeped in one of the arts, probably painting, literature or the drama.

THEATRICALS

ACTING is great fun. It may entail a certain amount of hard work, but there is no doubt that all the labour put into the show is well worth it.

In this section of the book, a few short funny monologues are given. The reciter, in rendering them, is advised to dress for the part, if he wishes to score a great success. A little paint and a suitable costume will not only help the audience to understand him better, but they have the psychological effect of giving him greater confidence in himself.

Charades, too, are discussed in this section. As is well known, they are great favourites for filling in the time at parties. A charade is so easily prepared and performed that its popularity is readily understood.

Of course, a humorous recitation, whether it be in poetry or prose, will always be welcomed at any social gathering. A selection is included for those who are looking for particularly good numbers.

In a collection of this kind, the items must necessarily be few; but readers who require further material will find all they require in the following volumes of *Foulsham's Home Library*, each 2s. net, bound in cloth:

Plays for Boys and Girls—Drama and Comedy in 1, 2 or 3 acts for Home, School or Concert.

The Best 100 Recitations for Boys and Girls.—This volume, unlike the average book of recitations for children, contains grave and gay pieces in prose.

The Best Short Prose Recitations.—A picked selection of humorous and dramatic works in prose, that will prove favourites with all audiences.

Another book which has proved exceedingly useful and popular is *The Sixty Best Humorous Recitations* (Foulsham), 1s. net, cloth.

HUMOROUS MONOLOGUES

THE GUIDE

The following monologue is intended to poke fun at the way many guides show visitors around buildings that are more or less famous. Should any such building of note exist in the neighbourhood where the monologue is delivered, it will help considerably if some humorous references are made to it. It will not be difficult to find a place where a passage may be introduced without upsetting the thread of the recital.

Ladies and Gentlemen.—You see before you a most wonderful building, very beautiful and majestic. Only last year, a number of old gentlemen—what you call antiaquariums—came here and pronounced it as the most noble, interesting and famous building for miles around. It was begun in the year 1066 by the well-known explorer William the Conqueror, and finished by a chap of the name of Julius Cæsar. Cæsar was a very rich man, who amassed a lot of money by making arterial roads. He was a knowing chap, was Cæsar, and I guess he finished off this place because he thought it would do nicely as a night-club or a cinema. Well, just as it was finished, he got a wire from Italy that something had gone wrong with his ice-cream business over there, so he went back home, never to return to England.

Now, ladies and gentlemen, before we go any further, I want you to notice that, on the left hand, there is the old moat. You'll be pleased to hear that the present owner of the estate, Sir Percival Piggins, O.B.E., who made a lot of money and became a gentleman during the war, has decided to make several improvements to this moat. As it is now, it's no use at all. It's not fit for boating, bathing, nor nothing, so Sir Perce is filling it all in and is going to make one of the finest dirt tracks of it in England.

On my right hand, I have—No, Sir, I heard what you said about " chilblains "; that's a very old joke, indeed. Quite unnecessary, seeing that I'm doing my best to destruct you. Well, on the right hand are the private apartments of Sir Percival Piggins, O.B.E. You can see a lot of statutes in the gardens. When he come here, most of 'em was broken, and people say that none of it had been touched since Julius Cæsar went back home. Sir Perce—a very nice gentleman he is—had the whole lot done up and made to look just like new. They might have been made yesterday, thanks to the repairs.

Straight in front of you is the main gate. Old folk used to call it the Saxon gate. Probably they kept sacks there or something of the sort; but it was a nasty cramped entrance, and when Sir Percival bought his new fifty-horse-power car, it wouldn't go through. So he had the Saxon gate knocked down, and the fine wide gate, that you see now, was built in its place. One thing about Sir Percival is that he's always prepared to *improve* the place and never sticks at suspense.

Right over the top of the gate is a very fine crest of an ancient family. If you look hard, you will see that it is made up of lions and buzzards. Beg pardon, sir, I didn't quite catch what you mean. I said "lions and buzzards." Well, what's that got to do with Slaters and the A.B.C.?

Over yonder, where the estate touches the road, are half a dozen stone columns. They're a bit knocked about and don't serve any useful purpose. But if you happen to pass this way in a fortnight's time, you'll find all the unsightly pillars cleared away, and a row of brand new petrol pumps in their place. There's going to be one pump for each column, so that the artistic effect will not be altered.

Now, on the top of the highest tower, there's what is called a bacon. In olden times, a light used to flash out from it at night and it could be seen for twenty miles around. Of course, a site like that is worth money, and Sir Percival Piggins is arranging with the *Daily Brag* to fix up an electric sign, like those at Piccadilly Circus, with something about insuring you on it. I don't quite know what it all means, but I'm told that it will be a very fine thing when it's done.

I'd like you now to follow me and come inside. We are now in the "what-you-may-call-it" tower. Sir Perce always tells us chaps not to mention its real name when ladies are present; but it's the same word as they used to call Queen Mary, the wife of William of Lemons—Yes, thank you, miss, I meant *Oranges*. It got that name, so history tells us, because all the windows overlook the roadway where the motor cars pass.

Just here is the staircase which leads up to the "look-out" on the top of the tower. Sir Percival Piggins is thinking of doing away with the winding stone stairs and putting in an escalator. It'll be a great improvement when it is done.

The trouble up to the present is that there is only sufficient space for a stairway up, and no room for one to come down. Of course, that's rather awkward.

All these oil paintings which you see hanging on the wall are real old pictures. They were bought in one lot at a sale in Houndsditch. There were no titles to them, so Sir Percival thought it would be nice to put his own name on that one there, and his grandparents' names on the others. It's pretty clear that he picked the best-looking chap for himself.

Over there is a fine statute of Boadecia. Do er you see 'er ? Yes, sir, that's rather a bad pun, but I always puts it in because the ladies like it. The statute was not there originally. Sir Percival bought it with some money he saved out of his income-tax. That statute there, nobody knows who it is; but I'm pretty sure it's Henry VIII, because there, at his feet, are the heads of his eight wives. Here is a rather fine picture of a man mounted on a black horse that is swimming across a river. The man is none other than Dick Turpin, and the river is the Turpintine in Hyde Park. We are doubtful about who that black person over there is, for we can't quite tell whether it's a man or a woman. Sir Percival says if it's a man it's the Black Prince, but if it's a woman, it's Black Bess. No sir, I don't think it could be Black Maria, as she was not extempore.

Now, we'll pass out this way into the flower gardens, and I must ask the gentlemen not to pick the flowers for buttonholes. If they must have something to give the ladies, there are a lot of nice rhubarb leaves in the kitchen garden. This tree, here, is worth looking at. In the spring, it's a mass of cherry blossom. Sir Percival—he's got an eye for business, you know—intends to turn the blossom into boot polish next year. What did you say, sir ? Is that a pear tree ? Yes, that's full of pears in the autumn. Is he going to turn them into soap ? Well, sir, I've not heard anything yet to that defect ; but I shouldn't be surprised.

Perhaps you'd like to peep in this window before we come to the end. You will see, ladies and gentlemen, that it's Lady Piggin's boudoir. The whole of the room has been done up and refurnished ; in fact, the furniture only come down from London last week. I don't know where it was bought because it arrived in plain vans. Beg pardon, sir, my eyesight is getting rather bad, but are those leaves I can see sprouting on the leg of that chair ? Well, I'm blowed, how funny !

Ladies and gentlemen, we've now come to the end. I trust you've all had an enjoyable time. Two things more; don't forget all I've told you, and don't forget the guide. Thank you kindly, sir . . . good lord—a threepenny bit!

THE MOTORIST

It's a downright silly world, this is, and I'll tell you why. Now, you've all got motor-cars, of course. As I look round, I see you all admit that you have. It would be mighty funny if anyone hadn't, in these days of easy payments. Half a guinea down and six hundred weekly doles of fifteen and threepence.

D'you know, I read in the papers the other day that with the advance of science we shall all probably live to be a hundred and thirty. That'll give us nice time to get through with the weekly instalments, before we bump over to the happy sphere *where everything is bliss and the rate collectors cease their troubling.* It's a fine thought, that, especially as we shall then be able to leave our cars in our wills, with the full knowledge that the day after the doctor fills in our death cards, the plain van won't arrive to take back our elegant little two-seater, four cylinder, seven-horse-power sports model. That will be a great comfort.

But to get back to what I want to say. It's a downright silly world, this. I always read all the motoring hints in *Home Snips.* You see, my wife gets the paper every week because she wanted twelve handsomely bound volumes of the world's best cookery books. They are so helpful, she says. You know them—take seven pounds of fresh butter, forty-two eggs and a gallon of milk. Froth all to a light cream. Rinse in cold water and hang on the line until dry.

Well, as I said, I always read the motoring hints, and if I were the chap who wrote them each week, I'd—well, I'd— I tell you what, I'd be downright ashamed of myself. Now what do you think of this? In last week's issue, our friend, who signs himself " 70MPH "—I rather like that nom-de-plume, don't you?; it sounds a cross between a telephone number and a size in collars. Well, Mr. 70MPH has the— I call it impertinence—to tell us that " Last Sunday he tried out a little two-seater, Streak Lightning Silvery Six, and found that it was better on the flat than when climbing. Its performance on a rise of one in eight was only fifty miles per hour, which was decidedly disappointing. The engine revved a little unevenly when the ninety mile mark was exceeded, and after the hundred mark was topped, there was a certain sway of body-work."

Now, I ask you, how can the readers of *Home Snips* benefit by that choice piece of information? What is it to them to know that the Streak Lightning Silvery Six exists at all? I haven't got one. Has anybody here? No, I thought not. Of course, mine's a five-h.p. Baby Bumber, air-cooled, hand painted tourer. Naturally, when I say mine, I mean the one I'm getting on the " pay-way." I think " pay-way " sounds so much nicer than " hire-purchase," or on the instalment system, don't you?

The sort of information the readers want is just the kind of stuff I could give them. What, I ask you, does " 70MPH " know about motoring, really? Anyone could drive a big car like his. You just sit down, get yourself comfortable, step on the gas, and away you go. When all the juice is used up, you stop, and there you are. Now, with the Baby Bumper, it's different. If you can drive her, you're a driver—a real good one. That's why I know I could write for *Home Snips* some red-hot tips. Excuse the poetry; quite an accident.

Just take a hint like this. It's really very useful. I wrote it out in the office this morning. " Should your carburetter fall to pieces, go back along the road just travelled and pick up the various pieces, put them together again as near as possible in the original order, and bind with string, twine, rope, tape, stamp-paper, or anything else that will do the job. If the carburetter will now do its work, you have done yours; if it won't, you haven't." Now, you see how nicely that meets the case in a nutshell, so to speak.

I've written a lot more in the office, as well. Only the other day, I put a number of splendid hints down on a piece of paper; but, unfortunately, I threw the paper away by accident when I was emptying my pocket of bus tickets— and other tickets. You see, I don't believe in keeping them, because the wife always asks a lot of questions when she finds two tickets with the numbers running together. They're dangerous things, bus tickets, that's what they are. However, to return to what I wrote. I remember it began by saying that you should always start with the hand-brake off. There's less drag on the wheels then. Now, a piece of information

G*

such as that is really useful, isn't it? Not like the stuff
" 70MPH " writes. All high-falutin'.

And there's another thing I'd like to say. Motoring hints
ought to be made brighter. They are too dull as they stand.
At the moment, when I'm at the office, I'm compiling a poetic
guide to road hints; but I don't want it known all over the
place, because some blighter like " 70MPH " will crib the idea
and bring out his book before mine. The hints start off like
this :—

  Here lies the body of William Jay,
  Who died maintaining his right of way.

You see, anybody reading this will know better than to stick
out for his slice of the road when something bigger is coming.
Quite likely, he'd never have thought of it before. Now for
another :—

  Here's all what's left of Harry;
  At the cross roads he didn't tarry.

I've written seven hundred and twenty-five of these motor
snips, and they're all as good as the two I've told you. Fine,
don't you think?

But that reminds me. I want to give you a piece of sound
advice. If you own a car, never get sozzled. I did once and,
getting home at about 2 a.m., I took the car to bed and put
my wife in the garage! Until the morning after, I never really
knew my wife.

Speaking of wives, the man next door is a funny chap.
The other day he was grousing, and then, all of a sudden,
he asked me a conundrum. " Why is my wife's tongue like
a motor-car ? " " Haven't the foggiest," I said. What do
you think the answer was ? " Because both of them run people
down."

But the people opposite, they're a bit funny, too. The man
told me he'd lost control of his car. I asked him how it
happened. He told me that he got behind with the instalments.

Well, I must be off. Toot, toot!

THE LADY BOARDER

*This monologue should be presented by an individual who is
required to play the part of a fussy but prim spinster, a little
past middle age. She should be dressed and otherwise equipped*

to suit the part. The scene is a room in a boarding house, and the dumb character is the lady who keeps the place.

Well, I'm very glad to find you can take me in, Mrs. Slithers. I like this room immensely. It's just what I want. Now, what are your terms? Fifty shillings a week, all included. Isn't that a little high? You see, I shall not be one of those people who are here to-day and gone to-morrow. I should like to settle down in this little place for ever. Couldn't you make a reduction as I shall be with you so long? Forty-five shillings, did you say? Why not make it two pounds, then we shall both be satisfied? Ah, that's splendid; I knew you would listen to reason, Mrs. Slithers. You have such a kind face, and I pride myself I can read people like an open book the moment I meet them. I'm certain, Mrs. Slithers, we shall get on very well together. I'm sure of that. So it's to be forty shillings. Good! I shan't be a bit of bother to you. People tell me I'm so easy to please. Now, Mrs. Slithers, what are the arrangements? Breakfast at eight-thirty. Oh, that's a trifle early; you see, my doctor has ordered me to take things easy. If it wouldn't make any difference to you, I'd like it at nine-thirty. You think you could arrange that. Oh, very good, that's nice. And could I have fruit for breakfast, sometimes, instead of bacon. I simply hate bacon. You see, I'm a sort of vegetarian; but, of course, I'm not a bit fussy with it. Oh, no, fussy people I can't stand at any price.

Lunch, you say, is at one. Well, now, isn't that a little too soon after breakfast at nine-thirty? But there, I don't suppose the waitress would mind if I had my simple little meal at two. It wouldn't be a scrap more work for her, after all is said and done. Is there any afternoon tea? None, did you say? Well, leave it to me, I can soon fix up something with the waitress, you may be sure. Do you know, at the last boarding-house where I stayed, all the staff thought no end of me.

Have you any facilities for doing any light washing—hankies and things? None at all. Well, that's easily got over. I can rinse them out in the bathroom and get the kitchen maid to let me run over them with an iron downstairs. You think she'll object? Not a bit. I know how to get round any kitchen maid. You think I ought to send them out to be done? Oh, not at all; it isn't worth all that trouble.

And, while I think of it, are the boarders quiet at night and do they retire at a reasonable hour? If there is anything I hate, it is to be kept awake after a tiring day. If anybody should make a noise, they will hear about it. I know how to deal with unreasonable people like that. At the last place I stayed, the landlady said that nobody had ever cowed her guests as I had done.

Yes, and while we're talking about things, I think I ought to tell you that I can't abide rice pudding; when I do take meat, I like the outside of the joint; in my tea, I usually have four lumps of sugar, and I won't drink it at all unless it is freshly made. I'm rather faddy about bread and butter; it's got to be cut thin and the butter must be really fresh. I bar all tinned foods except sardines. I don't want boiled potatoes everlastingly. I like them fried and mashed occasionally. And . . . I beg your pardon; what did you say? You are afraid I am rather exacting? Oh, not at all. I am as easy to please as anyone could be. I'm only telling you these things so that it will not be necessary for me to complain. I hate to have to complain. And, oh, that reminds me. I must have a feather bed—I absolutely can't sleep on anything else. Of course, you won't call that unreasonable, will you? No, I thought not. We shall get on together famously. What did you say? We shall get on, but it will be on each other's nerves. Mrs. Slithers. I believe you are trying to make trouble. I'm not in the least desirous of being a party to anything of the kind. I'm a plain, straightforward woman, anxious to fit in smoothly with other folk, and I think you misunderstand me.

Now, before I agree, finally, to the terms, may I ask if any of the other boarders keep animals about the place—or babies? I can't bear dogs, and I simply can't stand babies. What? You think I'm a trifle too exacting? Mrs. Slithers, you don't suppose that I have lived in boarding-houses all my life for nothing, do you? You wouldn't be at all surprised if I had! Mrs. Slithers, what do you mean?

HUMOROUS RECITATIONS

THE ACCIDENT

The motorist should have been more careful as he careered through the village; but he was not totally to blame. The old lady who was knocked down did not exercise all the care she might in crossing the road; but beyond being smothered with dust and dirt, and her clothes torn here and there, she had not suffered much.

The local policeman was speedily on the scene. "From all the witnesses," said the constable, "it appears that you were going along as though you didn't know how to drive."

"That's the height of nonsense," replied the motorist. "I'm an experienced driver. I've been driving daily for two years."

"What of that?" exclaimed the outraged woman. "I'm an experienced pedestrian. I've been walking daily for sixty-one years."

DAISY

He was married and did a bit of betting. He had other faults as well—there was a girl in the case. One morning his wife asked him at breakfast why he kept on mentioning the name "Daisy" in his sleep.

"Oh, that's quite easy to explain," he stammered in a confused way. "Why, Daisy is the name of a horse I backed yesterday. I won three pounds on it, and I was thinking that, if I gave you thirty shillings of it, you'd be able to buy yourself a nice new hat."

The wife collected the thirty shillings, and said no more until the husband returned home in the evening.

"You know that horse named Daisy which you backed yesterday—well, she 'phoned up this afternoon," said the wife, "so I told her that if she didn't drop out of the running, she'd be scratched."

THE CARLISLE "NON-STOP"

Before the Non-Stop to Carlisle left the London terminus, a passenger approached the guard. "I say, guard," he began, "I want to get out at Carlisle and I'm afraid I may go to sleep and not wake up. Here's five shillings. I want you to put me out at Carlisle without fail. I'm a very heavy sleeper, and if I do fall off, I shall want a lot of rousing. My wife says I swear rather terribly when I'm awakened; but if I do, just get on with the good work and take no notice. If I resist, well, you know what to do. Just bundle me out. I've a very important engagement at Carlisle, which I must keep at all costs. Now, do you understand?"

The guard said he understood perfectly and would see that he did not run beyond his station.

As the train slowed up into Glasgow, the passenger rubbed his eyes, yawned, and looked out of the window. "Good gracious!" he exclaimed, "that fool of a guard has not done as he was told." Our friend was the first to alight on the platform, and he lost no time in seeking out the guard and giving him a rather large slice of his mind.

When the passenger paused for breath, the guard interrupted a renewal of the attack. "You swear all right," he said, "but you can't swear a patch on the chap we *did* unload at Carlisle."

AN URGENT COMMUNICATION

All ex-soldiers will remember the old exercise of passing a message "along the line." A certain battalion, whilst in training, was lying in open order spread across a considerable portion of Salisbury Plain. The "reserve" was stationed some distance behind the right flank, and from the extreme left an officer sent the message: "Send reinforcements. We are going to advance."

Slowly the message went from mouth to mouth. Upon reaching its destination its wording had become slightly altered, as is not uncommon. And the officer on the right was extremely puzzled to hear: "Send three and fourpence. We are going to a dance."

TACT

A British workman one day inquired of his mate—a plumber—what was meant by "tact." Said the plumber:

"Why, tact is —well, yer can't get on wivout tact. It's a—sort of—well, I'll give yer an instance o' tact. I 'ad a job t'other day, down Arden Crescent. Gent there sent fer to 'ave 'is bath waste-pipe fixed. I goes dahn wiv me bag, skivvy lets me in, and ses as the bathroom's first door on the right up the stairs.

"I finds it O.K., opens the door, and sees the lady o' the 'ouse 'avin' a bath! Nah, this is where the tact comes in. Did I get excited? No! I pops back be'ind the door, ses 'Beg pardon, SIR,' and 'ops it. That was tact, that was—'n I got a extry five bob for it.".

THE BROOCH THAT WAS LOST

RACHAEL lived alone in a little flat, as many girls do. The world had treated her unkindly, and money was one of the things she lacked. However, an old aunt had left her a brooch worth five pounds—which was insured for a hundred. Rachael often mused over the brooch, and thought how, when the worst came to the worst, the hundred pounds would have to be collected from the insurance company.

In course of time, the worst came to the worst. Rachael was spending her last few shillings. What was to be done? Yes, the insurance company should be done. Rachael's mind was made up, and that afternoon she sallied forth into the highways and byways, wondering how to stage-manage the business.

She wandered down to the Embankment and looked at the waters, which were anything but clean. There, by the bridge, stood a little steamer which was about to set out on a hazardous trip to Richmond. It was just what she was looking for—the whole thing could be enacted on that little boat with perfect ease.

Rachael bought a ticket and took her place among the handful of passengers. About half-way up the course, she said to herself, "Now," and with that she got up and looked over the side of the boat. It was quite a simple matter to arrange the brooch and the pin so that it fell into the water—and it did.

In earlier times Rachael had been keen on amateur theatricals, and what she had then learnt stood her in good stead now. She threw up her hands and shouted, "Oh! my brooch has gone!" Kind people gathered round and tried to console her. Some even said they saw it fall, and one old gentleman assured Rachael that he would be able to recognise it again. This was after Rachael had described it to him.

The rest of the journey was a sad one, everyone being sorry for the girl who had suffered the loss. Names and addresses of witnesses were readily collected, and when the landing stage was reached, Rachael hurried back to the flat.

As she pushed open the front door, it wedged somewhat; but by pushing more it gave easily, and Rachael walked in. "It's the doormat that's got in the way," she said to herself. With that she bent down and lifted up the mat to put it straight.

Tucked under the mat was an envelope which had reposed there for some days. Rachael opened the envelope and read, "Dear Madame,—The policy covering your brooch expired yesterday. Unless it is renewed within fourteen days, etc. . . ."

The insurance had run out!

M. JAMIESON.

THE DINGY LITTLE ANTIQUE SHOP

Rose was just an ordinary girl, who worked all day long in an ordinary office. She dressed like thousands of other girls dressed, read the same soul-less novels, and went to the "pictures" regularly every Saturday night.

But there was one person who saw in Rose a vision of loveliness. To him, she was an angel sent from Heaven. She was everything that's perfect. He loved her, and his name was Adolphus Brown.

On Saturday nights, Adolphus Brown would shut up his little antique shop in the dingy back street, and escort Rose to the "pictures," where they munched chocolates.

Everything went swimmingly until one day a fat old gentleman—old enough to be Rose's grandfather—came upon the scene. The rest may be guessed. He fell in love with Rose, and countless money bags weighed down the scales in his favour. Rose's mother saw to it that Adolphus became a back number.

The wedding was not long delayed; nor was the funeral, for within a year, Rose was a widow. " Pictures " not only on Saturdays, but every evening in the week, had proved too much for the old gentleman.

Rose inherited all the money bags, but only as long as she remained a widow, which was not long. In less than no time, she married once more. It was the penniless Adolphus who led her to the altar on the second occasion.

They settled down and lived in a large house; they kept two or three servants and ran a car. Every luxury was theirs.

How was it done, since they were both poor? Oh, I forgot to say that, as soon as the old chap died, Rose squandered the whole of his money away, buying antiques at fabulous prices—from Adolphus Brown & Co.

PHYLLIS RAVEN.

GRANDMA'S ADVICE

" Help yourself, help yourself, little boy—do!
Don't wait for others to wait upon you."
Grandma was holding her afternoon chat,
Knitting and rocking away as she sat.
" Look at the birds, how they build their own nest!
Watch the brown bees, always toiling their best!
Put your own hands to the plough if you'd thrive;
Don't waste your moments in wishing, but strive."
Up in her face looked a mischievous elf;
" Don't forget darling," said she, " help yourself."

Afternoon shadows grow drowsy and deep :
Grandma was tranquilly folded in sleep :
Nothing was heard but the old farmhouse clock
Plodding away with its warning " tick, tock "!
Out from the pantry there came a loud crash ;
Pussy jumped up from the hearth like a flash.
Back to her chair strode the practical boy,
Steeped to the ears in jam, custard and joy.
Grinning, he cried, " Please, I've upset the shelf,
Grandma, I minded : I did help myself."

Author unknown.

MILESTONES

"Let me see, now, it's just a month ago to-day we were married, isn't it, duckie?"

"Yes, Bert, it's just a month! It doesn't seem five minutes though, does it, so quickly the time has passed. And yet, you know, Bert darling, it is horrible to think that there was a time when we were not together. Wouldn't it be awful if we were ever separated again!"

"Very true, darling; it's bad enough to have to be all day in the city, with you waiting at home for me to come back. I don't know how you get through the day. I suppose you just live for six o'clock to come."

"Have you your pipe and tobacco and your biscuits for lunch? Just a moment while I powder my nose, and then I'm ready to toddle along to the station with you."

Bert slips his arm into Joan's and they pick their way along the unmade road, avoiding the muddy puddles left by the builders.

"I've just got three minutes to spare, duckie, before the train carries me away from my little Joannie, and then I shan't see her any more until six o'clock to-night!"

"Here it comes! Think of me, hubbie dear, while you sit at your desk. And don't forget to change those curtain rings. They must be painted white, not brass. See?"

"Righto, good-bye." Kisses.

"Good-bye." She gets out a handkerchief, preparatory to waving it.

Joan turns slowly homewards, wipes a tear from her eye, with the aforesaid handkerchief, and thinks of the long hours from eight-fifteen to six-three.

* * * * * * *

(Several years elapse.)

"I say, mother, I'm getting fed up with the way you let the children use my handkerchiefs. There's never a clean one for me. Look at this, it's covered with paint that you haven't washed out. How can I go to the office with a thing like this?"

"Well, buy some new ones, Albert. You can't expect half-a-dozen handkerchiefs to last a life-time. And the children must have handkerchiefs to wipe their noses!"

"It's not their noses that I mind them wiping on my best handkerchiefs—it's the paint-pot that I object to. And, another thing, I'd like to tell you that my money doesn't run to buying handkerchiefs every day of the week. You don't seem to understand that now Bertie is going to school, we've got to scrape the money together somehow."

"Do be quiet a moment, Albert, can't you hear one of the children calling!" She calls upstairs. "All right, darling, I'll be upstairs as soon as father's gone. You'll be back at about eight, I suppose, as usual?"

"Yes, between eight and nine, and I'd like to ask you to see that there's a clean table-cloth on for dinner—not the one with all the holes in it. I might bring George and Maurice in for cards."

"All right!"

"Good-bye." The front door slams.

* * * * * * *

(Many years later.)

"Do you know, darling, what to-day is?"

"Of course I do, father."

"Yes, fifty years ago, to-day, you were my blushing little bride. And, by Jove, there wasn't a prettier little woman in the kingdom. Every day during those fifty years has been a day of joy. Never regretted it once."

"Keep your coat collar buttoned over your chest, father; these cold winds are trying to old folk like ourselves."

"Fifty years, and never regretted it once! It's a fine thing for a man to be able to say."

"And don't walk quite so fast. Take it easy or you'll get out of breath. It's a bit trying to walk fast now."

"Yes, half a century and never regretted it once! Splendid, for a man to be able to say."

DOROTHY MAXIM.

A WORKING-MAN GIVES HIS VERSION OF "THE JACKDAW OF RHEIMS"

Well, it was like this here. One day a lot o' chaps belonging to the Church 'ad a meeting, to discuss whether they'd down tools if they didn't get their wages put up. The chairman, 'e was a cardinal, all dressed in red, same as those pictures in the advertisements that tell you to wear wool next yer skin.

Well, as I was a-saying, before they commenced to talk

business, they 'ad a good dinner to make them sort of comfortable inside. Some cardinals, you know, enjoy their grub. Well, while they was a-feasting, a saucy little bird—no, I don't mean the kind o' bird you mean—I mean a bird what flies. Well, this bird 'ad the name of jackdaw, same as my name's Hambrose and yourn's Harthur. Well, this bird come it rather thick; it plops down on the table and marches all among the grub. Not satisfied with that, what does this little jackdaw do? Why, it perches itself on the old man's chair, and to cap it all, when the old man turns round and sort of frowns at 'im, why, he does a wink. Course, this was a bit too cheeky, and all them monks, who was a-wonderin' 'ow their rises would come off, got the wind up. They said to themselves, " if this 'ere bird puts the old boss in a temper why, our rises are as good as gone!" And, of course, they were right—a little thing like that would make all the difference.

Well, when all the big noises had filled 'emselves with food and drink up to their chins, they thought it was time to get on with the next bit of business. So, in comes a lot of nice little choir boys, if little choir boys can be nice—personally, I think they is a lot o' little demons. Well, in they comes and each struggles in wiv' something in their 'ands. One brought in a *ewer*, whatever that means. Another, he fetches in a bar of Sunlight. Another 'ad a bottle of *eu-dee-Kolognee* —that's the stuff that smells all right—and I forget what the others 'ad, but they all 'ad somefing. Oh, I remember what another 'ad. He 'ad a towel to wash yerself with.

Well, the cardinal chap 'e 'ad splashed himself with the soup, so nothing would please 'im but he must 'ave a wash. So he takes off his coat, rolls up his sleeves, and off his finger 'e takes 'is wedding ring and pops it down side of his plate. Course, there's nothing funny in all that; but now here comes the *dénouement*, as they say in Yankee-land. While the old gentleman 'ad 'is eyes full o' soap, the dreadful bird palms the ring and clears off. Course, that was like putting the tin 'at on their rises.

When the cardinal 'ad done his absolutions, he sez, " Where's my ring?" And nobody could tell him. Naturally, the old gentleman got a bit fresh. " Where's my ring?" he bawled out again. " Where's my ring?"

Now, the monks they got a bit funky. If that ring's gone, so are our rises, they thought, and, of course, they were right.

So they all began to look round and "hunt the thimble." What a pretty sight it must have been to see them poor fellers on their hands and knees, crawling around the floor, just as if they was getting ready for a game of over-backs!

Somebody sez to the cardinal, "'As it dropped in yer shoe?" So the cardinal looks in his shoe. Nuffink! Somebody else sez, "Is it in your pockets?" So the cardinal looks in his pockets. Nuffink! Another chap sez, "Is it in your permanent turn-ups?" So the cardinal looks in his permanent turn-ups. Still nuffink! In fact, they tried all roads and each time the answer was "Nuffink!"

"My hat," says the cardinal at last, "I'll learn the fellow what's pinched my ring. I'll learn him. He shall know all about it." Well, with that, the old boy begins to swear and and curse something dreadful. For a man of the Church he ought to have known better. He swore and cursed for about five minutes right off the reel. Then, when he had got all the curses off his chest, he looks up and sez, "Which is the chap what's got it in the neck?" The funny thing was that nobody was a pennuth the worse. "Remarkable!" muttered the old sport.

Well, things didn't improve. The cardinal, he walked about with a terrible frown, and all the monks they looked like nothing on earth, through fright. Everybody was a-lookin' everywhere and nobody dared go to bed that night. It was an awful time for the spiders and cobwebs; they all got damaged and blown about.

Well, early in the morning, a chap called the *sacred-stand*, or some name like that, he happened to clap eyes on the jackdaw. Poor thing, it 'ad lorst all its fevvers and it looked a proper mess, it did. "Lumme," exclaimed the chap with the rum name, "that's what done it—five 'undred pound to a farthin'." So he calls up all his pals and the cardinal, and sez, "'Ow about 'im?" "O'course," sez the cardinal, very pompous like, "that's the creeter what's got my ring. Now then, dicky, just you cough up that ring at once, if not sooner," he sez, kindly like, and with that the jackdaw leads all the fellers to 'is little nest, and there, sure enough, was the ring.

To cut a long story short, the cardinal he fell on the neck of the little bird, and when it died, they made it a saint. The monks they all got put on the trade union rate of wages, and everybody lived 'appy ever after.

WHY HE DIDN'T EXPLAIN

Some eight or ten years ago a silvery-tongued chap, who claimed to be a fruit-tree agent, swindled the farmers of Nankin county in a shameful manner, and one resident was so mad about it that he came to Detroit, searched the rascal out, and gave him a pounding on the street. After he got through his work, he told the fellow that he would lick him twice as bad if he ever put eyes on him again, and it was a threat to be remembered and nursed.

About three weeks ago, the Nankin man was travelling in Washtenaw county, and as he journeyed along the highway he met a traveller who so closely resembled the fruit-tree swindler that he halted and called out : " Here you are again, you bold-faced rascal ! "

" Yes, I'm here," was the calm reply.

" Well, so'm I, and I'm going to lick you until you can't holler ! I said I'd do it, and I always keep my word. Climb down here ! "

The stranger " clumb " without a protest, shedding his coat as he struck the ground, and a fight began. In about two minutes he had used up the farmer, and was coolly replacing his coat.

" See here," said the man from Nankin, as he wiped his nose with a burdock, " you fight better than you did eight years ago."

" Well, I dunno. This is my first affair with you."

" Didn't I wallop you in front of the Detroit post office eight years ago ? "

" No, sir ! I was in Australia up to a year ago."

" And you never saw me before ? "

" Never ! "

" And was never in Nankin ? "

" Never."

" Well, I'll be hanged ! Come to look at you I can see that you are not the man ! Why on earth didn't you explain, or ask me to ? You must have thought me mistaken."

" Oh, yes, I knew you were mistaken, but I had just discovered that I had driven seven miles on the wrong road and was wishing someone would come along and give me two words of sass. I didn't want any explanation about it. A rotten sweet apple will cure that black eye in three or four days, and salt and water will tighten your front teeth in a week or so. I feel fifty per cent. better, and I'm ever so much obliged. So long to you."

ACTING CHARADES AND HOW TO PLAY THEM

CHARADES provide admirable fun for young and old, alike. They need not be elaborately staged and acted in order to mystify the audience ; in fact, some of the best charades that we have taken part in have been presented in a very simple manner, yet they have proved extremely successful.

For the benefit of those who are not quite clear as to what a charade actually is, let it be said that a secret word is selected by the actors, and the audience, having witnessed the acting of the word, is required to guess what it is.

The guests, or house party, should be divided into two equal groups, and it is important to see that the two groups are as nearly equal as possible. If the company is a mixed one as regards age, then each section should contain the same number of grown-ups, the same number of youngsters, and they should also be equal in boys and girls, men and women.

A senior should be in charge of each group, and should take the part of producer. One party takes its place as audience, while the other leaves the room, and eventually acts a word chosen by themselves, leaving the audience to guess the selected word. To give them a reasonable chance, a word of two syllables is invariably selected ; then each syllable forms one act, and the whole word forms a third act of a miniature play, or series of separate scenes.

If the audience guess correctly, the two parties change places, and a further charade is performed ; if they fail to guess the word, then the original actors are allowed to perform again. A definite number of guesses, or a strict time limit should be arranged, otherwise the audience could go on guessing all night, whereas the intention is to act as many charades as possible.

Dressing up is not necessary, but if suitable costumes are available, they should be used. Fancy dresses are kept ready in many country houses, since amateur theatricals are generally popular with house parties. But the producer can do all that is necessary by explaining matters in advance.

The object of the actors is to puzzle their opponents, but this must be done in a reasonable manner, as it is essential to give them a fair chance of guessing correctly, if they use their wits. For this reason, it is usual in the case of a children's party, to act each syllable and the full word in a descriptive manner, but for grown-ups, or mixed parties, this would be too easy and would not prove interesting or amusing.

In such cases, the syllable or word must be spoken, generally more than once, and the brief act should be characteristic in addition—in other words, the particular syllable *must* be of great importance.

Take the following example in order to show what is meant. The producer announces that the word is of two syllables, that the scene is a parlour, and that all three acts take place in the same room. Then he withdraws, and some of the actors enter. One would be the mother of the family, another the father, or some young member of the family—some neighbours could be present. They discuss the expected arrival of the eldest *son*, a sailor, who has been on a long voyage and has been absent for several years.

The word dock must be introduced repeatedly—when is the ship due in dock, when can he get away, and so on. A youngster can ask what they mean by dock, what they do there, and other questions. It should be made quite clear that it is Saturday—the youngster could ask what would happen if he could not get away, as the next day would be Sunday.

Then the producer appears, and announces that this ends Act I, and that Act II will start at once.

The sailor son comes home, and they all ask him about his adventures. " Adventures ! " he cries. " Why, there was nothing like the dangers of your London streets—I took a taxi and we tore through the traffic ; tore up this street, tore round the corner "—and so on. He says that he feels quite ill, and declines to go out again by *day*, only at night when the streets are quiet. Then he faints, and a neighbour rushes off for the doctor.

Now the producer appears once more, and announces that this ends Act II, and that Act III commences at once.

The neighbour returns, bringing the doctor, who fusses over the sailor son—knew him as a baby, and so on. Nothing the matter but tiredness and nerves—a few days at home with his mother will do wonders. Go to church on Sunday—that will make him realise that we still have some peace in old England, in spite of the mad rush of our week-days.

The producer announces that the Charade is finished, and the audience is invited to guess the word.

Naturally most people will guess DOCTOR, but the words DOCK, TORE and DOCTOR were deliberately introduced in order to trick the opponents. You must treat them reasonably, but trick or puzzle them all you can. For this reason, experienced performers mix two, or even three words into a charade, as we have done in this case, where the real word is SUNDAY.

It will be seen from this example that the actual spelling of the word is of no importance whatever—the charade is based upon the generally accepted pronunciation of the word and its two syllables.

Words of two syllables are usually enforced, because a three-syllable word would need four acts and that would certainly mean that most of the audience would lose grip of the first act: That would not be fair.

Words of one syllable are no use, as that would mean only one act, and only one clue—you would have to give a very obvious hint, and thus spoil the fun, or alternatively you would make it almost impossible for the audience to guess correctly.

As the actual spelling of the selected word is ignored, it is very important to be fair to your audience. For instance, it is not reckoned " fair play " to introduce illiterate characters into a charade, merely in order to allow such a person to pronounce a word wrongly. You can have a charwoman in the scene, if that is natural, or if you intend her as " camouflage "; but if your selected word is HUSBAND, it would be deemed unfair if you made her say HUS for US, as your first syllable.

In the same way, you must not use FOOL for FUL, in such words as FAITHFUL; nor could you use FUEL. You must not act BABE and EYE for BABY; nor BED and IN for BEDDING. It is unfortunately only too true that many people do not sound the final G in words that end with ING, but you must not take advantage of this.

Another difficulty with the English language, in its colloquial form, is found in slurred syllables—for instance, SCULLERY is generally pronounced in two syllables, as SCULL'RY, but you must not act it like that in a charade. Similarly many two-syllable words are slurred into one syllable, and in poetry a letter is omitted in order to indicate this. For instance, a poet can use the word FLOWER either as a two-syllable word, or as a single syllable, according to the nature of his verse.

All doubtful words should be avoided in charades! There are, unfortunately, many honest difficulties to be faced by the producer, and one of these is the question of double words— that is, the joining together of two common words in order to form one compound word. You can safely use the word WINE-GLASS, though it is generally spelt with a hyphen, but you must not use PORT WINE, although it is really a compound word of the same character. Nor must you use any compound verbs such as SHOW OFF.

On the other hand, you need not keep to a rigid division of syllables, provided the usual colloquial pronunciation justifies your action. For instance, you can safely use SPANK and KING for SPANKING, and no one would question your fairness; but it would not be right to use WOE and MAN for WOMAN.

Naturally, your party knows what is taking place on the "stage," but it will certainly take your audience a few minutes to grasp your purpose, even if you are acting in costume. For this reason, it is not considered "quite the thing" to introduce the syllable or word very early in the scene—it does not give the less nimble members of your audience a reasonable chance. Introduce the syllable or word as early as you please, but only on condition that it is repeated at least twice nearer the end of the scene.

Be fair above all things; a victory is not worth scoring if its success depends upon an unlikely "catch." Puzzle them—trick them—but do it by skill, and then you will certainly enjoy this tussle of brain against brain.

JUNIOR SECTION

It may seem very startling to say so, but more than a million people will probably read this book. That being so, it may be reckoned that many thousands of boys and girls will peep inside the copies which their grown-up friends have bought. As we don't want them to be disappointed, we have provided this section specially for them, and we hope they will enjoy it. Seeing that the grown-ups will read it, for sure, it is only fair that the juniors should devour the other sections as well. They will find a good deal to amuse them, on almost every page.

FUNNY FACES

Try your hand at drawing funny faces, but do it in this special way: Take a sheet of paper about twice the size of this page, fold the top edge over the bottom edge, using the short sides, and cut along the crease. Then, take the two sheets and double them so that one side lies over the other. You now have a little booklet of four sheets.

With a pair of scissors, cut all the pages of the booklet into four equal horizontal strips, but do not run the scissors quite up to the folded edge of the pages. Leave about an eighth of an inch uncut so that the booklet cannot fall to pieces.

Now, draw a funny face on each of the four sheets, but do it in this way: arrange for a hat in every case to fill up the top space; for the face to take up the next two spaces, the eyes and nose being on the one above and the mouth and chin on the one below; then, on the lowest space of all, have the shoulders. See that the drawings come in the centre of each whole page.

By turning over the flaps at random, a change of face appears and the variety of expressions is endless.

It adds to the finish of the little booklet if it is pinned or sewn together along the back end, and, of course, if the faces are coloured they will be funnier still.

PAPER HATS

Lots of fun can be had out of paper hats. If you want to make a few for a party, or maybe for your little regiment of make-believe soldiers, this is the way to do it.

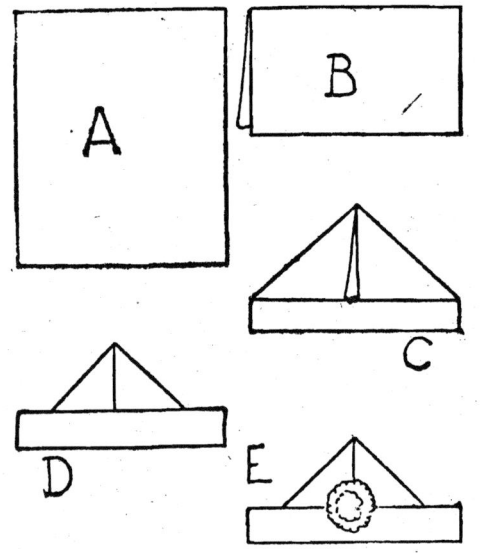

Get some large sheets of paper. Newspaper is hardly stout enough; brown paper is much better; but why not hunt out some gay-coloured papers—reds, blues, greens, etc? Let each sheet be not quite square—say a quarter more one side than the other, as Diagram A. Now fold as follows:

JUNIOR SECTION

(1) Halve the long edges and double the paper over so that the crease joins the two halfway points, as Diagram B.

(2) Bend over the two upper corners so that they meet down the middle, as Diagram C.

(3) Fold the lower edges so that they double over the triangular top, one at the front and one at the back, as Diagram D. The hat can now be opened out and worn.

It makes a nice addition if the hats are ornamented by having coloured rosettes or other gay decorations pasted on to them. The rosette shown in Diagram E not only serves as an ornamentation, but it helps to keep the hat from coming undone.

SOME OPTICAL ILLUSIONS

It is a well-known fact that the eye can be cheated, and a good deal of amusement may be derived by drawing diagrams which mislead our vision. We give here six sets of pictures which are purposely arranged so that, on looking at them, we jump to the wrong conclusion.

Take, for instance, A and B. Here we have two strips cut from a circle. Which is the longer piece? Naturally, you immediately say, "Both the same," merely because you have been asked. Your eye, however, told you it was A. In spite of what your eye told you, the truth is that B is the longer. Cut out of thin card two similar strips and shade them like these; then get your friends to tell you what they think.

Look at C. This diagram contains a number of vertical lines. They seem to bulge outwards, yet they are quite upright. The diamond spaces placed across them give them the bent appearance.

Now take D and E. Which is the larger space? E looks much more expansive, yet they are identical in size.

F and G are two more deceptive diagrams. F looks tall and G seems wide. Their boundaries are both squares of the same size, however.

H and I are old friends, largely because they are about as deceiving as they can be. Which has the longer vertical line? I, without a doubt, seems the longer; yet it is shorter than H.

What of J and K? Is the black space of K larger than

the white spot in J? In spite of what your eye says, they are exactly the same size.

Draw all these diagrams on separate cards, and show them to your friends. Take F and G, for instance, here they are

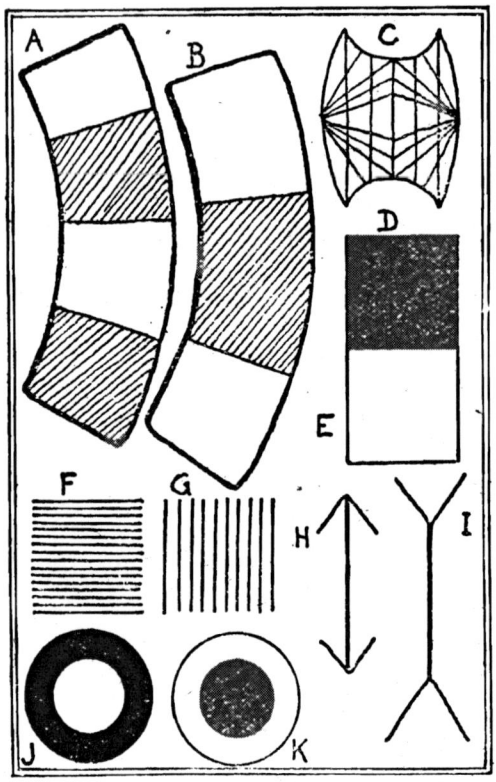

too crowded, which makes them easier to assess. But on separate cards, placed a little way apart, they become far more deceptive, and this is what you want.

DRAWING THE UNION JACK

Everybody in this country must have seen thousands of Union Jacks, but how many people can draw one accurately? Just try, yourself. Take a piece of paper and a pencil, and sit down: then, see what you can do. It is not sufficient to draw some crosses, one overlapping another; but you should be able to indicate where the narrow and the wide lines come, and what colour they are.

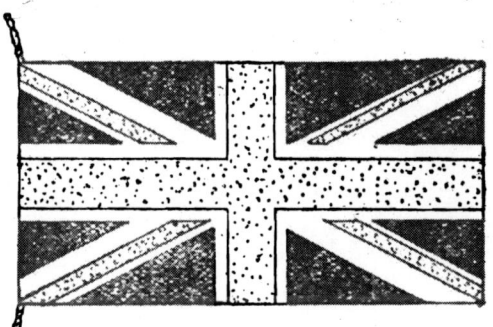

BLUE IS SHOWN ABOVE BY BLACK AREAS, RED BY DOTTED AREAS AND WHITE IS LEFT PLAIN...

When you have had a good try, compare your effort with the diagram.

MAKING A SECRET CODE

Occasions arise when it is necessary to send a secret message to a friend. Now, if the message is written in ordinary language, the paper may fall into a third person's hands, and the secret become known. Clearly, the way out of the difficulty is to adopt a code, the key of which only you and your friend know.

Codes may take many forms, and, though we will only outline a few obvious ones, those given will show you how to make others.

1. There are twenty-six letters in the alphabet. Instead of using them in their usual way, take them, say, three places further down the scale, so that C becomes A, D becomes B, E becomes C, and so on. Of course, you can adopt any number you like instead of 3.

2. The numerical code is a good one. First you must decide on a number to represent A, and then B becomes the number plus one, C the number plus 2, and so on.

3. Hieroglyphics offer all sorts of variations. Draw the letter I, put a dot on a level with the top of it and in front of it and call this A. Put the dot on a level with the bottom of it and in front of it, and call this B. Put the dots after the

How many points can you score?

See page 225.

JUNIOR SECTION

and they become C and D. For E, F, G, and H, similarly place dots round the letter J, this being the next letter in the alphabet to I. Continue thus as far as required.

So far so good, but any secret alphabet planned on the above lines can be deciphered by clever people. They begin by picking out the one-lettered words in the message, and they know that wherever a sign stands alone it must be your way of writing A, I, or O. Next, they look at the three-lettered words, and they come to the conclusion that THE and AND are the most frequently used words of three letters. By comparing the one-lettered and the three-lettered words, they can often tell what cyphers you are using for A, N, and D. So they proceed until the whole of your secret message is known to them.

There is a clever way of mystifying the would-be code reader who does not possess the key. Arrange a number of dummy signs which have no significance at all. Sprinkle them irregularly through the message; tack them on to the one-lettered words, on to the two-lettered words, and even put them as words by themselves. Your friend, when he gets your message, will first cross out all the dummy signs, and then begin the decoding proper.

HOW MANY POINTS CAN YOU SCORE?

This is a little game for kiddies only—no adults or grown-ups are admitted. Here are the rules: Open the book flat on the table and take hold of a pencil. Then, take turns with yourself and your friend to shut your eyes tightly. Jab at the Golliwog and hold your pencil still. Open your eyes and see if you have scored any points. The player who gets 25 points first is the winner.

These are the points:
- 5 for either eye, white or black.
- 4 for the white bib or collar.
- 3 for either hand.
- 2 for either boot.
- 1 for a black square on trousers.
- 0 for anywhere else.

(Please don't jab too hard or you may hurt him.)

AN INTERESTING SUM

Eight eights are sixty-four, of course : but the question here is " Can you write down eight eights so that they add up to one thousand ? "

Here is the way :

```
    888
     88
      8
      8
      8
   ————
   1000
```

Now you know how it is done, try it on one of your uncles or aunts.

ANOTHER SUM

Write down eleven thousand, eleven hundred and eleven. Before you read any further, get a piece of paper and see what you make of it. It sounds easy enough, and the first part is easy enough ; but what of the second portion ?

These figures explain the catch :

Eleven thousand = 11,000
Eleven hundred = 1,100
Eleven = 11

Total = 12,111

THE GOLDFISH AND THE GLOBE

Here is an amusing toy which can be made in a few minutes. Procure a piece of cardboard, about 3in. long by 2in. wide, and white on both sides—a piece of a postcard will do. On one side of the card draw a globe such as goldfish live in, but have it quite empty of fish. You may scribble a few lines to suggest that there is water in it if you like. Now, turn the card over so that the blank side is uppermost. In doing this be careful to see that the globe is turned upside down. On the blank side draw, neatly, a goldfish. Do it in red ink if you used black for the globe. Lastly, make two tiny holes in the middle of both sides of the card and insert thread through them, to form a loop at each end.

Hold the thread slack, one end in each hand between the thumb and first finger, and rotate the card until the thread is well twisted; then slip the loops over your thumbs and pull apart, moving your hands towards each other to permit the thread to rewind itself, and so on. In this manner, the

card can be kept spinning. As the card flies over, the eye obtains the impression that there is a globe with a goldfish in it.

Instead of the globe and fish, all sorts of variations can be devised, such as a canary and a cage, or your own name with alternate letters on one side of the card and the remaining letters on the other.

THE TRICK MATCHBOX

Obtain two matchboxes exactly alike, and, for preference, select a variety that is labelled both top and bottom. Take out the trays from the two boxes, and carefully unstick the blue paper placed round one of them, and also the bottom panel. Now fit the bottom panel as a top panel to the tray as yet untouched. Stick it round with the blue paper, and so enclose it completely. Before shutting it up finally, insert half a dozen matches—dead ones will do.

When a friend asks you for a match, hand him your trick box and watch his expression as he turns the box over and over to find the entrance.

SOAP BUBBLES THAT LAST

Every boy and girl finds amusement in blowing soap bubbles, but the worst of the game is that the bubbles burst almost before we have time to admire their beauty. That they are exceedingly beautiful, we are all prepared to admit.

Here is a recipe which will allow our bubbles to last thirty minutes or more if the air is still. Take a piece of good soap and make a very strong lather with it in hot water. When the water is cold, and much of the froth has gone, add about half as much glycerine as water. This solution will make strong bubbles that will float about in the air for a considerable while.

If you have any of the solution left over when you have done blowing bubbles, put it in a bottle, cork up tightly, and it will remain good for many weeks. Shake the bottle well when you use it again.

THOSE ROVING EYES

Here is one of those silly little things which cause a good deal of amusement. On a stout envelope draw a head as large

as you can make it. Let it be the classic features of Charlie Chaplin, a hungry alligator, a mischievous monkey, or anything you like. Colour the features, and slit the envelope above the head and below the neck. Also cut out rather large holes for the eyes. Next take a strip of paper, just wide enough to pass through the envelope, and about 8in. long. On the strip draw two thick, wavy, zig-zag lines, but see that the lines are always in view through the eyeholes, when the paper is drawn through the envelope. Paint the strip pink, red, yellow, blue, and green, but let one colour merge into the next. As the paper is drawn through the envelope, the lines will give the effect of moving eyes, and their movements will prove extremely funny.

CUT-OUT FIGURES

A good deal of fun can be obtained with a pair of scissors and a sheet of paper. When next you have some friends at

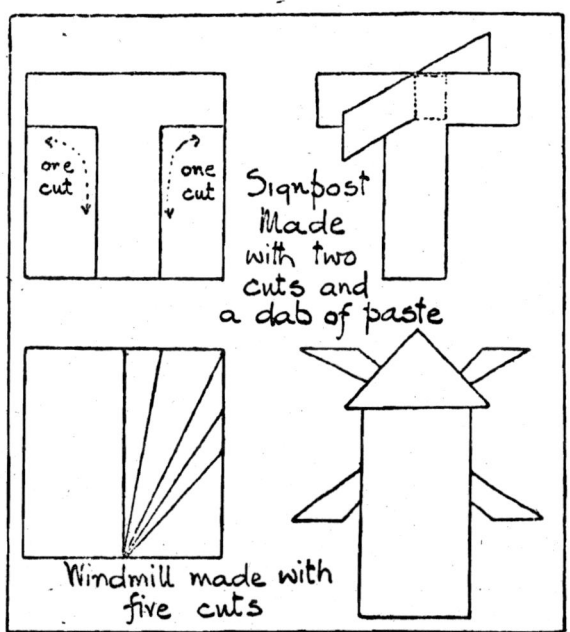

your house, provide them each with scissors and a square of paper, and challenge them to make the best design with the least number of cuts, or pieces of paper. A sheet three inches each way will do nicely, and if possible, select paper that is covered with squares. Provide a pot of paste in case some of the efforts need to be stuck, though you should make it clear that a design assembled flat on the table will be quite in order.

In the diagram, we show two typical designs, the first is of a sign-post, and the second a windmill.

THE WALNUT TORTOISE

Clever hands can devise all sorts of funny things out of waste material, and our small sisters and brothers love to see us build up playthings out of oddments. Here is one such article. Crack a walnut so that one half of the shell is perfect, and eat the walnut, of course. Now put the shell, dome side up, on a piece of thin card (a postcard is about the right

thickness) and cut out an oval to fit the shell. Leave four projections of card for the legs, and two extra for the head and tail. Run some fish glue round the flat rim of the shell and press the card into contact. When hard and dry, paint the card to match the colour of the shell, bend the legs slightly down and the head up. Thread a length of cotton round the neck and you have a fine little toy which will amuse a youngster for hours. If you make two or three of these walnut tortoises, the kiddies will be able to run races with them and have all sorts of fun and sport.

JUNIOR SECTION

THREE SHIES A PENNY

It is really wonderful what a lot of fun can be got out of home-made toys and games. Here is a simple little article which will provide endless fun. The ingredients in this case are one old man's straw hat—no, that's not right—one man's

old straw hat, one bottle of ink (red, green, mauve, etc.), six table-tennis balls, the use of one paint box, some string and one nail. If your father can't spare his last season's "straw," borrow an old bowler and make the design with coloured chalks.

But to return to the old man's—no, the man's old straw hat. First, take out the internal lining. Next, give the outside a coat of ink to make it look lively. After that, cut out a large oval from the crown. This should be about four by three inches, and the crown is now painted to look like a face, the opening being taken for the mouth.

The string and the nail are used for hanging the hat on the

wall. Now, here the fun begins. Take three of the balls and, if you are a big chap, stand six feet away; come closer if you are a girl or are small. The game is to feed the monster. His mouth is large enough.

AN AMUSING TABLE GAME

Take six rather large corks. Let them be wide in diameter and not standing too high. Push the point of a compass or an awl, if you have one, through the centre of each, and make the hole sufficiently large to grip a match tightly. A touch of glue may be necessary to keep the match in place. On each cork, print a different number, 1, 2, 5, 8, 10 12.

Now take some plain post-cards and cut rings out of them. The cut-out centres should be about twice as wide as the diameter of the corks. They must all be the same size, however.

Stand the corks, with the matches pointing upwards, on the table, about a foot and a half from the edge. Place them in a convenient little group. Give each player half a dozen rings. The game is to see who can throw the rings on to the match sticks and first score thirty points. No points are scored by a ring that capsizes a cork.

If you print the numbers on the bottoms of the corks and mix them well before setting them up for each player it will add to the fun, as nobody will know whether he or she is aiming at a high number or a low one.

A CURIOSITY IN WORDS

```
K A I S E R
S E R B I A
J O F F R E
F R E N C H
```

During the War, these four names were on everybody's lips. At first sight, there seems to be nothing very unusual about them, except that they all consist of six letters. But, draw a vertical line through the centre of the four words, so as to halve them all. Then, read down each half, taking two lines to make a word. We get exactly the same four words as we have by reading along the lines in the ordinary way.

JUNIOR SECTION

THE HANDKERCHIEF DOLL

Take a clean handkerchief and spread it out flat. Then, tightly roll up one of the long sides until the middle is reached, and follow by rolling up the other side, until the two rolls lie side by side (see A).

Next, take the farther end of the two rolls and double them over, so that they almost, but not quite, touch the nearer end (see B).

After that, bend the nearer end under the end just folded (see C).

When this is done, press on the handkerchief with one hand

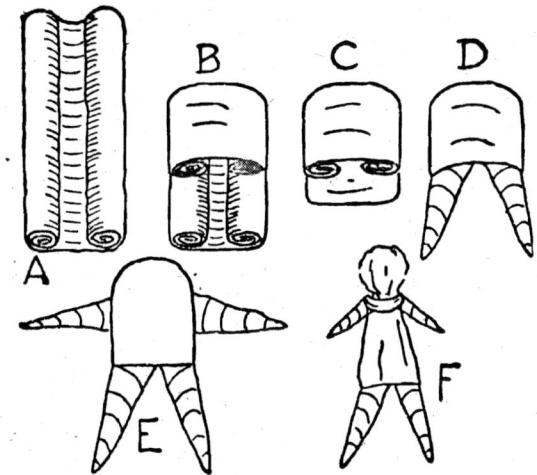

and, with the other, search for two corners, which will be found one in each roll, and pull downwards (see D).

Follow by finding the two other ends of the handkerchief, and pull them outwards and sideways (see E).

Tie these two latter ends around the mass of handkerchief, an inch from the end (see F), and you have an attractive doll—and all made in a minute.

GROTESQUE FACE MASKS FOR PARTIES

If you want some grotesque face masks and cannot get any from the usual sources, it is not difficult to make your own.

Obtain some tough but flexible paper—good typewriting

paper serves admirably, quarto size. Then, draw on it the faces shown in the diagram, or any others that your fancy dictates. See that the distance between the eyes conform with that of your own face, or your youngsters, and apply plenty of colour. Various inks serve best, but coloured

pencils will do, if you are in a hurry. Cut out the holes for the eyes, and it will save much time if the nose is drawn flat on the paper.

Trim each face to the shape shown in the diagram and fix a piece of string at each ear. Stick a piece of gummed paper where the string pierces the paper, in order to provide strength. You will then have some screamingly funny masks.

AN INTERESTING COINCIDENCE

Nobody is quite certain how the word " Shakespeare " ought to be spelt; one quite common method is " Shakspeare." Separate this word into the two portions " Shak " and " Speare." Count the letters; there are four and six, which may be read as forty-six.

Now turn to the Bible and look at the 46th Psalm. Count off the first forty-six words and you arrive at "Shake." Again count off the last forty-six, and you discover the word "Speare"!

THE RITE OF WRITING RIGHT

BY A PLAYWRIGHT

Write we know is written right,
When we see it written write;
But when we see it written wright,
We know 'tis not then written right;
For write to have it written right,
Must not be written right nor wright,
Nor yet should it be written rite,
But write—for so 'tis written right.

MISCELLANEOUS SECTION

THE GENERAL KNOWLEDGE GAME

ASKING questions is excellent fun and, where a gathering consists of grown-ups, there are few better ways of filling in the time. Duplicate a collection of about twenty questions, impose a time limit and set everybody to work. If you find difficulty in making up the papers, consult *What do You Know?* and *What More do You Know?* two volumes in Foulsham's "Knowledge Library," price 2s. each, cloth. Each book contains more than one thousand five hundred suitable questions and answers.

Here are three specimen papers, including the answers to the questions.

PAPER 1

1. For what do the following groups of letters stand? P.A., P.L.A., P.S.A.
    1. *P.A. stands for Press Association; P.L.A. for Port of London Authority; and P.S.A. for Pleasant Sunday Afternoons.*
2. When is St. Swithin's Day?
    2. *July 15th.*
3. What colour is a sapphire?
    3. *Blue.*
4. What is a love apple? What is an oak apple?
    4. *A tomato and a growth on an oak tree.*
5. Which shipping concern owns the "Berengaria?"
    5. *The Cunard Line.*
6. What is caviar?
    6. *The pickled roe of the sturgeon.*
7. Which is the highest point of England?
    7. *Scafell Pike (3,210 feet).*

MISCELLANEOUS SECTION

8. Who was the first President of the United States?
   8. *George Washington.*
9. For what is Lourdes noted?
   9. *Roman Catholics visit the town to be healed.*
10. What is the value of a groat?
    10. *Fourpence.*
11. What letter can be placed in front of the letters ENY to make an English word?
    11. *D, to make the word deny.*
12. For what do the letters, C.W.S., stand?
    12. *Co-operative Wholesale Society.*
13. What is the Southern Belle?
    13. *A Pullman train which runs daily between London and Brighton, in both directions.*
14. What coin is exactly an inch in diameter?
    14. *A halfpenny.*
15. Who wrote the Forsyte Saga?
    15. *John Galsworthy.*
16. What is a telemark?
    16. *The name given to a turn in ski-running.*
17. What is haggis?
    17. *A Scottish dish, comprising the pluck of a lamb or sheep, chopped with suet, highly seasoned and boiled in the stomach of the animal.*
18. Where is Tattenham Corner?
    18. *A point on the Epsom racecourse, nearing the end.*
19. Does the King's head on the coins and the stamps face the same way?
    19. *Yes.*
20. Which letters are vowels?
    20. *A. E. I. O. U.*

PAPER 2

1. What is meant when a man says he put a shilling on a horse "both ways" or "each way"?
   1. *He staked two shillings: one to back the horse to win and the other to back the horse to secure a place: i.e., coming in first, second or third.*
2. Why was Peter Pan different from other children?
   2. *He would not grow up.*
3. What do P.T.O., G.P.O., and N.C.O. stand for?
   3. *Please turn over; General Post Office and Non-Commissioned Officer.*

4. What cathedrals are situated in London?
   4. *St. Paul's and Southwark, and also the Roman Catholic (Westminster) Cathedral at Victoria.*
5. What are the Needles?
   5. *A rocky promontory at the western end of the Isle of Wight.*
6. Is Monmouth in England or Wales?
   6. *Now, it is in England.*
7. How do you pronounce Towcester?
   7. *As though it were spelt Toe-ster.*
8. What country is called the "cock-pit" of Europe?
   8. *Belgium.*
9. What is the meaning of M.C.C.?
   9. *Marylebone Cricket Club.*
10. Who is the Poet Laureate?
    10. *John Masefield.*
11. When is Boxing Day.
    11. *December 26th.*
12. Which is the nearest city to the City of London.
    12. *The City of Westminster.*
13. What is a jig?
    13. *An Irish dance.*
14. Who wrote "As You Like It"?
    14. *Shakespeare.*
15. What wine is made at Oporto?
    15. *Port Wine.*
16. Who shot an apple while it was perched on a boy's head?
    16. *William Tell.*
17. Where is Stonehenge?
    17. *On Salisbury Plain, close to Salisbury.*
18. What is T.N.T.?
    18. *A very powerful explosive.*
19. What is a female fox?
    19. *A vixen.*
20. Who has made the most motor-cars?
    20. *Henry Ford.*

PAPER 3

1. What prevents that sinking feeling?
   1. *Bovril.*
2. What is the guardian of the pore?
   2. *Wright's Coal Tar soap.*

3. What initial letter is on the front of the original and genuine Old Moore's Almanac?
   3. *The letter F.*
4. Whose pills are pink, and who are they for?
   4. *Dr. William's Pink Pills for pale people.*
5. What does Veno sell?
   5. *Lightning cough cure.*
6. What is a Bath oliver?
   6. *A certain kind of biscuit made at Bath.*
7. What are worth a guinea a box?
   7. *Beecham's pills.*
8. How can you get that schoolgirl complexion?
   8. *By using Palmolive soap.*
9. Who makes 57 varieties?
   9. *Heinz.*
10. What paper prints a daily column by Beachcomber?
    10. *The "Daily Express."*
11. What railway company has a terminus at Liverpool Street.
    11. *The L.N.E.R.*
12. What colour is a sixpenny postage stamp?
    12. *Purple.*
13. What is "Brymay" short for?
    13. *Bryant & May.*
14. How much does the 5% War Loan earn now?
    14. *3½%.*
15. What is the letter postage to France?
    15. *2½d.*
16. Can you return by train with a week-end ticket on a Saturday?
    16. *Yes.*
17. What cigarettes please?
    17. *Players.*
18. If you put £1 in the P.O. Savings Bank, what interest do you get at the end of a year?
    18. *Sixpence.*
19. About how many miles is Carlisle from London?
    19. *About 300. Exactly by rail it is 299.*
20. What does the stamp cost which is required (a) on a cheque made out for 5s. and (b) for £1,000?
    20. *Twopence, in both cases*

TABLE TENNIS

There is no need to discuss the qualities of this splendid game; but for the sake of those who are apt to forget, we will point out that, according to the usual rules, a game consists of twenty-one points, and that the service changes hands whenever the combined score is a multiple of five. Should both players reach a score of twenty, the game is decided in favour of the player who is first to score five subsequent points. Service in this case passes alternately from one player to the other.

Scoring is called aloud as each point is made, the server's score being called first.

Service must be by an under-arm stroke, the bat being behind the end of the table. The ball is required to fall in the server's half of the table before bouncing over the net. Should the ball touch the net, and pass over, it is termed "let" and does not count. This affects a serve only. If the same thing happens in play, after service, it is for the opponent to return the ball, if he can.

Where a considerable number of people are ready to play, table tennis may be the cause of good fun, in the following manner:

Arrange the players equally around the four sides of the table. The two who are centrally placed at the short ends of the table serve and reply in the usual manner and, immediately they have done so, they drop the bats on the table and pass along in a clockwise manner. The whole company moves up one space and this brings two fresh players to the centre of the short ends of the table. It is their duty, each to grab a bat and to keep the ball in play. Naturally, they must be very alert, seeing that once the ball has been served, it must be kept going.

A player who fails to return the ball properly is out of the game; but before leaving, he serves. Clearly, the greatest fun is when the players have been considerably thinned out and there are only a few left to get round the table. The last in is the winner.

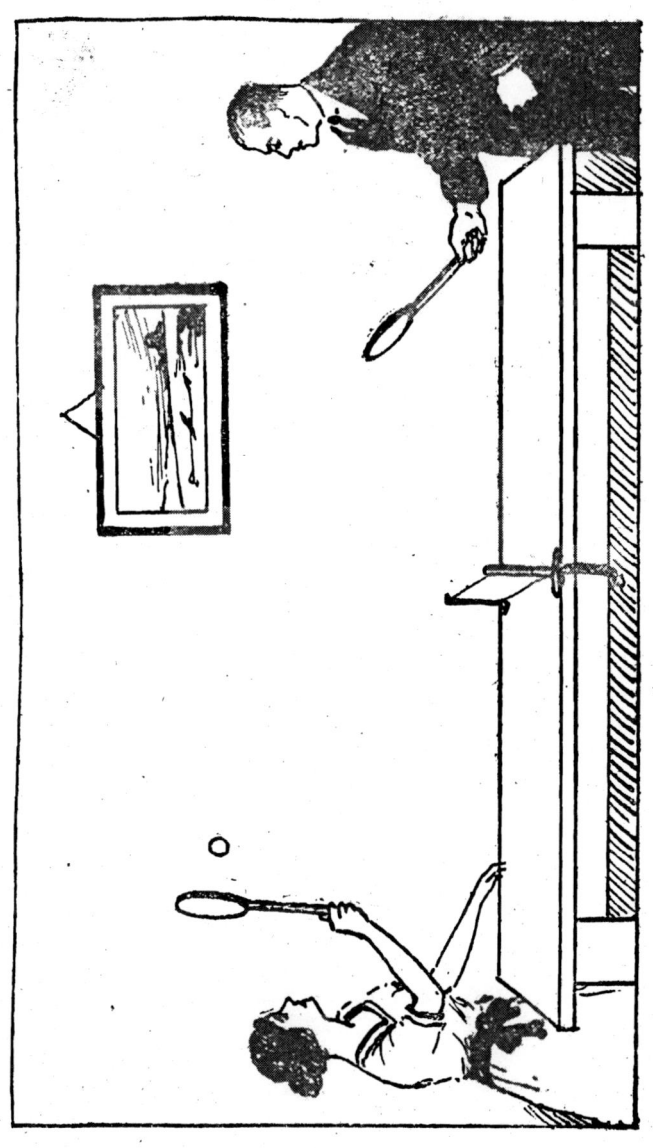

THREE GOOD GAMES OF DOMINOES

There are various ways of playing the game, but of these the three following will, we consider, best serve the purpose of this book.

RUNNINGS OUT
(Also termed the " Twosome Game ")

We have heard this game paradoxically described as " the simplest, and yet most profound of domino games." Be this as it may, it forms an excellent pastime for two or more players.

Before commencing the game, one of the players turns the dominoes upside down (so that the spots are completely hidden) and shuffles or mixes them until it becomes impossible for either to locate any particular card. If only two are playing, twenty-eight dominoes only are used. Next each picks a domino, when the highest number decides who has the " down," or first play.

The cards in question are now replaced in the pack, which is reshuffled by the player who has the " down."

Each then draws seven pieces, and these should be set on edge, lengthwise, facing each player—care being taken that none shall be able to see another's hand. The remaining cards must be placed aside, face downwards, as these will not be required in " Runnings Out " till the next shuffle.

The game may consist of from five to fourteen points, as fancy dictates.

After the " down," or first domino has been played, the game is to set a like number at either end (six to six, five to five, etc.) till the hands " run out." This is clearly demonstrated by the illustrative hands which we give later.

At the conclusion of the initial hand, the second player shuffles, and has the " down "—and so on, till the game is finished.

Should a player get rid of his hand, he must, on disposing of his last card, say " Domino." He then scores one point. If, however, he finds himself unable to play in turn (*i.e.*, to match the number at either end), he must cry " Go," or rap the table.

If no player can " go," their remaining dominoes are placed

MISCELLANEOUS SECTION

on the table, face upwards, and the spots in each hand counted. The player who has the smaller total then takes the point.

We will now deal with the two illustrative hands before-mentioned and, for convenience, term their holders A and B.

It will be a good idea to get out a box of dominoes and actually play these two hands, as described here :

A, who has the " down," notes that he has the double-six, six-three, six-two, six-blank, five-two, five-one, and three-blank.

B. has drawn the six-five, six-four, six-one, double-five, five-blank, double-three, and double-one.

A leads with the double-six.
B follows with the six-five ; when
A replies with the five-two,
B with the six-four, and
A with the two-six.

B next plays the six-one—and A at once knows that all the sixes are out, excepting the two in his own hand.

The game now continues as follows :
A—One-five.
B—Double-five.
A—" Go," for the reason that he has neither fives nor fours.
B—Five-blank.
A—Blank-six.
B—" Go."
A—Six-three.
B—Double-three.
A—Three-blank—Domino. A therefore wins the point.

It is obvious that a player should so dispose of his cards as to keep both ends open, thus avoiding the possibility of the " go " on his next turn to play. And, viewed in the light of his own hand, his opponents' leads should suggest much.

It is, however, an undoubted fact that the art of the game mainly lies in watching the number of cards of any particular denomination already played, and arguing from this the number (if any) likely to be in the hand of an opponent, and in the portion of the pack unused.

FIVES AND THREES

By reason of its variety and scope for finesse, Fives and Threes is in high favour with domino players.

The game consists of sixty-one points, and these may be scored on an ordinary cribbage board.

The "preliminaries and general tactics" are much the same as in the preceding game, "Runnings Out"; but, as our aim is simplicity of instruction, and as it is our desire to avoid anything in the nature of unnecessary "back reference," we will repeat these wherever we consider the learner will be helped by our so doing.

The dominoes are turned upside-down and freely shuffled or mixed—twenty-eight cards only, for two players.

Each player then takes a card, the highest deciding the "down," or first play.

The winner of the "down" next re-shuffles the set and selects seven cards, which he places on edge lengthways, with their faces towards him. The other players do likewise.

After the initial hand has been played, the shuffle and "down" combined are taken in turn.

The player who first disposes of *all* his cards must cry "Domino." He scores one for this—in addition to any extra points that may be due to him on the play.

Should a player not be able to play, he must cry "Go," or rap the table.

If, however, all have occasion to cry "Go," then the spots in each hand are counted separately, and the lowest total takes the point.

Now as to the object in view. It is to play those cards the exposed ends of which, added together, will make a number divisible by five or three, or both, *without a remainder*. For example—the first player sets down a double-five (crossways), for which he scores two points, there being two fives, with no remainder. The next promptly plays a five-two, and, the ten and two totalling twelve, scores four points—for four threes, without a remainder. The next player then matches the two with a two-three, but as the combined ends then total *thirteen*, he scores nothing. It is, however, a different proposition with another player, who plays a three-five, and brings the number up to fifteen—ten at one end and five at the other. For this he scores eight points—the highest possible—five for five threes, and three for three fives.

The art of the game chiefly lies in noting carefully the number of cards of each kind already played (remembering that there are but seven of each in the set) and, by this and other means, endeavouring to block one's opponents' play while keeping both ends open for oneself.

We will conclude with two illustrative hands, the players of which shall be A and B.

On an examination of A's seven cards we find he has the double-six, six-three, double-three, three-two, four-one, four-blank, and two-one.

B has the five-six, double-five, five-four, five-three, double-four, four-two, and double-two.

Again, we suggest that these hands should be actually played.

A sets down the double-six—thus scoring four points for the four threes. Having the six-three, he hoped that B could not play to sixes, so that with this card he would have made the total fifteen, and so scored eight.

B, however, goes with his six-five, but, the total being seventeen, makes no points.

A.—Six-three—no score.

B—Three-five—two for two fives. This leaves fives up A, having no fives, says " Go."

B then plays his double-five, making fifteen for eight—five three and three fives.

A—" Go."

B—Five-four to the double-five end—three for nine (four one end, and five the other). The play then continues:

A—Four-one, making the total six, and scoring two points for two threes.

B—" Go."

A—One-two—no score.

B—Two-four—again making the total nine, and scoring three.

A—Four-blank—one for the five.

B—" Go."

A, with no fives or blanks, is also compelled to cry " Go," and to challenge the count. On this, having eleven only to B's twelve, he scores one for the lower total.

N.B.—It will be seen that, on the play of the hands, A has scored seven and B sixteen towards the sixty-one points required for game.

MATADOR

This is an increasingly popular and somewhat scientific domino game, which comes to us from Spain.

Its title (though with what reason we fail to see) is derived from the Spanish *matador, matar* (signifying " to kill ").

It is customary to make the game 100 points up, but this may be varied as the players prefer.

As in the preceding games, the dominoes are shuffled and " down," or first play, decided by the highest card drawn. The holder of this then re-shuffles. The contestants next take seven cards each, and set them on edge, lengthways, in a row, with their backs outwards.

The player who shuffles always has the " down," and after the first hand this is taken in turn.

In matador it is not a question of matching the cards at either end, but of making the total "seven." There are in the set four dominoes termed matadors, all of which count seven—namely, the four-three, five-two, six-one, and, strangely enough, the double-blank.

These may be played at any stage of the game, need not match the last card down, and may be left with the end up which best suits the hand of the player.

All other cards must supply a number which will, when added to a domino already down, make seven—*i.e.*, a four-five card on the table demands a three at the four end, or a two at the five.

Should a player be unable to make seven, and have no matador cards, he must draw from the unused portion of the set, one card at a time, till he finds the domino which will supply his deficiency ; but, failing in this, he must continue drawing till he has taken into his hand all the cards but two. These then remain the " unknown quantity."

Though a player may be in a position to make a seven up, or may have one or more matadors in his hand, he need not produce these cards unless it serves his purpose so to do ; for he has the option at any point in the game of drawing from the set in the manner already mentioned.

If a player, having taken all the available cards but two, still finds himself unable to " go," he must rap the table, when his opponents proceed with the game, and probably open up one of the ends to further play.

The player who first disposes of his hand must cry " Domino " on his last card. He then proceeds to count the dots on the dominoes remaining in his opponents' hands, and, being the winner, adds their total to his score.

Should it occur that all players find themselves unable to

"go," the hands are then counted separately, when the possessor of the lowest total scores that of the higher—altogether ignoring that of his own hand.

When two totals happen to be equal, the combined number is noted and given to the winner of the hand that follows.

As the method of playing the actual pieces departs slightly from the ordinary domino lines, we propose concluding with two illustrative hands, which will not only show this peculiarity, but give the learner a glimpse of several other important aspects of the game.

We will, as in the preceding games, again term the players A and B.

A's hand is made up of the double-two, five-one, four-blank, double-three, six-blank, six-one, and double-blank—these two latter cards being matadors—while B holds the four-two, five-three, five-four, five-blank, six-five, four-three, and five-two—these last two cards also being matadors.

A, we find, starts with the double-two—a double being a good "down," as it restricts his opponent to a single number. The double-blank as a first down would compel a second matador.

B replies with the five-blank—so making seven, and still keeping the play to a single number, unless his adversary cares to produce a matador.

A, however, follows with the five-one, and

B produces the six-five.

A now thinks fit to set down the double-blank (a matador), forcing

B to play a further matador, the four-three.

A, having played the four-blank to this, causes

B to part with the third matador, the five-two

A, finding he has no fives, reluctantly gives up the fourth and last matador—the six-one—and from here the game proceeds as follows :

B—Five-four.

A—Six-blank.

B—Three-five.

A, finding he has no two's, draws a card from the unused portion of the set. This proves to be the two-three which, when played to the five end, enables

B to set down his four-two, and cry "Domino."

A has but one card left—the double-three.

B therefore scores six only.

From the foregoing it should be evident that much of the subtlety of the play is concerned with the attempt to force an opponent to draw cards freely from the unused portion of the set, in the interest of the final count. We trust it will be equally clear that this object may be considerably helped on by a full realisation of the important part played in the game by the four matadors.

A DICE GAME FOR TWO PLAYERS

SIXTY-ONE

This is a purposely-simple dice game, the interest of which might, under certain conditions, be considerably increased by a small stake.

To play the game, all that is needed is a dice and cup, together with a cribbage board and four pegs. Illustrations of these latter appear in "Cribbage," on page 103, where it will be noted that the board is pierced on either side with sixty holes (thirty up and thirty down, and in groups of five), with a sixty-first, or home hole, near to the point from which each player starts.

The scoring is done with the pegs, the players having two each. Once these are on the board, the back one only should be brought forward in recording the points, as the front peg is left to indicate the previous condition of the score.

The dice is thrown by each contestant, when the higher number commences the scoring. This is then in turn, and always starts from the outside of the board. The player who first scores sixty-one wins the game.

According to the dots appearing on the top side of the dice after the throw, so are holes pegged—but with the following exceptions:

On nearing the sixty-first, or home hole, the player must throw the exact number required to carry him out. Should he secure more, he must then move back his *front* peg to the figure indicated by the dice. And so on, till he is thrown into "Sixty-One."

Should a player exactly reach the 10th, 20th, 30th, 40th, or 50th hole, he must take out his pegs and start again. He need not, however, go back more than twice during a game.

FOX AND GEESE

This game is played on a Draughts board, with four white men for Geese and a black man for the Fox. The Geese are placed on the four alternate squares of the first row, as at Draughts, while the Fox can start from any of the corresponding squares at his own end of the board. The moves are made diagonally as in Draughts, but the Fox travels either backwards or forwards, as a king, while the Geese can only move forward.

The player of the Geese should endeavour to block the Fox in a corner, for he wins if he can get his Geese " home " to the four last squares of the Fox's territory. The Fox endeavours to capture as many Geese as possible, while keeping out of danger himself. The Geese move first.

It is very interesting to play a match of ten points up, the Fox counting one point for each Goose captured, the Geese one point for each one that reaches " home." Each player should handle the Fox and the Geese in alternate games.

AN EXPANDING TOY

This is just the sort of plaything that will amuse many youngsters for hours. You will see what to aim at by looking at the diagram.

Eight pieces of wood four inches long and an inch wide will be required. The material can be bought in long laths from the wood-yard, or strip-wood will serve. In addition two pieces of wood five inches long are needed for the handles. They must be two inches in width at the wider end and taper down to one inch at the narrower end. These will have to be cut and trimmed out of a piece of box-lid or similar material. At the wider end a round hole must be cut, large enough to allow a finger to be slipped through.

Now let the pieces be assembled. First arrange them as suggested by the diagram; then prick holes at the ends with a fine awl and push panel pins through the wood, so as to join up the two thicknesses at each corner. Turn over the projecting part of each pin and snip off all but sufficient to hold the wood.

At the far end, away from the handles, nail on two grotesque faces, cut out of stiff cardboard and coloured with pen and brush.

To use, place a finger and thumb through the two holes

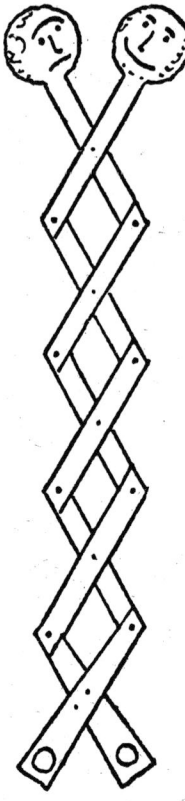

in the handles. Contract the hand and the lattice arrangement springs out its full length. Expand the hand and the lattice draws in. It is capital fun.

If a number of these toys are to be made, much labour can be saved by using garden lattice-work.

Colour all the wood with some bright, quick-drying paint.

THE CLOTHES-PEG FAMILY

Have you ever tried to make funny people out of clothes-pegs—we mean, of course, the pegs with a spherical top and

vo springy legs ? With a little ingenuity you can fashion
)me really curious doll-like folk. The pegs almost seem to
e designed for making grotesque people. The knob of the
)p serves admirably as a piece of headgear. Paint it red
r black and stick a little paper flower on it and it will look

just like a woman's hat. Or fit a flat edging of paper all
round it and it becomes at once a man's bowler. The part
immediately below the knob should be given up to the face;
and what faces can be devised with a little art and ingenuity!
The middle part is, of course, the body. Paste on a frill
of coloured crinkled paper and it is a neat skirt; or shape the
paper to look like a pair of trousers. A little trimming with
a pocket-knife of the tips of the pegs and you have supplied
the necessary shoes. Take half a dozen pegs and see what
lively little people you can make of them.

Lightning Source UK Ltd.
Milton Keynes UK
UKOW032229271212

204139UK00001B/41/P